D1431504

AMERICAN HOME COOKING

Rowman & Littlefield Studies in Food and Gastronomy

General Editor:

Ken Albala, Professor of History, University of the Pacific (kalbala@pacific.edu)

Rowman & Littlefield Executive Editor:

Suzanne Staszak-Silva (sstaszak-silva@rowman.com)

Food studies is a vibrant and thriving field encompassing not only cooking and eating habits but also issues such as health, sustainability, food safety, and animal rights. Scholars in disciplines as diverse as history, anthropology, sociology, literature, and the arts focus on food. The mission of **Rowman & Littlefield Studies in Food and Gastronomy** is to publish the best in food scholarship, harnessing the energy, ideas, and creativity of a wide array of food writers today. This broad line of food-related titles will range from food history, interdisciplinary food studies monographs, general interest series, and popular trade titles to textbooks for students and budding chefs, scholarly cookbooks, and reference works.

Titles in the Series

AMERICAN HOME COOKING

A Popular History

Tim Miller

ROWMAN & LITTLEFIELD
Lanham • Boulder • New York • London

Published by Rowman & Littlefield
A wholly owned subsidary of The Rowman & Littlefield Publishing Group, Inc.
4501 Forbes Boulevard, Suite 200, Lanham, Maryland 20706
www.rowman.com

Unit A, Whitacre Mews, 26-34 Stannary Street, London SE11 4AB

Copyright © 2017 by Rowman & Littlefield

All rights reserved. No part of this book may be reproduced in any form or by
any electronic or mechanical means, including information storage and retrieval
systems, without written permission from the publisher, except by a reviewer
who may quote passages in a review.

British Library Cataloguing in Publication Information Available

Library of Congress Cataloging-in-Publication Data

Names: Miller, Tim (Timothy Jon), 1970– author.
Title: American home cooking : a popular history / Tim Miller.
Description: Lanham [Maryland] : Rowman & Littlefield, [2017] | Series: Rowman & Littlefield
    studies in food and gastronomy | Includes bibliographical references and index.
Identifiers: LCCN 2016057276 (print) | LCCN 2017000530 (ebook) | ISBN 9781442253452 (cloth :
    alk. paper) | ISBN 9781442253469 (electronic)
Subjects: LCSH: Cooking—United States—History. | Gastronomy—United States—History.
Classification: LCC TX360.U6 M54 2017 (print) | LCC TX360.U6 (ebook) | DDC 641.01/3—dc23
LC record available at https://lccn.loc.gov/2016057276

∞ ™ The paper used in this publication meets the minimum requirements of
American National Standard for Information Sciences Permanence of Paper for
Printed Library Materials, ANSI/NISO Z39.48-1992.

Printed in the United States of America

CONTENTS

ACKNOWLEDGMENTS

I would like to thank Ken Albala, the content editor for this series, and Suzanne Staszak-Silva, the editor at Rowman & Littlefield, for the opportunity to write this book. I had been thinking for some time about the state of home cooking in America, and this book has given me the chance to investigate the history of home cooking and write about it.

INTRODUCTION

This book is a history of home cooking in America, so it is probably good to begin with a definition of just what "cooking" is. Unfortunately, in the past century or so our definition of cooking has become quite complicated. Cooking exists on something of a continuum. At one end of the continuum is cooking from scratch, preparing (for example) a salad from ingredients gathered in a garden. Toward the other end of the continuum is making something like cheese dip, where the contents of a few cans are poured into a bowl, the bowl is warmed in the microwave, and the dip is ready to serve.

While this is a book about home cooking, a precise definition of "cooking" is not terribly important for the purposes of this book. This is not a book that strongly advocates a return to home cooking, nor is it a eulogy for the demise of home cooking. Rather, this is simply a history of home cooking written with the knowledge that cooking, like most other activities Americans have participated in over the past few hundred years, has changed with the times. Today everyone has their own definition of cooking, and that, in itself, is a part of the story of American cooking.

The work of cooking is done in the kitchen, so much of this book is focused on that room. Looked at historically, the kitchen is something of a strange room, a leftover from a much earlier time. A few hundred years ago, before factories came along, homes were centers of production—almost everything was, literally, homemade. Clothes were homemade, starting with the gathering of the wool or flax and continuing with the spinning of the yarn, weaving of the cloth, and cutting and sewing of that cloth into clothes. Cheese and butter were made from milk taken from the family cows. Medicines were made from gathered and grown herbs. All of this was done within the home. Today the kitchen is the final remnant of all that production, the last place where we actually make something in the house. After we gave up making our own clothes, medicine, and everything else, we still have not given up cooking our own food.

There are, after all, perfectly good alternatives to making food. There are restaurants willing to sell us almost any kind of food we want. Grocery stores today do not just sell ingredients for food—they sell finished food as well, and a well-stocked grocery store sells everything from Chinese and Mexican foods to pizza and salad, which customers can select from an extensive salad bar. Those same grocery stores sell foods that aren't quite ready to eat but that require a minimum of work to finish. Frozen pizzas and TV dinners only require minutes in the microwave or oven, and frozen pasta needs no more than a quick dip in boiling water, with an accompanying packet of sauce that only requires warming. These foods need slightly more work than something taken from a restaurant, but far less work than food made from scratch.

This is a second focus of this book: to look at the alternatives to home cooking, including alternatives to scratch cooking. Two hundred years ago the average cook had no alternative to making a meal from scratch, but slowly, over time, alternatives developed. Convenience foods like canned goods or packaged mixes were invented. Restaurants became a legitimate option for a meal rather than a place bachelors or travelers stopped for food.

The twin focuses of this book, the home-cooked meal and the various alternatives to the home-cooked meal, have had something of a push-pull effect on Americans. On the one hand, there have been things that have pulled us toward the kitchen, such as a lack of alternatives to cooking or the idea that a woman's proper place is in the kitchen. On the other hand, there are all those alternatives that have pulled us away from the kitchen, like restaurants and processed foods that minimize the time spent in the kitchen.

While working on this book, my wife and I went on a diet called the Whole30. The program is fairly simple, marked more by what is not allowed than what is: no grains (so no wheat, corn, or oats), no dairy (no cheese, butter, or yogurt), no legumes (no soy, peanuts, or beans), no sweeteners (no sugar or honey, and no calorie-free sweeteners), and no alcohol (a few preservatives are also on the forbidden list). When I say *forbidden*, I mean the foods we ate could absolutely not contain any of those substances, even if "soy" came in as the last ingredient in a food with an ingredient list fifty items long. The main components of what we could eat were meat, vegetables, and fruits. There is no calorie counting on the diet, since the point is more to avoid foods that may cause digestive problems or food allergies than to lose weight, but we both lost weight anyway.

We also spent a lot of time cooking. As it turns out, almost all processed food—that is, anything not in a completely raw and untouched state—contains something on the forbidden list. I already knew that soy was an ingredient in many foods but was surprised at how often sweeteners showed up—it is almost impossible to buy deli meat or pork products that do not have sugar added to them (although we were able to find some at Whole Foods, with all the pricey shopping trips that implies). Most restaurant foods were also out, since contamination had to be avoided and restaurants usually prepare all of their foods in a common kitchen.

This meant that we had to cook all of our meals. When I say all, I mean *all*: three meals per day, unless we ate leftovers. Because we could no longer simply grab a frozen food and heat it up for dinner, or even open a box of cereal for breakfast, we had to plan all of our meals in advance and shop accordingly. Our shopping trips became an inversion of how our shopping time was spent before the diet: a half hour in the produce section, bagging the fifteen or twenty fruits or vegetables we needed from that area, and two minutes zipping through the rest of the store for the remaining few items.

I gained several insights while doing all that cooking. I realized that, while it was a pain to cook everything, it was still much less difficult than it would have been even a hundred years ago. Our refrigerator keeps our food at a constant cold temperature. The oven and stovetop heat up with a flick of a switch. Hot and cold water immediately flows into the sink and drains into a hidden sewer system. The dishwasher cleans several meals' worth of dirty dishes while I work on other things. Cooking today might take time, but the fact is that most of the time we spend cooking today is actually spent preparing food, not preparing for cooking by lighting fires, cleaning stoves, hauling water, or performing the multitude of other tasks our ancestors had to do just to get to the cooking.

Spending an hour or more per day cooking from scratch also gave me a new appreciation for convenience foods. My mother, who was born during the Great Depression, loved instant coffee, white bread, and saltine crackers. My siblings, who are all much older than I and who are baby boomers, generally avoid all of those things. A generational shift occurred around the time of World War II in terms of attitudes toward convenience foods. Those born before World War II, who grew up making meals from scratch, often viewed convenience foods as real time savers regardless of the excessive sweetness or saltiness that is inherent to processed foods. Those born after World War II grew up in a world where convenience foods have always existed, where those foods have tended to be cheaper than "from scratch" alternatives (in terms of both time and money saved). For those born later, there has always been a choice of using convenience foods or making something from scratch; for those born earlier, the choice was not always there. If one is in the situation of having to cook every meal from scratch, whether because of a special diet or a food allergy, convenience foods again begin to look like miracle foods.

This book is divided into six chapters that cover six large time periods, starting with the year 1800. The divisions are based on changes in the American food landscape and, while the precise divisions may be somewhat arbitrary and vague, the intention is to call attention to how our ideas about food, and how we consume food, changed over time.

The first chapter describes the cooking and eating situation in the year 1800. Without conveniences like refrigeration or running water, the cooking process was long and involved, and it was almost always done at home. Places to eat outside the home existed, but they were only for people who did not have a home to eat at.

Chapter 2 covers the early 1800s to about the 1870s, the years just after the Civil War. Almost all cooking was still done at home, but there were some advances, such as the introduction of canned foods and the cookstove, which moved the cooking process off the fireplace floor. Cookbooks became popular, offering both cooking recipes and guidance on how to run a household. Restaurants continued to be for travelers, bachelors, and men who could not return home for the noontime meal—certainly not a place for a family. Therefore, eating at home was still the only realistic option for most people.

Chapter 3 examines the late 1800s through 1945, the end of World War II. It is the longest chapter because it was a period of great changes to American foods—in some ways, the pieces of modern American cooking were put in place during this time. Researchers discovered the calorie and that foods could be divided into proteins, carbohydrates, and fats, but knowledge of vitamins would come later. That technical knowledge, combined with reform movements in society, led to the creation of home economics, a movement that, for the next fifty years or so, would be the dominant force when it came to food in America. Cookbook authors, radio cooking show hosts, nutritionists, food educators—all of them would be connected to the home economics movement in one way or another, most of them advocating that a woman's place was firmly in the home, cooking for her family. Food companies were there to help women by offering a growing number of convenience foods like mixes and breakfast cereals. Restaurants during this time became somewhat more reputable, especially those that catered to the upper class, but the problem with those restaurants was that they were far too expensive to be a real option for most households.

Chapter 4, which covers the end of World War II through about 1970, looks at the two conflicting ideologies that dominated home cooking during that time. The first ideology held that, essentially, when it comes to cooking, the ends justify the means: since the most important thing about cooking is putting a meal on the table, it does not matter if the meal is made from scratch, with fresh ingredients, or if the meal is simply assembled from a bunch of canned foods and mixes. This was the ideology promoted by the food companies that introduced a long list of new convenience foods like instant potatoes and frozen orange juice, and most home economists of the time were happy to go along with it. The second ideology, promoted by people like Julia Child and the counterculture of the 1960s, held that convenience foods should be avoided as much as possible and the best cooking was from scratch, using fresh ingredients.

Chapter 5 brings the story from the early 1970s to now, analyzing the uneasy relationship between those two ideologies, as well as the ongoing decline of home cooking. People today have far more general knowledge of food than our grandparents, and we commonly eat foods previous generations scarcely knew existed. We also cook far less, although we actually do have more leisure time than was available in the 1950s.

Chapter 6 is the last chapter in the book and looks ahead to the future. For historians, this is a dangerous activity, particularly when it comes to dramatic pronouncements about the imminent return, or the imminent disappearance, of home cooking (dramatic pronouncements rarely come true). With that in mind, I take a look at some current trends that will affect how we cook and where we get our food in the future. I do not believe there will be dramatic changes in cooking over the next number of years. The dramatic changes come from the accumulation of decades of smaller changes, as can be seen by looking at the first chapter, when almost everyone ate homemade meals and cooked from scratch.

I

COOKING IN 1800

In the beginning was the fire.

Using fire to do something to raw food—to roast it, to boil it, to bake it—is the oldest form of cooking. The ability to use fire was one of the differences between our distant ancestors and the animals they evolved from. In fact, primatologist Richard Wrangham has argued that using fire was not simply a difference between humans and other primates—it was the thing that helped move us along the evolutionary tree to becoming human. Cooking food makes it easier to eat and digest, and it also makes the food yield more calories. Once we started cooking, our brains changed. As Wrangham writes, "Cooking increased the value of our food. It changed our bodies, our brains, our use of time, and our social lives." [1] It was, literally, what made us human.

In the millennia since the first use of fire for cooking, humans developed tools to help with cooking. Metal pots and pans were particularly useful, but there was also the assortment of utensils for cooking with fire, like bellows and grates. These helped with the process of cooking, which was long and involved and, for Americans in 1800, always revolved around fire.

American houses in 1800 came in all shapes and sizes, from the mansions of the southern plantation owner or well-connected old-money scion to the crude log hut or lean-to of a frontier family. What they had in common, compared to houses of today, was what they lacked: plumbing, electricity, tight joins around windows and doors, all but the most rudimentary insulation, and thousands of other technological innovations that have come along in more than two hundred years. One modern author, comparing the comfort of today's houses with those built over a century ago, wrote that, rather than a haven to come back to after a day of work, back then "a house was a place of toil, a scene of production, the locus of food preparation and of laundering and of personal hygiene. During free hours, it was a place to get out of." The reasons to escape were myriad: "The ventilation, heat, and lighting were atrocious; it was hot in summer and cold in winter. Window screening . . . was not introduced until the late 1880s; before that time swarms of gnats, mosquitoes, June-bugs, and beetles moved at will through domestic quarters."[2]

The houses may have been sturdily constructed from stout timbers, or they could be rickety enough to blow over in the next windstorm. They all had a certain primitive air about them, though. Heating was done either by fire or through the ambient temperature outside. The bathroom would not be a separate room in the house until the late 1800s; until then, it was a shack out back.

The floor plans of the houses were fairly simple. The entire house was usually in a symmetrical, rectangular shape, so that the rooms on the left and right sides of the house generally matched each other in location and size. In larger houses a hallway might run down the center of the house, while smaller houses might only have a wall defining the center. Small houses might only have one or two rooms, while larger ones might have six rooms on the ground floor, with another even number of rooms upstairs. The frontmost rooms were intended for receiving the public, while rooms further back were strictly for family use. The symmetry of these early houses stands in sharp contrast to the asymmetrical, ramshackle-looking houses of the Victorian era, which will be examined in the next chapter.

Cooking inside the house was done at a fireplace built along one wall of the building. In houses with multiple rooms, the cooking was done in what we would call a kitchen and they often called a hall, but in many houses the cooking was done on one side of the only room of the house. The fireplace was, literally, just a fireplace: cast iron cookstoves would come later.

From the vantage point of the twenty-first century, it is hard to imagine cooking every meal over an open fire. Most Americans have some experience with cooking over flame, whether it is a gas stove, a barbecue grill, or an open campfire, but one point that is easy to miss is just how versatile a fire burning in a large, open fireplace can be. A pot of stew, hung from a long horizontal pole, can simmer above the flame while whole potatoes cook slowly, buried in the ash near hot coals. Lumps of bread dough, placed on a warm brick floor that had been swept clean, can rise for eventual baking. The cook could also warm herself before the fire on cold winter days.

Granted, the setup had glaring problems. It was inefficient with energy, sending much of the warmth from the fire straight up the chimney. Most food was cooked within a few feet of the floor, resulting in back-breaking work for the cook. The fire that was so warming in the dead of winter would be sweltering in the heat of summer, although cooking was often moved outside in warm months. In many homes all of this would change in the next few decades, but in 1800, American cooking meant cooking in a fireplace.

American kitchens in the early 1800s were usually simple affairs, consisting of the fireplace, a table or two for working, and some shelves. Compared to today's fireplaces, which are intended to either warm a room or just look cozy, those of the early 1800s were enormous, tall enough for a cook to bend over and enter, a few feet deep, and four or so feet wide. The fireplaces were even wider in larger homes with more mouths to feed. The intention was not to build a fire that occupied the entire space but to have enough room for one or two fires, with working space all around them. The working space could be used for noncooking activities as well. One woman who grew up cooking at one of those fireplaces remembered sitting in the fireplace with her sisters as they warmed themselves "while we looked up the chimney into a square of blue sky, and sometimes caught a snow-flake on our foreheads."[3]

Families with more money might have a more elaborate setup. Some kitchens included a stew stove built into the wall. As its name indicates, this stove was used for long-cooking dishes cooked in pots. At counter level was a hole the pot sat upon, while a low fire burned just below the pot, set into a small alcove in the wall. Some families also had brick ovens for baking bread. These built-in, specialized cooking areas were elaborate solutions to the cooking problems of the early 1800s that would be solved within a few decades by the development of the cookstove. Until then, most cooks spent much of their time literally inside the kitchen fireplace.

Illustrations from the early 1800s reveal just how primitive and un-adorned early kitchens were. One drawing of a northeastern artist's kitch-en in the 1830s shows one wall of the room that includes the fireplace. Several chairs of different styles, clearly used by the cooks to work or wait, are shown, including one pulled up before the fire. Candlesticks sit on the mantel while a bellows hangs from a hook attached to the mantel. Tongs and a grate lean against the inside of the fireplace, and a teapot sits on the ground near the fire. An iron rod is suspended above the fire with hooks of a variety of lengths hanging from it, one of which supports a pot that hangs just over the fire. The kitchen shown is typical of those of the time with an uncluttered workspace, the only tools being those that were metal, durable, and heavy. [4]

The vast majority of Americans in 1800 lived on farms, and a large amount of the food that came through a kitchen was grown on the proper-ty. Each family grew a variety of plants and kept a number of types of animals for both work and food. Some plants, like strawberries, were delicious to eat but impossible to store, while others, like potatoes or beans, lent themselves to storage so well that they appeared in almost every American garden. Staple crops such as corn and wheat would be grown by the acre and then taken to a mill to be ground into flour.

Animals provided a variety of useful items. A dairy cow gave milk, from which cream, butter, and cheese could be made, and at the end of her life meat and a useful hide could be procured. Chickens gave eggs and meat, and pigs, sheep, and goats also gave a number of different raw materials to work with.

The farms were not usually self-sufficient. Some ingredients and tools would have to be purchased from a store or neighbor. Salt, used for both seasoning dishes and preserving foods, would have to be obtained else-where, as would most tools and utensils, whether they were made of metal or pottery (wooden utensils could, of course, have been easily made). Nonessential ingredients such as raisins, nuts, sugar, coffee, or tea could also be purchased from the store.

Then, as now, Americans ate three meals per day, although the main meal (which was also called "dinner") occurred at noon rather than in the evening—the shift to having the main meal in the evening was a result of the factory and business life of the mid-1800s, when working family members could no longer return home for the midday meal. Breakfast was sometimes leftovers from the previous day, but when new food was prepared it was not much different from the breakfast foods of today, with the notable exception of cold cereal—that would come at the end of the nineteenth century. One Englishman traveling through Indiana in the 1830s reported stopping at a house for breakfast (taverns and other places that typically served food to travelers were often few and far between, so stopping at the nearest house while traveling was extremely common). He detailed both the preparation of the meal and the meal itself. "A kettle and two frying pans were put on the fire, and two others over some ashes, removed from the general mass by means of a shovel, and placed on the hearth," he wrote. "Into one of these pans some small loaves were placed, which had been prepared before hand, and covered with a lid, on which hot ashes were placed; and in the other, batter-cakes, called flap-cakes, were prepared. In one of the frying pans on the fire bacon was dressed, and in the other potatoes; so, in less than half-an-hour, a breakfast of the best the house could afford was prepared."[5] Pancakes, bacon, fried pota-toes, fresh bread—this is the same sort of meal that can be found today at any Waffle House or IHOP. The traveler described something of a large breakfast, but also one that was intended to serve a number of guests.

Lunch, the heaviest meal of the day, could feature many more dishes. Writing about the midday meal in New England during the 1700s, which likely did not change much by the early 1800s, a modern historian wrote that the meal "included meat, often beef, with cabbage, squash, peas, beans, or root vegetables, and condiments such as vinegar and pickles. Fish, butter, cheese, and molasses rounded out the fare."[6]

Supper was a lighter meal in most households. One European traveler wrote that, when traveling through what he called the "backwoods" (southern Indiana, where it might be ten or fifteen miles between houses), "pork, or as they call it hogs-flesh, together with venison and hommony (boiled Indian corn), was my usual fare, and a blanket or two, on the floor of the cabin" was his bed. He clearly did not think much of the food but "was amply compensated for this want of luxuries by a degree of open-ness and hospitality, which indeed the most fastidious could not but have admired." Indeed, he wrote that when leaving the house in the morning, the host sometimes "accompanied me four or five miles, in order to put me in the track leading to the road."[7]

In fact, many of the foods prepared in the early 1800s were not much different from those that can be found on American tables today. Washington Irving's "The Legend of Sleepy Hollow," his 1820 story of the Headless Horseman, includes many descriptions of food. At one point schoolmaster Ichabod Crane attends a potluck dinner and marvels at what he sees: "There was the doughty doughnut, the tender oly koek, and the crisp and crumbling cruller; sweet cakes and short cakes, ginger cakes and honey cakes, and the whole family of cakes." He goes on to describe "apple pies, and peach pies, and pumpkin pies; besides slices of ham and smoked beef; and moreover delectable dishes of preserved plums, and peaches, and pears, and quinces; not to mention broiled shad and roasted chickens; together with bowls of milk and cream."[8] That passage contains the second written mention of the doughnut, although, in the context of the story, Irving is clearly looking back in time and listing foods that were well known in rural New York.

In general the foods of the early 1800s were not complicated. Many of the foods listed by Irving in the passage above would have required no recipe for an experienced cook to make well. Although some foods, like roasted meat, were forgiving enough that a cook could make it almost any way she wanted, many foods required at least some sort of recipe to turn out well, although the cook might know the recipe by heart if she made the dish often enough. A family recipe book, written in a number of women's hands and dating to 1731, provides examples of the types of recipes women needed to have available. The first twelve pages of the book contain recipes for pickling everything from pigeons to peaches to walnuts, and the variety of foods indicates the importance of pickling as a method of preserving foods. Pickling required a recipe because the cook would probably not pickle a given food very often and also because, unlike with most other foods, she could not simply taste the food to see whether it was good, since it might take weeks for the pickling to finish. The next bunch of recipes in the book is for preserves, and, again, a recipe would be needed to make sure the proportions of ingredients were correct in order for the preserves to be good. A section on baked goods follows, including recipes for cheesecake, sugar cakes, and biscuits; baked goods are another type of food needing specific ratios of ingredients to turn out well.[9]

Today we take for granted that most foods are available year round. This is true because of worldwide food distribution systems that were developed in the twentieth century; before that, people ate what was fresh, preserved what they could, and sometimes simply did without certain foods. "Doing without" could, on occasion, mean fooling oneself. A recipe for Mock Apple Pie, published in a cookbook in 1870, substituted soda crackers for the apples, noting that it was "a good recipe for Spring use," spring being the time when preserved apples from the previous year had probably gone bad, before the new crop was ripe.[10]

Methods of food preservation were limited. Some of the general-purpose methods popular today that can preserve many different types of food, like freezing and canning, either did not exist or were unavailable to most Americans. As mentioned above, some foods could be pickled. Alcoholic drinks were popular both because of the alcohol content and because the alcohol ensured the drinks would not go bad, and a wide variety of fruit-based drinks, like brandies and wines, were available. The same was true of vinegars, since the process for making vinegars was almost the same as that of alcohol, and vinegar will also keep without refrigeration. Other foods had to be kept in their own way. One cookbook advised keeping apples on the floor of a cool, dry place; when winter came the apples should be placed in barrels with lime or plaster, handled "as carefully as eggs, not even breaking the stem." Those intended to be kept as long as possible "had better be wrapped in a newspaper."[11]

In the days before nutritional science, bread was seen as a basic necessity of life, and there was a preserved version of bread that was usually referred to as hard tack. "Biscuit" is a more apt name for it, since that word contains the basic cooking instructions: in Latin *bis*, or "twice," and *coctus*, or "cooked." Hard tack was first baked in a hot fire for a short period of time, and then baked for a much longer period of time in a low fire in an effort to cook out every bit of moisture from the dough. If cooked and stored correctly, the hard tack could last for months, although it took some work to make the hard tack edible again—soaking in liquid was a requirement if the diner did not want to break a tooth. Hard tack was a standard food for those traveling across the country or serving in the military, and one Civil War veteran recalled that his company knew fifteen ways of preparing it for dinner.[12]

One point that should be made about those methods of food preservation: preserving food at that time meant changing the food. An apple that had laid for months in a barrel with lime did not taste like a fresh apple. A pickled cucumber did not taste like a fresh cucumber. Salted meat did not taste like fresh meat.

There are two ways to react to that truth. One way, pursued by the modern food industry, is to use technology to overcome this obstacle. The food industry has poured enormous amounts of money into finding better ways to preserve food. For many foods, freezing has been something like a miracle. A frozen strawberry, defrosted, does taste something like a fresh strawberry. Frozen broccoli is a good replacement for fresh broccoli. The food industry has also spent a considerable amount of money and time creating a distribution system, using technology, to make it so fresh foods are always available to consumers. For much of the year we do not have to buy frozen strawberries because fresh strawberries are also available (they may be as hard as rocks, but they are still available). Fresh broccoli is always available at the store. With this distribution system, food preservation, for many different types of foods, is superfluous.

The other way to react to that truth, the way people in and before the early 1800s did, is to simply shrug one's shoulders and make dishes to fit the available preserved foods. Yes, it was impossible to keep an apple perfectly fresh all winter long, but an apple packed in the lime barrel could be used to make a good apple pie. Chipped beef on toast, a dish that is still sometimes prepared, was originally a way to use beef that had been preserved by salting and drying it. It may not have been possible to preserve a food with no change in taste or texture, but when the resulting food could be pickles that crunched when bitten into, cherry brandy that made one's tongue curl with tartness, or a panful of frying bacon, there was surely little complaining on the subject. Many of those preserved foods, in fact, tasted so good that they are still quite popular today, including sauerkraut and smoked ham.

The cookbooks from a time period can give a window into more than just the popular foods of the time, and the cookbooks of the early 1800s are no different. One important piece of information that can be gleaned is the simple fact that there were not a lot of cookbooks from that time. The American printing industry was still fairly primitive, especially when it came to books written by Americans. The first cookbook printed in America, in 1742, was a copy of a British cookbook with recipes dating back to 1727, and British cookbooks remained popular for much of the rest of the century. Amelia Simmons's 1796 cookbook, *American Cookery*, is usually seen as the first American cookbook because it incorporated foods unique to America. Although most of the recipes in *American*

Cookery are similar to British recipes, Simmons does include some that use pumpkins, winter squash, cranberries, and cornmeal, all foods originating in the Americas. The book also called for pearl ash, a leavening for baked goods first used by Americans. [13]

Looking through the recipes in *American Cookery* can be a bewildering experience. Many of the conventions of cookbook recipes, such as listing the ingredients before the instructions for making a dish, or standardized measurements for cups and tablespoons, were developed decades later. The recipes in the book assume the cook has a considerable amount of knowledge regarding cooking. For example, the complete recipe for "Gingerbread Cakes, or butter and sugar Gingerbread," is "three pounds of flour, a grated nutmeg, two ounces ginger, one pound sugar, three small spoons pearl ash dissolved in cream, one pound butter, four eggs, knead it stiff, shape it to your fancy, bake 15 minutes." [14] There is no information on what form the ginger should be when it is added (chopped or grated?), how much cream should be used, whether the eggs should be beaten before adding them to the batter, and what consistency the batter should have when ready. There is also nothing on how large the cakes should be or how hot the oven should be. All of this, the author assumes, a cook would already know.

And cooks of the time *would* have known all of this. They grew up cooking with their mothers and sisters and knew the basics of the process. Since the cookbooks of the early 1800s do not outline all the steps involved with making a dish, the cookbooks were likely used as a reference by cooks looking for a new dish, not by those looking to learn the entire cooking process. The recipes that are confusing to us today are communications between people who were adept at cooking in a very particular time and place. Any cook from the time who read the gingerbread cake recipe would know just how close to the fire in the fireplace she should place the cakes. The information that it should take fifteen minutes to bake the cakes would give a clue to the cook as to the proper relative temperature, since the time to cook anything is a function of how hot the fire is.

Another way the recipes in *American Cookery* are bewildering is the size of the finished dishes. The gingerbread recipe above calls for three pounds of flour, which would be about ten cups of flour, or enough flour for three modern cakes baked in a nine by thirteen pan. A recipe for preparing "a round of Beef" calls for a single piece of beef weighing fourteen to sixteen pounds. A recipe for chicken pie calls for six chickens.[15] Some of the reason why so much food is called for is because households were larger back then, since they included both children (a dozen children was not unusual) and hired workers who lived at the house. Some of it was also because certain dishes were expected to last for days. Baking was a long process that used quite a bit of fuel, so those gingerbread cakes would feed people for days after they were made.

Dealing with food took an enormous amount of time and energy, since almost everything consumed came from the farm itself. The effort involved with preparing food before it touched a diner's plate can be divided into three types of work. First, there were raw materials coming in from the outside that needed to be processed for storage. One example of this might be a cow or pig, freshly slaughtered. Slaughtering was usually done in the autumn because raw meat spoiled more slowly in the cool weather and because the dearth of grass meant that animals would need to be fed during the winter months, an expense that was easily avoided by slaughtering some of the animals. In the days before refrigeration, preserving meat meant smoking, salting, or drying, options that required effort on the part of women. Another example of raw foods that required processing were fruits and vegetables that, at harvest time, could generate bushel baskets of produce that needed to be processed almost as quickly as they came in. While the canning process would not be developed until the mid-1800s, women used a variety of methods to preserve food, ranging from pickling to potting (for meat) to making hard apple cider. Some foods, like berries, were preserved to make the diet more diverse, but others, like meat, were essential parts of the diet. Ruining hundreds of pounds of salted meat could mean the difference between a fat and a very lean winter. Indeed, food preservation was so important that on slave plantations, where there were plenty of workers, the white plantation mistress, rather than slaves, was solely responsible for food preservation.[16]

Another type of food preparation that happened every few days, which meant that it cumulatively took quite a bit of time, was preparing some of the standard items that appeared at most meals like bread, cheese, and butter. Bread was made only a few times a week because it took quite a bit of fuel for the fire, and so it was more efficient to make many loaves rather than a few. Cheese and butter came from the milk produced by one or two milk cows, and although the amount of milk varied throughout the year, there would always be some milk coming in to be processed. The fresh milk was poured into pans, where, over the next few hours, the cream rose to the top, ready to be skimmed off and used for butter or cheese.

A third type of work involving food was, simply, making meals. This work was also involved and required time and effort. The author of *American Cookery*, from 1798, began a recipe for chicken pie with "pick and clean six chickens . . . take out their inwards [*sic*] and wash the birds while whole then joint the birds."[17] Again, American households were much larger back then and might include hired hands or servants and grandparents and other relatives, and all of this contributed to the amount of work involved in simply preparing three meals a day.

And then there was the cleanup afterward. If a woman were lucky, a water source was just outside her door; if not, she might have to walk to obtain it. Everything was cleaned in order of its dirtiness: the cleanest dishes and plates were first, while the worst cooking pots would be saved for last, and the water might have to be changed out during the process. It is an obvious point, but the development of drains and sewers went hand in hand with the development of running water, so if water had to be manually carried into the house, it also had to be carried outside. Usually this simply meant pouring the water just outside the back door, but that involved a careful trip to the door to avoid slopping the water onto the floor. After cleaning, objects made from wood or pottery could be left on towels to air dry, but metal flatware or cast iron pots and pans would need to be dried immediately to avoid rust or corrosion.

The cooking and cleaning was, of course, work done alongside all the other work the typical housewife of the early 1800s was responsible for in the course of a day or week. Taking care of children, cleaning the house, washing clothes, helping sick family members, making cloth and clothes—all of these were things women were in charge of.

Women often had a difficult time keeping up with all the work, but, at that time, men also did a considerable amount of work. They were in charge of all crops outside of the garden (which was the woman's domain), all animals larger than a chicken (except the milk cow, the dairy also being the woman's responsibility), and keeping up all buildings on the property. While farming was labor intensive, it was only intensive during certain parts of the year, and during the slow times (like the winter) many men kept busy in workshops making things like shoes or clocks.

If there was too much housework for a woman to keep up with, there was always the option of getting someone to help. Farm families are traditionally large, since the children, once they get to a certain age, can be helpful workers, and most young women learned to cook while helping an older female relative, whether it was a mother, sister, aunt, or grandmother.

Hiring labor was also an option, particularly because there were so many young people around. One girl who lived in New England in the early 1800s was sent off to a neighbor for a week when the mother of the house was unable to do her work. Completely in charge of the house, the girl fetched water away from the house, boiled potatoes and brewed coffee for breakfast, made beans and biscuits for dinner, cleaned up after all the meals, got the family's twin girls ready for school, and took care of an aged relative living with the family. The girl was ten years old, and she received fifteen cents for the week's labor.[18]

Slave-owning families often had slaves work in the kitchen. Slavery will be discussed more in the next chapter, but well-to-do families in the North (before slavery was gradually outlawed) and in the South often used slave labor in the kitchen. In the North slavery gradually ended, so this ceased to be an option in the first few decades of the 1800s, but the habit of using slaves in the kitchen continued in the South through the Civil War.

Restaurants are ubiquitous today, offering a wide variety of food from the inexpensive to the pricey. With restaurants being such an important part of the modern food landscape, it may be surprising to learn that restaurants as we know them today did not really exist in America in 1800, and it would still be a few decades before their development.

Certainly, there were places to eat away from home. Taverns were a popular choice, particularly for men, but the food and drink served at the tavern were usually not the reason why people visited. As one historian wrote about Midwestern taverns, businessmen "patronized the inn for relaxation and socialization, but likely of greater significance was the possibility of collecting bits of information useful to their businesses or making important personal contacts." Local farmers also stopped by, sometimes for food and drink, but often because the local tavern was the site of community events, meetings, or even court trials.[19]

Boarding houses existed in every city and most towns, places where people (usually men) rented a room and ate three meals a day (included in the price of rent) in a public area. While it is fictional, Herman Melville provided a classic example of this type of establishment in *Moby-Dick* with the Try Pots, a seaside boarding house with a dining room that served only chowder in two varieties, clam and cod. The clam chowder "was made of small juicy clams, scarcely bigger than hazel nuts, mixed with pounded ship biscuits, and salted pork cut up into little flakes; the whole enriched with butter, and plentifully seasoned with pepper and salt." The narrator proclaimed it "surpassingly excellent" and then ordered the cod version, which he also enjoyed. But he then described the problem with this situation: "Chowder for breakfast, and chowder for dinner, and chowder for supper, till you began to look for fish-bones coming through your clothes." He also noted that the milk at the Try Pots had a strange "fishy flavor" that puzzled him until he saw the milk cow feeding on the remnants of fish.[20]

The mania for chowder at the Try Pots fits with *Moby-Dick*'s focus on manias in general and is probably an extreme version of the type of food served at boarding houses. However, the fact that hotels and boarding houses routinely included meals with the cost of lodging attests to the fact that there were few other real choices for those who wanted to eat away from their homes. Many of these locations were focused on feeding those who, for one reason or another, could not eat at home, either because they were traveling or because, as unmarried or widowed people, they had no home to return to and only rented a room at a boarding house.

Restaurants in America developed because they were needed, but in 1800 the conditions that allowed restaurants to develop had not yet come to pass. One problem was that, in 1800, America was an overwhelmingly rural country, and a restaurant needs a nearby population of diners to exist. The largest city in the country in 1800 was New York City with a population of sixty thousand people; the second largest, Philadelphia, had forty-one thousand; and the third, Baltimore, had twenty-six thousand people living within its borders. The top ten cities had a combined population of 216,000 people, in a country of more than four million people, not including Native Americans.[21] Over the next few decades, the country's population grew dramatically because of natural increase as well as immigration. American cities swelled as most immigrants chose to settle in urban areas, expanding the number of people available to eat at restaurants.

A second precondition for the development of restaurants has to do with our perception of a restaurant: it is not so much somewhere one has to eat but somewhere one chooses to eat. Boarding-house dining rooms were full because the meal was part of the price, and roadhouses located along country roads had patrons because travelers had to stop somewhere while they traveled and the locals were interested in hearing the news and gossip. The travelers and boarding-house tenants had no other real options when it came to eating. Restaurants, though, would be born when people who wanted other options came along. That group, decades into the nineteenth century, would be the middle class, a group that barely existed in 1800.

At the turn of the nineteenth century, people ate at home because there was no other choice. They ate meals made from scratch because processed foods, other than preserved foods, also did not exist. Women prepared the food because they worked around the house rather than away from it. Things were the way they were largely because there were no other options. During the 1800s Americans would begin to get some of those options.

2

THE EARLY TO LATE 1800S

The young American country changed considerably during the nineteenth century, and its relationship to home cooking changed as well. By the end of the period Americans still ate most of their meals at home and women did all of the cooking, but cooking began to become more modern. The combination of new ways to preserve food (most notably canning) and new transportation systems like steamboats and railroads meant that local food distribution systems became regional, and even touched on being national, a move that, in some ways, made food dangerous to consumers. A growing middle class read literature that advised them on how to cook foods and also explained why women should not just be in charge of food and the entire household but also were ultimately responsible for the entire family (and a woman's failure to do her job could lead to dire consequences). While the American food landscape by the late 1800s still looked very different from how it looks today, pieces of it were moving into position, transforming the America of the late nineteenth century into a more modern place.

Several trends in American culture profoundly affected cooking in the nineteenth century and will be discussed at various places below, although an overview at this point will be helpful. First, industrialization took hold in America in the first few decades of the century as a factory-building boom took hold, mostly in northeastern states. The Industrial Revolution had swept through parts of Europe in the 1700s, and so American factory owners used technology borrowed, or perhaps stolen, from Europe (particularly Britain). Some industries, like the cloth industry, became completely dominated by factories, producing bolts of cloth so cheaply that few Americans continued to make their own cloth, although most would continue to sew their own clothes well into the twentieth century. Other industries would take decades to be transformed by the Industrial Revolution. The factories affected home cooking by offering new products, particularly canned goods, that were mass-produced, often hundreds or thousands of miles away from the consumer.

Factories relied on good transportation to move raw materials to the factory and finished products away from the factory, and during this time there was also a revolution in transportation. By the 1820s steamboats moved up and down many American rivers and canals were built to link rivers and other bodies of water, and in the 1850s railroad tracks began connecting areas together, although it was not until the 1870s, after the Civil War, that a boom in railroad construction saw tracks crisscrossing the country. Developments in transportation enabled food producers to move their products faster, more cheaply, and farther than ever before, so that by the 1870s meat from Texas cattle regularly appeared on dining tables in Chicago and New York City.

The factories created a new class of people, the working class (people whose wages were scarcely enough to keep them alive), but, by employing people like managers and accountants, it also enabled the growth of the middle class. The growth of the middle class is another trend that affected American cooking because the middle class developed a particular set of values and ideas that profoundly influenced other Americans. These ideas will be referred to as those of the Victorian Age, although it is somewhat clumsy to name it after a British queen. Victorian ideas influenced most areas of American daily life, including the utensils used in the kitchen and attitudes toward kitchen help.

Kitchens changed in several ways during the nineteenth century. Most became more efficient but also more complex, filling up with new gadgets, cooking utensils, and dinnerware. For Americans living on the frontier, and for those who were very poor, the kitchen remained a large fireplace on one side of the main room of the house. For others, particularly those in the upper or middle class, kitchens, like the rest of the house, changed during the 1800s.

One of the most important changes in American kitchens was the development of the cast iron cookstove. Cookstoves first became popular nationally in the 1840s, although they had been used in some areas of the country since the 1700s. Cookstoves completely changed the cooking process, but using a cookstove involved tradeoffs. In some ways it made the cook's job easier, but it also added work to the job.

To modern eyes, cookstoves were extremely complicated. Stoves today have three parts: the cooktop where pots and pans are heated, the oven that encloses the food to be cooked, and a set of dials or buttons for controlling the cooktop and oven. Cookstoves had a multitude of areas for cooking food and controlling the fire, not all of which were immediately obvious. One enclosed area might be for baking, another for roasting, and a third for letting bread rise, and the three areas might be at any height between the knees and shoulder of the average cook. The flues, rotating handles for directing heat, could be located at the front or side of the cookstove, again at almost any height. Needless to say, training was needed to control a cookstove.

Cookstoves had two main purposes: to raise the cooking area off the floor of the fireplace, and to have a fire that was more precisely controlled and regulated than what was possible in a fireplace. The contained nature of the stove meant that coal was usually used as fuel rather than wood. The fire itself was in a firebox, and by opening and closing flues in different parts of the stove the cook could direct heat to different areas of the stove, each intended for a particular kind of cooking (a water reservoir was also a standard addition to the stove, the water being warmed by the excess heat of the stove). The efficiency of the stove was a major factor in its popularity; as one 1869 book described it, "With proper management of dampers, one ordinary-sized coal-hod [bucket] of anthracite coal will, for twenty-four hours, keep the stove running, keep seventeen gallons of water hot at all hours, bake pies and puddings in the warm closet, heat flat-irons under the back cover, boil tea-kettle and one pot under the front cover, bake bread in the oven, and cook a turkey in the tin roaster in front."[1] The complexity of a cookstove comes through in that quote as the author describes six different areas where food could be warmed or cooked.

As one might imagine, using a cookstove required a cook to relearn the cooking process. Unlike a fireplace, the fire in a cookstove was hidden deep inside the stove, requiring the cook to check it every so often. The firebox was small, making it difficult to move fuel around within it. The flues were complicated to use.

And there was the cleaning. A fireplace certainly had to be swept regularly, but the cookstove, with its pipes and compartments, took cleaning to a new level. The entire cookstove had to be cleaned and blacked weekly, and, since coal produces much more smoke than wood, the stovepipe also had to be cleaned regularly. Historian Ruth Schwartz Cowan, in her book *More Work for Mother*, uses cookstoves as an example of an invention that did, indeed, make more work for the woman of the house, not the man. While fireplaces also needed to be cleaned, since the fireplace provided heat for the house, the fireplace was not viewed as the woman's responsibility—cleaning the fireplace was a man's job, not a woman's. Since the main purpose of the cookstove was cooking, and cooking was a woman's job, cleaning the cookstove became solely the woman's responsibility, a lengthy task added to her already long list of daily and weekly chores. [2]

Cookstoves did, however, have undeniable benefits. The work surface was above the floor. The stove's water reservoir produced hot water with no additional work on the part of the cook, other than keeping the reservoir filled. The stove used a much smaller volume of fuel than cooking in the fireplace with wood, an important consideration for urban families without much space for storing fuel.

Another benefit of the cookstove was that it was, to some extent, portable. Many families had a summer kitchen set up in a building away from the house in order to move the perpetual kitchen heat elsewhere, and although the stove, made from cast iron, was very heavy, the stoves do seem to have been moved in the spring and fall. Mark Twain wrote an amusing essay on the topic titled "Putting Up Stoves," and although his essay describes moving a heating (not cooking) stove in from the woodshed, where it had been in storage, the general description of bruised fingers and blackened clothes also likely describes the process of moving a cookstove.

Cookstoves replaced the old kitchen fireplace, and in many houses this happened in a very literal way. Illustrations from the 1800s show two approaches to placing a new cookstove. In some kitchens the cookstove was positioned squarely inside the fireplace; the smokestack fed directly into the existing chimney. In other kitchens the old fireplace was either bricked up or screened over, and the new cookstove was placed a few feet away from the wall with the smokestack running into the wall to join the existing chimney. Placing the cookstove away from the wall rather than directly in the old fireplace was the more popular option, since the stove would be difficult to clean inside the fireplace.

Illustrations from the time show what American kitchens looked like. One picture, from 1854, is amusingly titled "Shake Hands" and shows a cook, standing erect at her kitchen worktable, smiling warmly and extending a hand to the viewer even as she is in the middle of preparing a meal. A shelf of vegetables, including a bucket of celery, standing up, sits on a shelf beside her, while a plucked chicken and plate of butter, with butter knife, sits on the table before her. A pan of apples and bucket of water sit on the floor. Behind her a cookstove, only a few feet high, roars with a fire, a kettle and pot bubbling on top. Behind the cookstove is the old screened-off fireplace, itself extending up to the shoulder height of the cook.[3]

In the first few decades of the nineteenth century architects began publishing books of house plans featuring a new style of house that would eventually be known as the Victorian style. This new style was popular among middle- and upper-class families, who often used published plans as a basis for their own houses, even if the house was built from plans drawn by a local architect.

In some ways the Victorian style was a reaction to older house styles, and in other ways it was a response to a changing family demographic. The older house style, as described in the previous chapter, was essentially a symmetrical box with an equal number of rooms on each side of the house. The Victorian style broke apart the symmetry; a porch (or veranda, as it was usually called) might appear on one side of the house with nothing to balance it visually on the other side of the house. Older house styles featured a small number of large rooms while Victorian houses were composed of a large number of smaller rooms. These smaller rooms fit well with families whose members might change over the course of years as children grew and left the house and older relatives moved in. Without an overall sense of symmetry, rooms could be easily added to one side of the house as the family grew, and rooms could also be closed off as members moved out. A large house with a large family required lots of work just to keep the house running, and that often meant hiring servants, which in turn could increase the number of people living in the house. The complexity of the house, and the changing numbers of people living there, was reflected in the activities that took place in the house. In

the early twentieth century, when the Victorian house style was still popular, one writer observed that in the course of a day "the house is by turns
not only a boarding place for the family, but a maternity hospital, a
contagious ward, a factory, a laundry, a hotel, and the scene of number-
less other industries."[4]

The kitchen in a Victorian house was located at the back of the home
and often included a pantry as a separate room. In the cooler months the
pantry was useful as something akin to a walk-in cooler, particularly
since the room was usually against an outer wall and included a window
that could be opened.

Illustrations of model kitchens from the late 1800s show, if not the
reality, at least the ideas that were becoming popular regarding kitchen
design. In 1865, the last year of the Civil War, *The American Agricultu-
ralist* magazine portrayed what it called "A Convenient Kitchen Sink" to
its rural readers. The sink was wide, with slats positioned over it to one
side for quickly draining dishes before moving them to a slanted drain-
board just beyond the slats. On the other side of the sink was a worktable,
hinged to the wall with a moveable stand so that the table could easily be
dropped flat against the wall. Shelves above and below the sink provided
storage space for pots and pans. Oddly, the sink included taps for hot and
cold running water, conveniences that were then only available in a few
East Coast cities. Overall, the sink is made to be a useable workspace.[5]

Eleven years later the same magazine provided another illustration of
a model kitchen, one that showed how ideas were changing. While the
illustration does not include a stove, it shows two walls of the kitchen,
which presumably included most of the cook's workspace. A sink with a
single hand pump providing water is set into a countertop in one corner,
with closed cabinets beneath and beside it. An open door leads into a
pantry, with a passthrough cut into the wall beside the sink, making it
easy to move ingredients that might need to be cleaned before using. A
worktable sits beside the door.[6]

Southern kitchens were affected by the plantation system. While the
actual number of plantations, where dozens or hundreds of slaves
worked, was very small in relation to the total number of white families,
plantation owners dominated southern culture. They were the town leaders, the mayors, senators, and governors, and other southerners deferred
to them. Those lower on the social ladder frequently adopted the plantation owner's tastes and preferences. The plantation owners had an out-

sized effect on other southerners, and that effect extended to kitchen design.

As it was with other parts of the plantation, the plantation kitchen ran on slave labor. The typical cook on any plantation was not the owner's wife; rather, it was a black slave. Small farmers who owned a slave or two had a considerable amount of interaction with their slaves, but as the plantation grew this interaction changed to an enforced distance. The black house servants worked in the master's house, of course, but the majority of slaves were kept to the fields and slave quarters, away from the house. The kitchen was inescapably a place where slaves worked, though, so to keep the distance between black and white worlds, the plantation kitchen was physically moved out of the house to a nearby building.

The Big House kitchen, as it was called to differentiate it from other kitchens on the plantation, was a one- or two-room building that sometimes included a loft for the cook's family. Its existence as a separate building points to the fact that plantations usually had an excess of workers. In some ways the Big House kitchen was not unusual in America, as many families built a summer kitchen in a separate building in an effort to keep the heat of the kitchen away from the main house. The difference for the Big House kitchen was that it was used year round, and so it always required the cook and servants to deliver warm, finished dishes to the master's house, even in the dead of winter. Even on plantations that were financially successful, cooking in the Big House kitchen was usually done in a fireplace, not a more modern cookstove. A cookstove was much more efficient than a fireplace but cost money that most plantation owners were unwilling to spend, or, rather, they preferred to spend that money on buying more slaves. If cooking in the Big House kitchen was more difficult than it could have been, it was always possible to assign more slaves to the work to make up for the difficulty.

The drawbacks of the Big House kitchen became obvious after the Civil War, when the slaves were gone and the white mistress had to do the cooking herself. One woman, writing to a friend in the North, complained that at her place the kitchen was forty yards from the house and two hundred yards from the nearest source of water. Northerners, who had long since outlawed slavery, had no tradition of cheap labor and tended to turn to technological innovations to improve their lives, as the southerner's letter attests: "We have no wood house, washing machine, cooking stove—in short, none of the conveniences that you Northern people have been so long accustomed to, and worse than all, we have no money to fix these things."[7]

In 1878 Samuel Clemens, more commonly known as Mark Twain, took a tour of Europe with the intention of writing a book about the experience. That book became *A Tramp Abroad*, and toward the end of the book Clemens, homesick for America, includes "a little bill of fare" for what he calls "a modest, private affair," a meal he will eat all by himself. It is a list of all the foods he misses and runs a full page in the book, seventy-nine items in small type spread out over two columns.[8] The idea that he could eat all the food listed at one sitting is ridiculous, but the list does provide some insight into the American stomach of the time period.

The list is interesting for a few reasons. It includes dishes any home-sick American of today might put on a similar list, like fried chicken, hot biscuits, "Roast turkey, Thanksgiving style," and apple dumplings (he apparently became overwhelmed by thinking of desserts, because the list ends with the phrase "All sorts of American pastry"). It also contains dishes that are, at best, uncommon today. There is quite a bit of game listed, including canvasback duck, prairie hens, opossum, and raccoon (the last two referred to by the more backwoods "possum" and "coon"). Cherrystone clams make the list, as do frogs and terrapin soup.

The inclusion of all the game on the list points to a fact of American eating that has largely disappeared today: until the twentieth century we were a nation of game eaters. The abundance of wild animals available for Americans was a central difference between America and Europe and sometimes shocked early settlers. The earliest travelers occasionally re-ported seeing flocks of thousands of game birds and equivalent herds of buffalo. The tradition of eating game, particularly in sparsely settled ar-eas, continued through the 1800s but became weaker over time for at least two reasons. First, settlement often meant a decline of the wild areas game needed to exist, so there were simply less of these animals around. Second, as more and more Americans moved to urban areas, there was a paring down of the foods available to them. Growing gardens and hunting for game were activities of rural Americans; city dwellers obtained their food from markets. Although markets in the largest cities, like New York City, displayed a dizzying variety of foods throughout the year, markets in smaller cities, and smaller neighborhood markets in large cities, would have less variety of food available to the average consumer.

Getting back to Samuel Clemens's list, the simplicity of the vast majority of the items on the list is striking. Clemens includes vegetables such as asparagus, radishes, pumpkin, and squash with no qualifiers; he simply lists them without indicating whether they should be steamed, roasted, fried, or prepared in some other way. A few foods are listed with simple accompaniments such as "American coffee, with real cream . . . Sliced tomatoes, with sugar or vinegar . . . Green corn, cut from the ear, and served with butter and pepper." Some of the reason for the simplicity of these items is the fact that Clemens, as a man—and a rich one at that— rarely (if ever) was involved with cooking, although he had traveled widely as a young man and surely knew how to cook basic items. But the list also reflects the simplicity of large swaths of American cooking at that time. While the era's food preservation methods resulted in foods that were nothing like fresh foods, the fresh foods were probably quite impressive, even better than fresh foods today.

While that last assertion may sound surprising—how can fresh foods differ between time periods?—Clemens provides an example of a vegetable that has generated decades of complaints from consumers: the tomato. In the early twentieth century some growers modified tomatoes to ship them to distant markets. Tomatoes were engineered to be bright red with no blemishes so they would look good to consumers, and they were made to have thick skins and a solid body so they could handle being shipped hundreds or thousands of miles across the country. The taste of the tomato was very much a secondary consideration, and the changes wrought to the easily shipped tomato resulted in a tomato without much taste. This is the chief complaint from many consumers who have eaten fresh tomatoes from the garden. Today, store-bought tomatoes taste nothing like garden tomatoes.

In the 1800s, though, there was nothing else available. Fresh tomatoes were not available for most of the year, but when they were available, well, they were likely to make most people's list of favorite foods. And there was another difference between the tomatoes people had access to back then and the tomatoes we have today: they had many more varieties.

The produce section of most grocery stores today offers only a few varieties of tomato, usually differentiated by size and color. There is the standard palm-sized tomato, maybe a plum tomato as well, packages of smaller cherry tomatoes, and, at some stores, containers of still-smaller grape tomatoes. If the store really has a selection, there might be some yellow tomatoes. That is the extent of the selection at most grocery stores today.

The varieties back then were wilder in taste and color. How do we know, today, what they had back then? Because collecting and growing those seeds, called heirloom seeds, has become popular. Heirloom seeds are varieties of seeds that lay outside the parameters of what the big seed companies became interested in during the twentieth century. Common, everyday people planted them, year after year, and perhaps traded them between neighbors or within a community. In the past number of years groups have started collecting those seeds, cataloging them, growing them, and trading and selling them to other people.

The varieties of heirloom fruits and vegetables available are impressive. Tomatoes range from large beefsteak tomatoes to tiny grapes, in colors that vary from pale white to solid red to nearly black. One type of watermelon has a green skin speckled with yellow, with a golden interior, while it is possible to find a green pepper that ripens to a chocolate brown color, as well as decorative, inedible corn where each kernel is a different color.[9] Although some varieties of heirloom fruits and vegetables were created in the past hundred years, many more have been around since at least the early 1800s.

All of this points to the fact that, in the modernization of the grocery store that took place in the first decades of the twentieth century, a kind of choice was lost. The produce section of the typical grocery store today has far more types of vegetables than any American had access to at one time in the 1800s, but this abundance obscures the fact that gardeners back then, and many consumers, had access to more varieties of a given vegetable than most consumers do today. This type of variety was a fact of life in the 1800s.

One last observation about Samuel Clemens's list of American foods he missed while in Europe: many items have a geographic qualifier. Biscuits, wheat bread, bacon and greens, and peach cobbler, he wrote, should all be "Southern style," which indicates that, by the mid- to late 1800s, the South had a particular style of cooking associated with the region. Several dishes have very specific points of origin. "San Francisco mussels . . . Baltimore perch . . . Lake trout, from Tahoe . . . Prairie hens,

from Illinois . . . Missouri partridges . . . [and] Boston bacon and beans"
are on the list.

Clemens traveled widely both as a young man, when he went West
with the gold rush and worked on the Mississippi River as a riverboat
pilot, and as an adult, when he toured the country on speaking tours, so
the geographic qualifiers can be interpreted as foods he ate in particular
places: trout he caught and cooked while visiting Lake Tahoe, or prairie
hens he shot and roasted in Illinois. More likely, though, they refer to
foods from those particular places that were preserved in some way and
then exported to other areas. The riverboats of the 1820s, and then the
railroads of the 1840s and 1850s, were able to move relatively fresh foods
around the country quickly. Writing in the 1860s, Thomas De Voe, who
produced an encyclopedic account of foods available in a few cities on
the East Coast, observed that a food producer "is often hundreds of miles
in one direction, while the consumer may be as many hundred in another,
from the mart at which the productions were sold and purchased." His
description makes the movement of food around the country sound like
the body's circulatory system, as "the products of the North, South, East,
and West" move to large central markets, to be purchased by wholesalers
and then shipped to "other cities, towns, or villages, or on the many ocean
or river steamers or other vessels, as well as in foreign countries."[10] This
is a far cry from the globalism of today, where a single pineapple may
travel thousands of miles and cross numerous national borders, but it was
a step in that direction.

The increasing distance between food producers and consumers introduced a new wrinkle of complexity into the American food system. If
someone grows the majority of foods he or she eats, they can be fairly
sure that what they're eating is both safe and genuine (that is, the catfish
they fry up is catfish rather than some other type of fish sold as catfish). If
someone buys most of their foods, they have to trust that the food they
buy is safe and genuine. As Americans began buying more and more of
their food rather than raising it, trust became an issue.

Essentially, the omnivore's dilemma had returned. This phrase, coined
by researcher Paul Rozin and famously used as a book title by Michael
Pollan, refers to a central problem for omnivores. Herbivores, which can
eat only plants, do not have many choices in what they can eat and
usually rely on their senses of smell, sight, and taste to tell whether a
plant is known to them and safe to eat. Since they eat live plants, spoilage

is not an issue. Omnivores, though, can eat anything, and therein lies a danger: we can easily consume something dangerous.

Americans of the early 1800s largely had this figured out, as they usually ate foods they were familiar with, had raised themselves, and so knew to be safe. There were, of course, occasional problems, particularly when moving into new areas. Early settlers to the Midwest sometimes became ill after drinking milk from cows that had eaten white snakeroot, a plant that was native to the Midwest but unknown in the East. The resulting sickness killed thousands of settlers, including Abraham Lincoln's mother, before the cause of the illness was discovered. Food spoilage was another existing problem, since in warmer months it was difficult to keep foods from going bad, so stomach problems were an issue. By and large, though, rural Americans could be assured the foods they ate were generally safe because they had raised them themselves, and they knew the signs that indicated food might be going bad.

For increasing numbers of urban Americans, though, food safety became an issue. Foods were being shipped longer and longer distances, and the connection between producer and consumer became one that was filtered through many middlemen, any of which could be less than scrupulous. Shoppers had to watch for counterfeit foods that were, at best, imitations of the genuine article and, at worst, deadly.

The classic nineteenth-century text on the subject is Fredrick Accum's *A Treatise on the Adulterations of Food and Culinary Poisons*, which, as the extended title explained, applied to "bread, beer, wine, spirituous liquors, tea, coffee, cream, confectionery, vinegar, mustard, pepper, cheese, olive oil, pickles" and a whole host of other foods. Accum was a German chemist who spent nearly thirty years in London, where he gave lectures, sold chemicals and lab equipment, and wrote a series of books on everything from mineral analysis to wine and bread making. His book on the adulteration of food was published in 1820 and, although he wrote for a British audience, his findings also likely applied to foods available to Americans during much of the nineteenth century.

In his *Treatise*, Accum took a chemistry set to the food available to him in London and found that much of it was entirely counterfeit or contained unwholesome additions. He found blackthorn leaves that were substituted for black tea leaves, and roasted peas for coffee. Lead, which was then recognized as at least causing stomach problems, was added to poor-quality wine to help its flavor, to Gloucester cheese to give it a reddish color, and to cayenne pepper to keep it from fading in the light. He found black pepper that included a substance made from oil, clay, and cayenne pepper, and white pepper that started out as black pepper but was "steeped in sea water and urine, and then exposed to the heat of the sun for several days" before it was dried and rubbed.[11] Clay also appeared in cheap confectionaries, which additionally contained copper to give them a green hue. Some of the information in his book came from lab experiments, and some of it came from interviews with grocers and other researchers. He found a printed guide for distillers that advocated keeping the rum cask, which was used to fill containers for customers, stocked with a mixture of real rum and inexpensive molasses brandy to maximize profits, since the fake "cannot be distinguished, but by an extraordinary palate."[12] Accum's intention in writing the book was clearly to alert people to possible dangers in their foods, but the book may have actually helped spread unwholesome practices: by describing how real food could be replaced by fake versions, he was also letting potential perpetrators know exactly how to do it. However, Accum's presentation of the material makes it evident that much of the substituting was endemic to the grocery trade and that anyone who sold food knew of ways to trick the customer, so that the challenge to the customer was to buy only from those who were trustworthy.

The most important innovation in food preservation of the nineteenth century came to America, like most technological developments of the time, from Europe. Canning was invented in France in the midst of the Napoleonic Wars, refined and popularized in Britain, and then finally exported to America, where the words *can* and *canning* were first applied to the product and process, respectively.

Frenchman Nicolas Appert is usually considered the father of the canning process. Born in 1750, he worked with food all of his life and was employed, at various times, as a cook to a duke, a prince, and a princess. When he was thirty-one years old, he opened a confectioner's shop in Paris, and in his spare time he worked on new methods to preserve food. The ability to preserve food in one way or another is probably as old as cooking itself, but the methods of food preservation used in late eighteenth-century France had the drawback of changing the taste and texture of food. The first step in using salted meat, for example, is soaking the meat in water for hours to try to pull the salt out of the meat.

Appert focused on preserving food in bottles. He quickly hit on the basic steps of canning still used today: place the food in a clean container, seal the container, and heat the container to a high-enough temperature to kill the microbes inside. The devil was in the details, though, and it took him years to determine the best way to bottle food. He tinkered with the process for fourteen years before closing his Paris confectioner's shop and moving to a small town outside of Paris so that he could spend more time on his experiments.

Part of Appert's problem was the primitive medical and scientific knowledge of the time. He worked decades before germs were an established part of science; at the time, the idea that anything so small it could not be seen could make a human sick was laughable. Killing microbes is a central part of the canning process, though, so the lack of knowledge complicated Appert's efforts. Appert knew, for example, that heating the sealed bottled was an important part of the canning process, but he did not quite understand why. Years later, as canners produced larger and larger cans of food, they eventually reached a point where the food inside was contaminated and deadly: the can had been heated in the manufacturing process, but the food inside had not been heated long enough to kill the microbes at the heart of the can. In 1852, ten-pound cans of meat sold to the British navy were found to be spoiled when opened. After that, canners eased back on the size of their cans. [13]

In his workshop outside of Paris, Appert did make some headway. He sold bottled foods to the locals and interested the French navy in his canning process. Food preservation has always been an issue on ships, particularly those that sailed into the hot and humid tropical waters of the French colonies. The fragile glass bottles did not work well on ships, though, so the navy asked him to try canning food using a more durable substance, like tin.

It is at this point that a central problem in Appert's life becomes apparent: he lived at the right time but in the wrong place. Tin was the obvious substance to make cans from, but it would have to be imported, and France was then involved in a long-running war with Britain. Tin was simply unobtainable in the amounts Appert would need. The British, with a worldwide trading empire, would have been able to obtain enough tin, but the French government had made it known to Appert that they considered his process an important enough national asset that it should *not* be taken to Britain. French officials gave Appert some money, but it was not enough to start much of a business. As food historian Sue Shephard has discovered, though, Appert secretly worked with a British broker to patent his process and then sold the patent, making some quick cash for himself. Appert did later make some money with his canning business, but when he died, at age ninety-one, he was penniless and buried in a pauper's grave.

In the long run it was the British who really developed canning in tin. Bryan Donkin, who would become the leading canner in Britain, read Appert's patent but concluded that using glass bottles plugged with porous corks introduced too many complications into the process. Instead, his company used tin and clever marketing. In 1812, before his factory was built, he sent a few cans on a ship bound for Jamaica with instructions to eat the canned meat and soup during the voyage. When the ship returned nine months later the captain declared that the canned food had been as delicious as fresh food and provided a testimony to that effect, which was well used in advertising the company's products. A few years later William Underwood, an English immigrant, brought canning to America. One of his bookkeepers introduced the word *can*, so Americans use that word rather than the British word *tin* to describe canned food. [14]

Although canned foods arrived in America in the first decades of the nineteenth century, it would be decades before they had a real effect on home cooking. The cans and solder used to seal the cans introduced unnatural tastes into the food. Knowing the food would end up with a strange taste, producers often used lower-grade ingredients, giving consumers even less of a reason to trust food they could not see to begin with.

Canned goods were obviously revolutionary in their ability to stay relatively fresh for a long period of time. Canned foods were revolutionary in a second way, though, one that looked to the future of store-bought food. When they were introduced, all foods were bought by the consumer in bulk—nothing was prepackaged, so the consumer could easily see, smell, and even taste all the food he or she bought, rejecting anything that did not live up to expectations. This was impossible with canned foods. They had to be bought on faith. In order for canned foods to become accepted, their quality needed to be guaranteed or, at the very least, higher than that of the noncanned variety.

An early canned-food success was sweetened condensed milk, developed by Gail Borden Jr. Borden had worked at numerous jobs during his life, including newspaper editor and surveyor, and he also spent time tinkering and inventing. After the Donner Party tragedy in the mid-1840s, when a group of settlers, stuck in the snow of the Sierra Mountains, had resorted to cannibalism after running out of food, Borden worked on developing new methods of preserving food. He made a meat biscuit from dried meat and flour that was promising enough to be given a special commendation by judges at the 1851 Great Exhibition in London, but not popular enough to actually be picked up for distribution by any company in Britain. On the way back from Britain his ship was hit by storms severe enough that the cows on board, used to supply fresh milk, stopped producing. One baby died as a result.[15]

This seems to have given Borden the impetus to work on canned milk—that, and the fact that he had spent six years of his life and thousands of dollars developing a meat biscuit no one was interested in. Milk was a popular drink, particularly for children, but it could not be canned—the canning process ruined the milk, browning and burning it as it cooked in the can. Borden set about finding a way to can the milk while keeping it looking and tasting like milk.

If you have ever tried to drink sweetened condensed milk, you know that Borden did not quite succeed in his quest. He used a vacuum condensing process already used by the Shakers to preserve fruit—in fact, he used some vacuum pans borrowed from some Shaker friends—and he produced a form of milk that was thick and syrupy sweet, not quite like milk straight from a cow (to be fair, though, the milk that almost all Americans drink today is also nothing like milk straight from a cow).

In 1858 his New York Condensed Milk Company began selling cans of milk door to door, just like most milk was sold in cities back then, and while his product did not look like the milk New York dairies sold, it turned out that this was a blessing for Borden's company. New York City was then in the throes of the "swill milk" controversy, the city's newspapers having revealed that city dairies fed their cows the mash left over from the city's distilleries. The mash was cheap, since it was a by-product of the brewing process, but it had almost no nutritional value, and the milk produced by the cows was thin, watery stuff—so lacking in milkfat that the milk could not be used to make cheese or butter. Borden's canned milk looked like a good alternative to "fresh" milk to many New Yorkers. A few years later sales picked up again with the start of the Civil War, as the government bought canned milk for its troops.[16]

By this time consumers had the ability to can foods at home, but the process was considerably more complex than today because the combination of wide-mouth glass bottles and rubberized lids was still in the future. One cookbook from 1861 gave instructions for canning apples in either a tin can or a corked glass bottle. For the metal can the cook should fill the can with apples, seal it tight, and then poke a small hole in the top of the can with an awl. Water is added to the hole, enough so that the can would be filled when heated in the water bath (when the apples would expand with the heat), at which point the cook should drop liquid solder onto the hole, sealing the can. If the seal is perfect, the ends of the can will shrink when cooled, in a process similar to the "popping" sound home canners know to listen for; if the seal is not perfect, it "will certainly burst the can," as the author of the cookbook explained. The process for canning in a bottle is simpler, since the bottle is sealed once, before heating, with a cork. Hot air pushes out past the cork during the heating phase, while the cooling phase pulls the cork tighter into the bottle. [17]

Other methods of preserving foods had been developed, although perhaps not very successfully. Some Civil War soldiers reported that a block of what was called desiccated vegetables sometimes appeared with their rations. As one veteran recalled, it was "an ounce in weight and two or three inches cube of a sheet or block of vegetables . . . apparently kiln-dried."[18] When soaked in water it expanded enormously and appeared to consist of "layers of cabbage leaves and turnip tops stratified with layers of sliced carrots, turnips, parsnips, a bare suggestion of onions,—they were too valuable to waste in this compound,—and some other among known vegetable quantities, with a large residuum of insoluble and insolvable material which appeared to play the part of warp to the fabric, but which defied the powers of the analyst to give it a name."[19] Wars tend to spur the development of new methods of food preservation because militaries need enormous amounts of food and are far more concerned with keeping soldiers alive than they are with providing palatable food, and this concoction of dried vegetables—the veteran notes that it was often referred to as "desecrated vegetables"—is no exception.

The number of cookbooks available to American cooks increased during the 1800s, although the trickle of cookbooks published then was nothing like the torrent of today. Still, cooks had more choices as the century wore on. The middle class grew over time, and these people had money to spend on books, including cookbooks.

Some of these volumes were straightforward cookbooks. Mary Randolph's *The Virginia Housewife*, from 1824, simply contains recipes grouped by the categories that are familiar today, including beef, sauces, and vegetable dishes. The book is unusual in that it was explicitly regional, containing a state in the name of the book, but otherwise the contents, and many of the recipes, would be familiar to cooks today.

A second kind of book became popular during the 1800s, largely because of changes taking place in society that directly involved the middle class. This was a book that was something of an all-around guidebook to managing a home, one that usually included recipes but also had advice on such topics as managing servants, laying out a kitchen, and shopping for groceries (or "marketing," as the activity was then called).

This type of book became popular because some parts of society were changing. The middle class, still small by today's standards, was growing and becoming influential. As families moved up and into the middle class, they found that not only could they afford to have servants but they were also expected to have servants. Unfortunately, many newlywed wives had little to no experience in either managing servants or running a household, and these women were the audience for a book that told them everything about their new jobs.

One part of this job was shopping. In 1867 Thomas De Voe published *The Market Assistant*, a guide to, as the extended title described, "Every Article of Human Food Sold in the Public Markets of the Cities of New York, Boston, Philadelphia, and Brooklyn." Part of the reason he wrote the book was to aid women with servants who were tasked with shopping for food. As he described it, fifty years previously (that is, the 1820s and 1830s), the shoppers at the markets were the active heads of the household, either retired men or younger housewives whose husbands worked jobs outside the house. At daybreak the older men moved through the markets, searching for the best cuts of meat and freshest fruits and vegetables available from the vendors. Later in the day came the housewives, each of whom "would not trust anybody but herself to select a fine young turkey, or a pair of chickens or ducks."[20] These two groups, the older men and the housewives, both had a considerable amount of experience in selecting food at the market. By the 1860s, though, De Voe complained, "We now find many heads of families who never visit the public markets, who are either supplied through the butcher or other dealers in our markets, or by their stewards or other servants . . . of course, [those buyers] purchase the various articles of those who will give them the largest percentages" (that is, they buy their goods from those who will give them the largest kickback).[21] De Voe wrote his book as a guide for those who did not know much about buying at a public market but who did not want to simply trust others to do it for them. This explains the title of the book: a market assistant was someone hired to purchase food at the market.

Many of these guidebooks for new housekeepers were written in a straightforward manner, filled with advice for working with servants or managing a house. Many others, though, also promoted a particular worldview when it came to women's roles. The roles for women were not new, focused on tending to the home and family, although the ideology behind the roles was new.

The new ideology came about, in part, because the location where many men worked changed during the 1800s. At the beginning of the period women generally worked in the home or close to it: they cleaned the house, they tended the garden, they gathered eggs from chickens in the coop. Men generally worked outside the house, in the fields or in a workshop in an outbuilding, and they took care of larger animals. These locations were physically in close proximity. The chickens the women tended might be at the end of the same building the horses slept in. The garden butted up against the wheat field. Jobs sometimes moved from one gender to another. Men began the task of slaughtering a hog by killing it, hanging it up while it bled, and then lowering it into scalding hot water, but as the meat was cut from the animal it was brought to the women, who were in charge of preserving the food. Men harvested raw cotton and gave it to women, who spun it into thread, wove the thread into cloth, and cut and sewed the cloth into clothing.

During the 1800s, though, more and more men took jobs away from the home entirely. They worked at a factory or a store miles away, and after leaving in the morning they did not return until late afternoon or evening. Their working life was physically far from the home.

This very real distance caused a shift in ideas about the proper places for men and women, and what those places were like. Men worked away from the home in the often cutthroat business world, a world where poor decisions could mean debt and ruin for the family. Women worked in the home, but because the outside world was hectic and dangerous, the home, which, logically, should be the opposite of the outside world, became a safe haven, a calm island for the harried husband to return to after a difficult day at work.

Ideologies can provide a justification for doing things long after the need to do those things has disappeared, and to some extent the ideology espoused by the Victorians did just this. In the 1700s the family as an economic unit made sense, as everyone in the family had a role to play, and the loss of any of those people, even a ten-year-old child, could cause economic problems for the family as a whole. All family members older than a handful of years could play a part in helping out around the farm. In the 1800s, with the shift to having the father of the house as the main, or often only, breadwinner for the family, those old roles did not make quite so much sense. If there was no work for children to do, what were they to do with their time? Could most of the household tasks, those traditionally done by the woman of the house, be performed by someone else? Why did she have to be in charge of all the cooking, cleaning, and all those other tasks?

The Victorians responded to all of these questions with an ideology that affirmed, over and over, the importance of the woman of the house. As the house lost its productive capacity, as it no longer was the place where things were routinely made, it gained a new prominence in Victorian ideology: it became the central heart of the family, and the woman of the house was the person in charge of it. This was a big job.

A single book from the time period, *The American Woman's Home*, provides a good example of this Victorian ideology in action. Catharine Beecher and Harriet Beecher Stowe published this book in 1869. Harriet had previously written *Uncle Tom's Cabin*, an anti-slavery novel that quickly became the most popular book in America after the Bible. *The American Woman's Home* was an instruction manual for taking care of a home, five hundred pages of detailed advice that ranged in topics from cooking and cleaning to taking care of children and managing servants.

To the modern reader, two things are striking about *The American Woman's Home*. First, the book contains a lot of science, some of which is couched in language that is decidedly old-fashioned but was likely cutting-edge for its time. In a chapter on ventilation, the reader is informed that people breathe about twenty times per minute, pulling in half a pint of air with each breath, consuming "one hogshead of air every hour. The membrane that lines the multitudinous air-cells of the lungs in which the capillaries are, should it be united in one sheet, would cover the floor of a room twelve feet square."[22] A chapter on the importance of a healthy home includes illustrations of the lungs, capillaries, and different parts of the heart. These drawings are accompanied by detailed descriptions of just how blood circulates through the body, how air makes its way into the bloodstream, and how carbon dioxide is expelled from the lungs. The book's authors seem to consider this last gas extremely dangerous; pages and pages are devoted to warnings that unventilated houses could lead to the death of family members from what the book refers to as "carbonic acid." The science included in the book does not simply spring from the authors' minds; they bolster their writing by referring to experts like "Johnson, a celebrated writer on agricultural chemistry" or "Miss Ann Preston, one of the most refined as well as talented and learned female physicians."[23]

These examples point to the second striking aspect of *The American Woman's Home*: its topics are extremely wide ranging. The traditional areas of cooking, cleaning, and childcare are addressed, but also gardening, caring for animals like milk cows and geese, and constructing organizing systems. The detail on some topics is impressive. A chapter on the importance of early rising includes a discussion of artificial light, which the authors are firmly against: gaslight is "unhealthful" while coal light is "poisonous."[24] A chapter on fires includes information for burning wood, coal, oil, gas, kerosene, and candles.

By naming the book *The American Woman's Home*, the book's authors make clear that all of this is woman's responsibility, and the combination of the science with the variety of topics must have made being a Victorian homemaker a daunting task. In the same way the owner of a factory was ultimately responsible for everything that happened at the factory, from worker productivity to paying salaries to making sure the toilets worked, a homemaker was responsible for everything that happened within or around the home. In a section on food the authors wrote, "The person who decides what shall be the food and drink of a family, and the modes of its preparation, is the one who decides, to a greater or less extent, what shall be the health of that family."[25]

According to the book, potential dangers to the family were extreme and varied. The authors warned of children who were fed "sugar and molasses, cakes and candies . . . thus weakening their constitutions, and inducing fevers, colds, and many other diseases."[26] Coffee and tea were a "cause of much of the nervous debility and suffering endured by American women; and relinquishing them would save an immense amount of such suffering."[27] Card playing and novel reading were also dangerous. The authors advised that reputable people, such as "editors, clergymen, and teachers," should read widely so as to know the good and the dangerous novels, although this in itself was dangerous—these people would be like "physicians . . . visit[ing] infected districts."[28]

Danger lurked almost everywhere, and the woman of the house was responsible for watching out for it, in large part because the man's responsibility had shifted to only include his work life. This was a major change. Various types of danger, resulting in death or maiming, had existed long before this change had come along, but the responsibility had not hung solely around the woman's neck. Before the change, boys as young as seven or eight went off with their fathers to help as best they could, and, since much of the work revolved around large animals, the threat of being trampled by a cow or horse was very real. The responsibility for watching boys was the father's. Now, with the father working away from home, the responsibility lay with the mother, and while the house may not have been quite as dangerous as the farm, real dangers were still present.

Mother did have some help, though, if she were upper or middle class, and this Victorian ideology assumed she was. This help came from the working class, since it supplied the servants who helped the mother cook, clean, and take care of the house. Far from being helpful, though, the literature of the time portrayed servants as an endless source of frustration. The Beecher sisters, for example, characterized them as "to a large extent thriftless, ignorant, and unscrupulous."[29]

The frustration came from a number of sources. The servants were often young women who were inexperienced and immature, and who might be working their first job. Many servants were recent immigrants to the United States with no experience in many of the jobs required of them, such as managing cookstoves or cooking American foods. There was an overall shortage of good workers, so moving from one position to another in quick succession was not an unusual experience for many servants, even if having a series of short-term servants was exasperating for an employer.

The constant complaints about servants, while reflections of reality, also served to enhance a woman's status in two ways. First, a woman's complaints about household servants surely mirrored her husband's complaints about workers in the business world. Even if he did not manage employees, he likely worked with people who were also sometimes lazy, inexperienced, and prone to taking a quick succession of short-term jobs. As the 1800s progressed, the world of business became the fascination of America, and even though the Victorian home was supposed to be a haven away from the outside world, a bit of the sheen of the problems of the outside world may have helped women's status.

A second way the complaints about servants could enhance a woman's status was by reinforcing the idea that she was indispensable to the functioning of the household. Although the family might be financially successful enough to afford servants to do most of the work of the house, those servants could never replace the woman of the house, since, as women constantly complained, the servants were often untrustworthy and prone to running off and getting other employment. Her role as mistress of the household was safe.

In the early to mid-1800s, places to eat away from home remained exactly that: places to eat that were not home. Boarding houses, hotels, taverns, and restaurants were generally seen as options for people who, for one reason or another, could not eat at home.

The quality of the eating experience varied considerably, largely because the quality of the business varied considerably. In more sparsely settled parts of the country, travelers routinely ate and bedded down at whichever cabin or lean-to appeared at midday or sundown—both travelers and homesteaders seem to have had the expectation that all comers would be accepted, although not for free. Sometimes travelers ate whatever was available, and sometimes special food might be procured. One traveler reported eating salted meat at one house and added, irritated, that "they had no fresh [meat] 'unless we would wait *till they killed a pig*'" (emphasis in the original). [30]

Other places offered a much higher-quality experience, particularly at hotels in larger towns and cities. One visitor to a large hotel in Terre Haute, Indiana, in the 1850s reported that roast beef was always served at the dinner meal, along with, usually, "chicken pie, veal pie, beef steaks, roast lamb, veal and mutton cutlets, boiled ham, pigeons, roasted veal or roast pork." Peas and beans, squash, hominy, sweet potatoes, and ears of corn were sometimes served, and pie of one sort or another was usually served for dessert, along with ice cream and "cholera bombs," which was another name for watermelon at a time when many people thought cholera was contracted by eating infected food.[31]

The same traveler reprinted the bill of fare from a hotel in Cincinnati, Ohio, at a time when the city was quite prosperous (it was often called "Porkopolis" because it was a center for pork production for the region). The hotel was large, and the traveler counted one hundred people in the dining room at the same time. The meal was the noonday meal, which at that time was the largest of the day. The bill of fare includes fourteen entrees, another fourteen side dishes, and a variety of soups, vegetables, pastries, and desserts.[32]

Hotels usually had an attached restaurant because rooms were rented on what was called the American plan, where the room came with three meals a day. The European plan, rare in America, charged residents only for the room so that they could pay extra to eat in the hotel's restaurant or dine somewhere else. The ubiquity of the American plan meant that residents who paid for meals, regardless of whether they actually consumed them, subsidized the restaurants. Later in the 1800s this subsidization would result in hotel restaurants that were some of the most luxurious in the country—the Waldorf-Astoria in New York City, for example, regularly hosted visiting royalty and put on an annual horse show.[33] The American plan resulted in less of a demand for independent restaurants from travelers, who were already paying for three meals a day at their hotel.

By the mid-1800s, beyond the hotel restaurants there were only two types of real options for those dining out. The first was establishments that catered to working men who could not go home for the midday meal. These places were only open during the middle of the day and were exclusively focused on serving men. One notable aspect of those places was their relative equality: diners sat shoulder to shoulder at long tables while they ate, a businessman seated next to a ditch digger. The food was usually not very good, but it was quick and readily available.[34] The second option for diners was restaurants that served wealthier patrons. These places were open in the evening and were very respectable, but they were too expensive for any but the wealthy to dine at more than once a month or so. As will be explored in the next chapter, supper for two could easily cost a member of the middle class an entire week's wages. Even for those who could afford them, the fact was that there were not very many upper-class restaurants to choose from. In the 1880s New York City was a center for both wealth and population in this country, but it still had barely more than a handful of restaurants where upper-class families could spend their evenings.[35]

Neither of these options was realistic for members of the working or middle classes, who continued to dine at home for the vast majority of their meals. To a certain extent, this was a chicken-and-egg problem. There were no good options for eating out, so few people ate out, but so long as people did not eat out there would be no good options. This would begin to change in the 1870s, but until then, dining in was the only option many people had.

By the late 1800s, then, America had a food distribution system that was beginning to reach across the rapidly expanding country. Farmers were becoming distant from consumers, which meant that middlemen were taking a bigger and bigger cut of the food dollar, and this distance introduced a certain element of danger for consumers. Cookbooks showed women how to cook new dishes, but many of them also explained to women that they were now responsible for all aspects of the home, and therefore for their family's health. Some convenience foods appeared to help women do their job, and the cookstove took cooking off the fireplace floor, but women remained the ones who did all of the cooking, which could still be a long and taxing job.

In the next few decades, though, those women would find more and more help coming from food companies in the form of convenience foods such as canned condensed soups and mixes. They would also get some assistance from a new group of women who were committed to helping women do their job in the most efficient way possible. This was the members of what would eventually be called the home economics movement, who were there to help women but at the same time to let them know that a woman's proper place was in the home, cooking and cleaning and doing all the jobs women had been doing a hundred years before.

3

THE LATE 1800S THROUGH 1945

In the few years spanning the turn of the twentieth century, a group of women in Boston worked to answer the question of which was more cost effective: making food at home or having it delivered, fully prepared, from a caterer or restaurant. The women were with the Association of Collegiate Alumnae, and their study was conducted at the School of Housekeeping, a facility connected to the Women's Educational and Industrial Union of Boston. The study, which they worked on periodically for three years, was eventually published in the *Labor Bulletin of the Commonwealth of Massachusetts*, and the study's assumptions and conclusions illuminate many of the trends surrounding home cooking at the turn of the century.

The authors, in introducing the study, referred to the age-old servant problem, the idea that most servants were not dependable, skilled, or experienced, to the point that employing a servant ended up being more trouble than just doing the work oneself. The authors noted that this problem had been more or less solved in the area of laundry work, not because servants were better at laundry than they were at other tasks but because the trend for laundry work was to simply send it out to be done by someone else. Since this had worked for laundry, why could it not be done for cooking? The authors wanted to see.

They approached the problem from a few different directions. One approach was to compare the cost of making specific foods at home against buying those foods already prepared. Calculating the cost of the purchased food was easy—it was simply what one paid for the food. Calculating the cost of homemade food, though, was much more difficult.

The cost of the raw, unprepared food ingredients was fairly straight-forward. When one attempted to calculate the other costs involved with making food, though, things became complicated very quickly. Consider the cost of fuel involved with cooking. At that time three fuels dominated the cooking landscape: coal, oil, and (a newcomer) gas. Coal was popu-lar, but it took time to make a coal fire hotter or to cool it down, and coal stoves required a considerable amount of time to clean every week. Oil was an easier fuel to use, and gas was the easiest of all, since the fire could be controlled with a knob. But how should fuel cost be calculated? Coal-burning cookstoves were made to perform a multitude of tasks with only a single fire. Cooks routinely prepared several dishes at once, using one fire to simmer soup, roast a chicken, and warm bread dough to rise. That fire was sometimes also a primary method of warming a part of the house. How, then, could the fuel cost involved in just simmering the soup be calculated? Determining the labor cost was also tricky. The solidly middle-class authors had no doubt that the cook would be a hired servant, but they had no guidance on how much that person might be paid, since labor statistics were still in their infancy (that is, they knew how much they might pay a cook, but not what a state, or national, average was). The type of pay the cook received further complicated matters. Many cooks were paid by the week, not by the hour, so calculating just what fraction of that pay went into preparing a roast, or baking a cake, was almost beyond the ability of the authors of the report. In order to make the report, they finally settled on a labor cost of eight-and-a-half cents per hour of cooking.

In addition to comparing the costs of buying and cooking specific foods in isolation, the authors of the report also compared the costs in-volved with buying and preparing three meals for three full days. In November 1899, and then again in May 1901, the women first purchased enough prepared food to serve a family (eight to ten people in 1899, fifteen people in 1901) three meals a day, and then, a week later, they made all three meals in a kitchen.

The women's various experiments revealed three things. First, it was cheaper to make the food at home than it was to prepare it, although the difference was less in 1901 than it had been in 1899. In 1899 buying prepared food was about 55 percent more expensive, while two years later it was only 30 percent more expensive. The authors attributed the change to a slight drop in the price of prepared food and hoped that the trend would continue as prepared foods became more and more popular.

A second thing the studies showed was that it was, in fact, possible to purchase a fairly wide variety of prepared foods, enough to feed a large family different foods throughout the course of several days. Bakeries sold a wide variety of baked goods. Grocers stocked "crackers, biscuits, sweet cakes and cookies which are ready for use. Besides canned meats many grocers sell freshly-cooked ham, sliced and ready to serve." Caterers were another source of prepared foods, offering "freshly-cooked meats of all kinds, breads, rolls, plain and fancy cakes, pastry, puddings, jellies, soups, salads, sauces, both hot and cold, croquettes and cutlets, and so on through a long list of articles which furnish sufficient variety to supply any table."[1]

A final conclusion of the report was that, while it was more expensive, purchasing prepared food was faster and required less labor than making it oneself. This, of course, has always been the trade-off between making food and buying it already prepared.

The results of the tests are frankly not very surprising. What is interesting, though, are some assumptions surrounding the tests and the rather obvious desires of the study's authors regarding the conclusions.

The experiments were inherently urban based. In determining the cost of the food, there was no discussion of growing one's own food; it would obviously have to be purchased from a store. Of course, only an urban area could supply restaurants or caterers to purchase prepared food from, so that portion of the study had to assume an urban location. Although the prepared foods were made outside the home, there was no discussion of the possibility of consuming the food anywhere other than the home. Even if the prepared foods came from a restaurant, there was no consideration of eating at the restaurant (cleanup costs were calculated for both store-bought and homemade foods). For most people, meals were only eaten outside the home when the occasion required it, such as when traveling or working during the day; restaurants were not places where entire families took their meals if they could help it.

Everyone associated with the experiments seems to have initially assumed that home-cooked food would always taste better than that prepared outside the home. "It was a decided surprise to the family [that is, the people assigned to eat the food] to find that the food cooked outside of the house was so good," wrote the authors. "The meats in particular were very well cooked. Although they had to be re-heated they were not dried or toughened. The soups, too, were extremely good. Tea and coffee and a few other things were much better when made at home. But while admitting that the articles from outside were good the majority of the family preferred the home cooking."[2]

In a section of the study that analyzed cost differences between making bread at home and buying it from the bakery (which concluded that it was cheaper to make at home), the authors seem to assume that store-bought bread was not just more expensive but also not as good. In describing why store-bought bread was not as good, the authors employ a curious kind of logic that blames both the consumer and the baker for the situation, a way of thinking that was typical of the time period. "There is no common and accepted 'standard' of what really good bread is," the authors wrote, "and naturally, in the absence of such a standard," bakers would make whatever was cheapest and easiest for them to produce.[3] This situation would continue until consumers pressured bakers to make better bread; therefore, it was the responsibility of consumers to improve the quality of store-bought bread.

A note about this lack of standards: Americans' ability to talk about food in terms of good or bad flavors and textures, and to judge food, would only develop in the last part of the twentieth century, particularly with the rise of shows like *Top Chef* and other cooking competition shows. Until then, our judgment of food was limited to technological standards. The home economists of the early twentieth century, who would quickly become a dominant force in American cooking, judged food almost solely by its nutritional content and its appearance; taste and flavor were rarely discussed. The Duncan Hines series of restaurant guides that were popular at midcentury judged restaurants by their cleanliness and how the food looked. This dismissal of the taste of food in part helps explain the increasing popularity of processed foods during the twentieth century.

Back to analyzing the Boston study. The results of the experiments were clearly disappointing to the study's authors. Rather than simply accept the results, the authors argue that there are situations in which it might be better to buy prepared food than to make it. In doing so, they detail a possible future in which home cooking would eventually fade away. In a section that compared the costs of buying precooked meat against cooking it at home, the authors concluded that it was cheaper to make it at home, but they asked, "Might there not be conditions under which it would be as cheap to have it done outside? For example, the time of the housekeeper [which here refers to the woman of the house, not hired help] might be spent in teaching, writing, or otherwise in earning money which would exceed the increased expense of ready cooked food. It would then be economy for her to devote her time to these more remunerative occupations, and to supply her table with ready cooked food."[4] This seems fair enough, as it essentially anticipates women in the workplace, earning money but having far less time at home for cooking. The report then takes that logic to a radical conclusion. "If enough food could be cooked outside [the house], might it not be possible to do away with the cooking equipment in the house?" If the stove, icebox, sink, and other cooking equipment were removed from the kitchen, then there would be no need to employ a cook, no cook to feed, no fuel to burn in cooking, and no wasted food, all of which would be additional cost savings. There would, in fact, be no need for a kitchen, as "even the room itself would be available for other purposes." The report then summed up this line of reasoning: "Hence, by saving equipment, service, fuel, space, and food, might not the extra output for ready-cooked articles be more than counterbalanced? When arrangements for delivering food hot and ready to serve are perfected, it may be found entirely feasible to adopt this method of providing for the family table, and one feature of the domestic problem will be solved."[5]

These women, writing at the turn of the twentieth century, predicted a future in which women worked for money and balanced the time they used and the money they earned by buying the family's food, precooked, from outside sources, which they then had delivered to the home. This home had a dining room but no kitchen—an unnecessary requirement, since nothing was actually cooked in the home. Writing at that time, this vision of the future surely must have seemed to have been a distinct possibility. It never came to pass, of course, not because of events that came later but because of cultural and business trends that were rising at just the moment the women prepared their report.

Before looking at those trends, though, it may be helpful to look at just how much had changed for women during the nineteenth century, particularly when it came to the work they did in the home. In the early 1800s the types of work women did were the same as those done by their mothers and grandmothers, and it was necessary work—the work men and women did to support the household was done by them because there was no one else to do it. Much of women's work was the same work they would be responsible for in 1900, such as cooking, cleaning, and taking care of the children, but there were other responsibilities as well. They functioned as a nurse and doctor for the family, having a store of medical knowledge that included how to treat various ailments and how to make medicines. To do this, they kept a garden where they planted medicinal herbs alongside peas and carrots. Other jobs women performed in the early nineteenth century included making clothes, which in those days started with making the cloth the clothes would be made from. They managed the dairy, making sure the milk cow was milked regularly and converting that milk into butter and cheese as needed, and they gathered eggs from the chickens. All of this kept the average woman, as might be expected, quite busy.

As the Industrial Revolution caught fire in the United States, and as more and more Americans lived in urban environments, women began to shed some these functions. An early job women gave up was making cloth. The process was long, involved, and complicated, requiring tools like spinning wheels and looms and, of course, access to a raw material like cotton, wool, or flax. The first textile factories were constructed in the United States in the first few decades of the nineteenth century using technology borrowed from Great Britain, who was far ahead of America in developing innovative technology. The number of American factories boomed during a trade embargo with Britain, when British-made products were hard to get, and this resulted in an abundance of cheap American cloth—so cheap, in fact, that many women, particularly in the eastern United States, stopped making their own cloth. Why spend weeks making homespun when store-bought cloth was pennies a bolt?

Giving up making cloth was likely not a difficult decision for women—it was a fairly simple trade of a little money for a lot of time and effort they would no longer have to expend. Giving up the dairy and chickens took more time and involved the transition to urban living, where keeping milk cows and chickens became impossible. Giving up the function of doctor and nurse took even more time and today is not completely gone, as in many families it is the woman who is expected to take care of sick children (or at least to be able to read symptoms and know treatments).

One aspect of medical knowledge women gave up deserves a closer look in the context of this book, since it is almost like cooking: the task of making medicines. In the early 1800s women were responsible for making medicines to treat sick family members, but by 1900 this was gone, as medicines were usually purchased from drug stores or other businesses.

This was not because store-bought medicines were more effective than those made at home. A revolution in medicine took place in the early twentieth century as drugs based on chemical compounds replaced older formulas based on biological components such as herbs, and the new drugs were both much more effective and impossible to make at home. That revolution took place after 1900. Until then, store-bought medicines were often based on older home remedies.

This is not to say that store-bought remedies were just like homemade remedies, only that they were generally no more effective. The patent medicines that became popular during the nineteenth century were notorious by the beginning of the twentieth century due to their ingredients and their outrageous claims. Patent medicines could be purchased that promised to cure polio, tuberculosis, cancer, and any other disease in existence. Mostly, they were good at pain relief. The drugs often contained high percentages of alcohol, chloroform, cocaine, or opium derivatives. Many women were addicted to patent medicines, since it was improper for women to drink alcohol but consuming medicines was fine. Other than pain relief, patent medicines were no more effective than home remedies, although they could pack a powerful wallop.

The home remedies of the time were usually fairly simple, and the recipes existed as something of a subset of cooking recipes. The connection between cooking and medicinal remedies seems to have been fairly clear in the 1800s, as cookbooks routinely included a chapter on cooking for the sick and infirm, and the chapter usually included some medicinal remedies as well. An example of one of these recipes comes from an 1869 cookbook that included a recipe for a throat-soothing Elecampane and Hoarhound Syrup. "Put a pint of hoarhound in a quart of water, and let it draw by the fire," the author wrote, followed by the instruction to "put a tea-cupful of dried elecampane root in a pint of water, cover it close, and let it boil till all the strength is out; strain it and the hoarhound together, and put them to boil with a pound of sugar; when it is a rich syrup, pour it in a pitcher to cool, and bottle it. Take a table-spoonful at a time when the cough is troublesome."[6] There is nothing in the recipe an experienced cook in 1800 could not have handled, and, indeed, that cook could have had a pot of soup simmering on the fire right beside the medicinal concoction.

As food historian William Woys Weaver has pointed out, the recipe for Elecampane and Hoarhound Syrup printed above is most likely a home adaptation of a popular patent medicine from the mid-1800s. As Weaver writes, the cookbook that recipe came from also includes recipes for "Deshler's (Nipple) Salve, Huxham's Bark Tincture, and Warner's Cordial, all adaptations of old patent medicines."[7] In 1869 cookbooks still routinely included medicinal recipes like these, but by 1900 they did not. What changed over the course of a few decades? What made women give up one activity—making medicine—they had done for generations but keep another activity—cooking food—firmly in the home, particularly if the two activities were so similar?

The answer is complicated and involves some factors that were specific to medicine but not to food, but a short answer is that, when it came to medicine, businesses had a definite interest in shifting the production of medicine away from the home and toward the factory or pharmacy. When it came to food, though, business interests were mixed, as some companies needed home cooking to continue while others had an interest in moving it out of the home. In fact, some companies had different divisions that pushed in opposite directions, with some groups working to continue home cooking while others worked to lessen it. The medicine industry did not have this division within itself: all aspects of it had a vested interest in discontinuing the home production of medicine.

There were a number of factors involved in the shift from making medicine to buying it, some of which are directly applicable to the question of why home cooking still exists and some that are not. A few factors that are not applicable, and point to the differences between food and medicine, include the outrageous claims and high pain-killing potency of the patent medicines. Even if they did not cure anything but pain, patent medicines certainly made the consumer feel as if something was happening in a way that homemade medicines just could not match. Store-bought medicines also gained a sheen of respectability from their association with experts, as many patent medicines included a doctor's name in their labels. Moreover, most medicines had a relatively long shelf life. Some were small candies, like lozenges; some were steeped in alcohol, which killed any microbes that tried to grow; others were in powdered form and needed to be mixed with water before administering. A single purchase could last for months. Another difference between food and medicine is that when a medicine is needed, it is usually needed immediately. The sufferer of a toothache, migraine, or severe cough could not wait hours or days for a remedy to steep. Certainly, remedies could and were made in anticipation of cough or flu season, but if a remedy went bad or was rapidly used up, store-bought medicine was a quick and easy replacement.

While the process of making medicine was very similar to the process for making food, there were a few crucial differences between the two activities, and those differences aided medicines in their shift away from being made in the home. One difference was the volume of ingredients required for each process. We consume an enormous amount of food in the course of a year, particularly when compared with how much medicine the average person uses. Shifting the location of food production to outside of the house requires several trips per day to pick up the food (or have it delivered). Because the volume of medicine even the sickest person might consume is so much smaller, shifting the production of medicine to the pharmacy only means the occasional trip to buy medicine. Another difference between food and medicine lies in the nature of the ingredients. Different illnesses require different medicines. One modern author estimated that between two and three hundred medicinal ingredients appeared in home remedy recipes and, since some of those recipes were adopted from medicines originally made by Native Americans, the ingredients could be very specialized, only available in certain locations or at particular times of the year, making them difficult to obtain.[8] It was often just easier to go to the pharmacy to buy a finished medicine for an ailment rather than trying to find a source for an unusual ingredient in a remedy.

Both food and medicine producers used advertising to promote their products, sometimes in the same places. For example, the January 1901 issue of *Good Housekeeping* included advertisements from both food and medicine companies. Hale's Honey of Horehound and Tar, which was "palatable, harmless, and it cures," occupied ad space right alongside Diamond Condensed Soups (which were "a rare treat"). Vapo-Cresolene, a competitor to Vicks VapoRub, both cured and prevented "Bronchitis, Influenza, Measles, Catarrh, Coughs, Scarlet Fever, and other contagious diseases," at least according to the advertisement (advertisements like this would result in the 1906 Pure Food and Drug Act). That ad appeared only a few pages after one for Nestlé's Food, which was an early baby food, and Liebig Company's Extract of Beef. [9]

While both food and medicine producers advertised widely in local and national media, there was a crucial difference in just what was advertised. Medicine producers always advertised a finished product, one that could be bought, as is, at a pharmacy, and used with minimal preparation. Food producers, however, advertised both finished (or nearly finished) products and products intended to be used as ingredients in cooking. The Nestlé's baby food was a nearly finished product, requiring only the addition of water. But the magazine also included advertisements for cocoa and gelatin, both products that cannot be used in their unfinished state. In this way food producers promoted two different views of food: food could be purchased and used "as is" from a store, but it could also be used as an ingredient in home cooking. Food companies' overall attitude toward cooking from scratch since the late nineteenth century has been ambivalent. Convenience foods like condensed soups and pancake mixes usually have higher margins than commodities like flour or oranges, and so the companies would rather just sell the convenience foods, but basic commodities bring in a considerable amount of money, and so the food companies still sell those as well.

The medicine companies never had this ambivalence: they sold medicine, not ingredients for medicine, so all of their advertising revolved around persuading people to buy a finished product, not an ingredient. This was the single message coming from the industry. That the medicine companies never got into the ingredient business probably has to do with how pharmacies functioned at that time, since pharmacies sold many of the ingredients called for in medicinal recipes. As will be described later, grocery stores experienced a change in how they sold food in the early twentieth century as the shopping experience moved from one where clerks physically retrieved all items on a customer's shopping list to one where the shopper herself put her selections in her basket or cart. With the later system customers had to be educated, through advertising, on which brands to purchase at the store. With the earlier system the education focused on the storeowner or manager, who bought particular brands for the store to then sell to the consumer. Educating the consumer was pointless because they had no choice on which brands they would buy; they bought whichever brand the clerk gave to them. Grocery stores switched over to the new system, but pharmacies stuck with the older system when it came to the raw ingredients they sold, so educating the customer on which brand of horehound to buy was useless. They would buy the brand that the pharmacy stocked. However, pharmacies did usually have a variety of finished medicines on sale, so that a magazine advertisement for Hale's Honey of Horehound and Tar would probably result in increased sales at pharmacies that stocked that medicine.

A further difference between food and medicine was the variety of nonfood companies that relied on the continuation of home cooking. These companies ranged from those that made kitchen cabinets and tables to appliance producers (a growing field as more and more houses were wired for electricity) to those that made small gadgets such as egg beaters or even spatulas. The kitchen was a separate room of the house, one that required different furniture and fixtures than other rooms, and many industries had an ongoing interest in continuing its existence. There was no equivalent in the world of medicine. Making medicines at home required no specialized equipment or tools, so no industry developed around supplying those to consumers, and no industry existed to continue to explain to consumers just why they should continue to make medicine at home.

In the late nineteenth century a new advocacy group formed that would have an enormous effect on ideas about home cooking: the home economists. What the home economists did will be explored more fully below, but one of their main goals was to professionalize housewives. The home economists did not want to move women out of the house, into a professional job; rather, they wanted housewives to approach their work like their husbands approached theirs, with an emphasis on efficiency and expert knowledge. The home economists' world was centered on the home and family, and they derived quite a bit of power from this connection by arguing that their focus was the basis for society. In their work they focused on the traditional women's tasks such as cooking, cleaning, and taking care of children, all of which, they argued, was squarely within a woman's sphere of responsibility.

Their attitudes about medicine were a bit more complicated. An example of the home economists' approach to medicine can be seen in an article from the April 1903 issue of the *Home Science Monthly* titled "Nursing in Mumps and Chicken-pox." These were two common childhood diseases at the time, and the author, who had a master's degree in nursing, discussed how to handle children afflicted with the diseases.

Much of the article is concerned with the care of the sick and discusses topics such as which foods should be prepared for the patient. The recommendations are typical for the time, mostly focusing on nutritious liquids such as beef broth, milk, and raw egg. For mumps the author does not recommend any medicine, but medicines must have been available because she recommends using a curved glass tube for feeding or giving medicine to the patient. The author also does not suggest methods to help treat chicken pox other than advising mothers to reduce the itching for the patient by using talcum powder or petroleum jelly.

The absence of medical advice beyond what was needed to keep the patient from scratching their chicken pox points to an unspoken tenet of the home economics movement: medicine was not within women's sphere of duties. A hundred years before women had been responsible for all aspects of health care, from sitting with the afflicted to cooking and cleaning for them to determining which medicine was best and producing that medicine. By the late nineteenth century, though, anything to do with medicine had shifted away from women to doctors, who, traditionally, were men.

Certainly, women still often determined which medicine to buy and administer, as they continued to do today, particularly when it comes to treating their own children. There is, however, a striking absence of medical advice in much of the women's advice literature before and after the turn of the twentieth century when it comes to specifics on medicine. Books aimed at new homemakers that covered all aspects of keeping a house often had a chapter on caring for the sick, with extensive advice on foods and cleaning and the importance of fresh air, but they rarely had much to offer when it came to medicines. Much of this is because of the internal logic of the home economics movement.

Home economics relied heavily on scientific ideas applied to women's jobs at homes, and by relentlessly promoting a scientific, educated approach to housework, the home economists set themselves up as experts on that topic. This was not unusual for the time period, as practitioners of many different professions worked to establish themselves as experts in their fields. Doctors, lawyers, teachers, accountants, and many other people established professional organizations in the late nineteenth and early twentieth centuries, doing so in order to work toward common goals like standardizing practices or passing laws requiring licensing for those in the profession.

By defining themselves in this way, professionals carved out areas of expertise. Sometimes the claiming of areas of expertise was easy—lawyers, for example, had a fairly simple time defining themselves as experts in the area of law. Doctors had a more difficult time claiming medicine, given that there were many practitioners who could claim health matters. The college-educated practitioners had to contend with folk practitioners who might have apprenticed with an older folk doctor, and the different areas of knowledge in which health workers could further specialize complicated this. Some concentrated on botanical knowledge, advising the afflicted on various plant-based concoctions that could help, while others might use ideas based on electricity coursing through the body.

The struggle over defining just what constituted proper medical knowledge, and what was improper knowledge, continued into the first few decades of the twentieth century, and in the end the college-educated professionals won out. Those doctors were the true experts in medical knowledge, not the folk practitioners, not the nurses who helped the doctors with patient care, and certainly not the housewives who had traditionally tended to the afflicted.

By the time the field of home economics was established in the last years of the nineteenth century, the struggle over medical knowledge was in full swing, but by then housewives were out of the running. Medical knowledge, the home economists seem to have decided, required an education far beyond what they planned for American housewives. Furthermore, when the home economists surveyed the possible topics they could become experts of, medicine was already firmly claimed by others. Claiming medicine would have been a fight they did not want to take on. It was much easier to claim cooking and cleaning and leave the medicine to others.

Thus the home economists, who would become the loudest voice in the early twentieth century in favor of the continuation of American home cooking, were silent when it came to making homemade medicines. Even though the process for making medicine was the same as that for cooking food, and even though there were many medicinal recipes in existence, the production of medicine moved from the home to the factory in the late 1800s, never to move back. In this sense, the medicine makers won a victory that the food producers, even today, have never quite achieved.

The home economics movement lies at the center of cooking in the late nineteenth and early twentieth centuries. It was a movement by and for women that would have an enormous influence on Americans' perceptions of cooking, particularly home cooking, and would affect women's education and their prospects in the world of business, while at the same time vigorously proclaiming that a woman's place was firmly in the home.

In many ways the domestic science movement was very much of its time. It can easily be categorized as one of the many reform movements that began during the Progressive Era, in the fifty years or so between the 1870s and 1920s. While progressive reform movements were as varied as efforts to end political corruption, get women the vote, and enact laws to regulate businesses, the reform movements tended to share some similar goals. There was usually some effort at controlling something, whether it was corrupt politicians, immigrants who had no desire to learn English, or large corporations that put who-knows-what into the foods they sold. There was also an admiration of science and expertise; for example, Progressives wanted educated experts running cities in the same efficient way they managed companies like Standard Oil or Carnegie Steel. Together, these two ideas—control and expertise—transformed American cooking as domestic scientists worked to control the foods Americans cooked and make scientific experts of the women who prepared those foods.

The domestic science movement had its roots in a number of developments in the last few decades of the 1800s. Women were attending college, obtaining a better education than ever before, particularly in the hard sciences, and some of these pioneers had a profound influence on the women who came later. For example, in 1870 a Vassar graduate named Ellen Richards was accepted as a special student to the Massachusetts Institute of Technology—"special" because the school had never before had a female student. She did well enough to set up a "Women's Laboratory" in 1876 in an unused building on the MIT campus, teaching various aspects of chemistry to students, most of whom were training to be teachers. One course she developed was Household Chemistry, where students analyzed the chemical makeup of various foods, observed the reactions that made bread rise, and performed experiments on cleaning products. Richards trained a generation of women who would go on to become domestic scientists.[10]

Scientific advances also spurred the domestic science movement, both in the area of specific scientific research and as a more general science-oriented, rational approach to cooking. The Europeans were at the forefront of nutritional research, although by today's standards nutritional knowledge was quite basic. The era's research showed that food was composed of three basic elements, which were proteins, carbohydrates, and fats, and all foods gave some amount of energy, which was calculated in calories. Beyond this there was not a lot of knowledge, and some of the ideas promoted by domestic scientists, who latched on to this basic nutritional knowledge like grim death, look more than a little odd today. Without knowing about the existence of vitamins or the importance of fiber, a handful of candy, so high in life-giving calories, was considered better to eat than a bowl of fresh fruit or vegetables. The domestic scientists were among the earliest proponents of using scientific research in planning meals, but they were also an early example of a group that publicly asserted more knowledge on the subject than they actually had.

The scientific approach the domestic scientists took to cooking attempted to rationalize and standardize the entire process, which required a considerable amount of effort. The format for recipes was changed so that instead of a simple narrative that described the steps involved in making the dish, recipes began with a list of all necessary ingredients, followed by instructions on using the ingredients. Measurements were standardized so that instead of calling for a lump of butter the size of a walnut, recipes called for a certain number of tablespoons or cups of an ingredient. Of course, this required that measuring tablespoons and cups were always the same size, which meant that, going forward, the cups and spoons used for measuring would not also be used for serving food— a special set of cups and spoons would always stay in the kitchen, used solely for measuring ingredients. Using cups and spoons for measuring ingredients, it should be pointed out, was internationally unusual—the United States is the only country that uses recipes where ingredients are listed by volume rather than weight, a quirk that forced another step in the standardization process. Some ingredients produce the wrong measurement if they are put into the measuring container incorrectly. Flour needs to be sifted before measuring because packing it tightly into the container will result in too much flour, while brown sugar should be tightly packed when measuring.

In their efforts at standardization, the domestic scientists were aided by new technologies and business innovations. First gas and then electric ovens were equipped with a knob that regulated the temperature. No longer did cooks need to judge the heat of the oven by waving a hand into the oven and then adjusting the fire accordingly; now they merely had to turn the knob to the correct number (at first) or to the correct temperature (later). Ingredients also became standardized. Before the late 1800s all cooks kept a yeast "starter" somewhere in the kitchen to use for bread. The starter was a semiliquid concoction of flour, water, and a bit of the previous batch of yeast, which would grow by feeding on the flour and water until the next batch of bread was made. The starter also included various strains of bacteria that affected the taste, texture, and nutritional value of the bread. When it was time to make bread, the cook used most of the starter for the bread but added more flour and water to the container, beginning the cycle all over again. With this setup, some batches of starter had been alive for decades or even longer. The strength of the starter was variable, resulting in bread that might rise quickly or could take more time. In the late 1800s food companies began offering dried yeast to consumers, a product that had two advantages: The dried yeast could sit on the shelf for weeks or months without feeding, without losing its potency (it only had to be mixed in warm water to activate), and the yeast had a certain level of potency. It was standardized. A cook following a recipe could know that, if she used a certain amount of purchased yeast, the bread should rise a certain amount over a given period of time. The standardization of ingredients was a necessary step in standardizing recipes, and the domestic scientists came along at the right time for that to happen.

Both domestic science and home economics, as the movement was later termed, were oddly mislabeled. The two terms give the impression of a movement that focused on all aspects of the home while the reality was that the movement touched briefly on many aspects of the home while concentrating mainly on cooking. An example can be seen in the contents in a leading domestic science magazine, *Home Science Magazine*, from August 1903. Of fifteen articles that were not regular columns, five had titles that directly mentioned food. Several of the remaining ten articles dealt with food in some way, such as "Domestic Science in Scandinavia," which examined cooking schools in Sweden, or "The Equipment of an Ocean Steamer," which included details of the cooking facilities on board. The rest of the articles either dealt with taking care of children or were so ephemeral as to be filler, such as "An Old Diary with a Modern Theme," in which the author, after looking through one of her journals from decades before, lamented the changing, busy lifestyles of the modern day. In spite of the focus on cooking, domestic scientists continued to pay lip service to the other home-oriented topics, because by doing so they could claim that all areas of the home lay within their domain.

This focus on cooking came from the fact that so many early practitioners had entered domestic science through cooking school. Cooking schools lay at the intersection of two careers that were then readily available for women, cooking and teaching (cooking schools often had specific courses for women who were going to teach cooking themselves). Of the two careers, teaching was the more desirable, since it was a profession, whereas a cook was a servant. However, cooking was also seen as the duty of all housewives (or at least those without servants), so attending cooking school prepared a young woman to teach cooking in her professional life and also to cook at home for her family.

Cooking was also a desirable focus for domestic scientists because it could be so, well, scientific. European, and then American, researchers had made charts of individual foods that showed how much protein, carbohydrate, fats, and calories were in every conceivable type of food, and also how long it took to digest those foods. These were hard, scientific numbers that domestic scientists loved to repeat and analyze in magazine articles and books. The other home-related topics must have appeared quite mundane and pedestrian in comparison. Sewing had not changed much since the introduction of the sewing machine, although the ready-to-wear market, which was created with the need to outfit hundreds of thousands of soldiers quickly during the Civil War, was eating into the old necessity of making one's own clothes. Medicinal knowledge had shifted from the women themselves, in the mid-1800s, to doctors. Women's magazines contained a steady stream of articles on the topic of taking care of sick children, articles that were usually focused on a particular disease, but since medicine was still in something of its modern infancy, the advice was often simplistic. A 1901 article in *Good Housekeeping* advised caretakers against using any sort of water around a sick person confined to bed, although the author did not explain why. To relieve a patient's pain, "It is heat, not moisture, that quiets pain," the author wrote, subsequently going on to recommend using hot plates or sand bags to calm pain, or woolen blankets.[11] Regarding other potential home-related topics, cleaning must have seemed to be as much of a chore to write about as it was to do. Keeping household accounts and running a household efficiently were subjects that domestic scientists did seem to enjoy writing about, but one could only go so far with them, and magazine articles and book chapters on those matters tended to focus on advice for young homemakers, since older women usually had their own systems (which were often terribly inefficient, as these writers frequently pointed out).

Many domestic scientists had cut their teeth at cooking school and then went on to a teaching career themselves, one that sometimes included writing cooking articles or books. In the early years of the movement, in the 1890s, domestic science was still not as professionalized as it could be, nor did it reach very far into American society. While many domestic scientists saw their job as just a job, a way for a woman to work outside the home, some perceived it as a true reform movement, one that would change America by changing its eating habits first. In order to do this, the movement needed to reach far more people, but first the leaders of the movement believed they had to professionalize.

A push toward professionalization began at what would be the first in a series of conferences at Lake Placid, New York, in the fall of 1899. The movement had gone by a number of different names by then, domestic science being one of them, but after discussion all previous names were found lacking. The reformers needed something serious and to the point, something that clearly encapsulated what they perceived their focus to be. After more discussion, they settled on "home economics." While the "home" part of this is understandable, since that was clearly their focus, "economics" is a bit puzzling to us today, since economics deals with money and finances, which was not generally the focus of the domestic scientists. However, in 1899 the word *economics* was at the tail end of a redefinition. Until the mid-1800s *economics* meant all aspects of household management, from managing money to directing the hired help to making and cleaning clothes, but after this the meaning gradually shifted to dealing solely with finances. Thus, "home economics" makes sense as a title to replace "domestic science," to some extent, except that the home economists were much more forward looking than backward looking. They may have also chosen that name because it sounded cut-and-dried;

as author Laura Shapiro has pointed out, they wanted to stay as far away from the negative connotations that went along with the drudge work of cooking and cleaning as they could. [12]

Attendees at the Lake Placid conferences worked on plans that ensured that home economics would touch the lives of generations of American women far more than domestic science ever had. A goal of home economics was to professionalize housewives, but the approach had been too scattershot, since they had only trained women who entered cooking schools. What they needed was a way to train all women from the beginning of their educational lives, not just in their adult lives. Their plan, as any reader who took a home economics class in high school can guess, was to teach the subject in public schools.

This had been tried before, and early pioneers had experienced some pushback. A public school in Boston opened the country's first teaching kitchen in 1885, a facility that was utilized as the template for other teaching kitchens in other cities. Although many students approved of the teaching kitchen, some parents complained that their daughters were being trained for jobs as servants, not respectable careers that required a real education. [13]

Cooking for pay was a lower-class profession, and home economists tried to keep as far away from lower-class associations as they possibly could by stressing the science involved with home economics. Consequently, science was often front and center in home economics education. The home, students quickly learned, was a place full of scientific interactions. Bacteria grew on dishtowels, chemicals in foods reacted together to make gasses or smells, kitchens could be designed using scientific methods—why, it seemed that science was everywhere in the home. And not just science but all aspects of academia could be found in a household. The home encompassed everything from economics (it cost money to run a home, after all) to literature (women's magazines were full of fiction about young married couples starting out with their first household) to architecture.

At this point home economics education took something of a strange turn. The home economists wanted to get their curriculum into colleges, but women's colleges like Vassar spurned them—cooking and cleaning were just the sort of topic those colleges had spent most of their existence staying away from. This was, after all, an era when many men did not see the point in allowing women into college if they were just going to quit their jobs when they got married anyway. The last thing the women's colleges wanted to remind people of was the routine housework many people expected their graduates to turn to after marriage.

Coeducational colleges, such as state colleges and universities, were much more open to home economics as a course of study, although, again, there was early pushback against the idea. Classes in cooking or household management might be fine for high school students or for women preparing for a career in cooking, but home economics hardly seemed the equal of literature or engineering as a proper course of study for college students. The home economists pushed their way in by stressing the science involved in home economics. Students used microscopes and Bunsen burners just like biology and chemistry majors did, and they calculated the calorie, protein, and carbohydrate components of a meal just like math majors worked on solving math problems. The only difference between all of those other majors and home economics was the stress on the home. Otherwise, this was real science.

Once college presidents realized this, their eyes were opened to just how useful home economics could be for solving a growing problem at colleges and universities across the country. More and more women were pursuing degrees, to the point that some departments (particularly those in the humanities, like literature) were swamped with female students. Male students, in turn, were moving away from the humanities to other departments, like engineering. The way male college administrators saw it, they needed to do something with all those female students to bring male students back to the humanities. [14]

The usefulness of home economics in solving this problem came from its ubiquitous nature: home economics encompassed every academic discipline. It was chemistry, biology, economics, journalism, and much more, all focused on the home. Thus, if a female student wanted to major in chemistry, she was told to major in home economics with an emphasis in chemistry. If she wanted to major in journalism, she should major in home economics with an emphasis in journalism. The same thing happened for all majors—assuming the student was female. Home economics became the default major for female students.

As might be expected, the introduction of home economics departments at colleges across the country seemed like a godsend to the home economists. Not only was home economics becoming a standard course of study, but enormous numbers of female students were also expressly directed to major in home economics. Finally, the home economists were succeeding in their goal of professionalizing housewives.

And things kept going the way of the home economists. In 1914 Congress passed the Smith-Lever Act, which set aside money for extension work. In 1862 Congress had authorized the creation of land-grant universities (called that because the money came from selling public land) in each state. Among other things, these universities were to establish research-oriented agricultural departments. Schools such as Purdue in Indiana, Cornell in New York, Kansas State University, and Pennsylvania State University were set up and did good research, but, as one might imagine, there was something of a disconnect between the academics who did the research and the farmers who could use the knowledge and technology. The Smith-Lever Act made that connection by creating a system of extension agents whose job was to inform farmers about new research. The act was more far-reaching than simply funneling information from the schools to the farmers; the intention was to help everyone in a farm family. Agriculture agents gave lectures to farmers and ranchers on new research. The 4-H program was set up to help train children and young adults about leadership. And for the farm wife there was, in its first-ever mention in a piece of federal legislation, home economics. The Smith-Lever Act established home economics as, essentially, the female equivalent of farming, that most traditional of American occupations. [15]

This bolstered the reputation of home economics and also boosted the job prospects for home economists. With the Smith-Lever Act each extension office across the country employed a professional home economist to teach farm wives about nutrition and cooking. Food companies, too, employed home economists to work on research into new foods and to create recipes that required those new foods. Women's magazines and newspapers hired home economists to write about women's topics.

All of this made a home economics degree desirable for women. The real value of home economics to the women of the early twentieth century is debatable, though. A degree in home economics was certainly a ticket to the working world, with several possible avenues available. A young college graduate could enter the corporate world by working in the home economics department of a food company, she could be employed by the government by working at an extension office, or she could teach at any one of the many schools that offered home economics classes. As is obvious from our point of view, though, home economics also limited women's choices. A female college student who wanted to study chemistry, biology, or journalism would have had to fight quite hard to stay out of the home economics department (and colleges often made this physically difficult by intentionally placing the department near facilities, like cafeterias or dormitories, that were specifically made for women). Women who worked in the home economics department of a Birdseye or General Mills would have found it nearly impossible to ever transfer or advance out of that department, unless they wanted to become a typist or secretary.

Two ironies were present in the home economics movement as it developed over the course of a few generations. One irony came from the disconnect between the home economics perception of women's work and where home economists ultimately worked. Home economics firmly saw a woman's place as being in the home. An original and continuing goal was to professionalize housewives, but, as it turned out, home economics professionalized a large number of women straight into the workforce. For many women, home economics was a ticket to a paying job, away from the house. Yes, many of them might have quit their jobs when they married or became pregnant, but some of them also moved back to the workforce, in one way or another, once their youngest children were in school.

It should be noted here that home economics, with its focus on food and cooking, did not train women for the job that would seem to be a natural fit for that subject matter: that of a professional chef (that is, someone who cooked in a restaurant; with its orientation on the family and home, home economics did well in preparing a woman to be a paid cook in a household). Just as the waitstaff in restaurants was traditionally female, the cooks at restaurants were usually males who had either worked their way into the position or (at larger establishments) had some cooking school training in cooking dozens or hundreds of dishes during a given mealtime. Restaurant cooking jobs, with a very real gender barrier for women, were in no way a target for home economists, who tended to shy away from a fight like that.

A second irony inherent in the home economics movement lies in the contradiction between the home economists' approach to education and their approach to housework. The home economics curriculum was based on as much hard science as was possible. Majoring in home economics meant taking classes in chemistry, biology, and math—yes, the classes were oriented toward the science of the home, but they were real classes with a scientific background. On their way to professionalizing housework, though, the home economists also made it much easier to be a housewife. By relentlessly focusing on standardization and the simplification of the cooking process, they made cooking much less complicated than it was previously. Recipes spelled out all the information a cook needed, including the temperature of the oven, cooking time, precise instructions for mixing ingredients, and standardized measurements. The amount of knowledge a cook needed was now much less than her grandmother had needed to prepare a given dish. One no longer needed a lifetime of experience—merely a well-written recipe. What this meant was that housewives did not actually need the elaborate training home economics programs were providing.

As a movement that placed itself firmly in the path of almost all women at one point or another in their education, and that just as firmly promoted the idea that a woman's indispensable place was in the home, cooking nutritious meals for her family, home economics changed American cooking. In some ways, though, it is difficult to measure just how much of an effect it had. Part of the reason the home economics movement was popular was because it espoused ideas that were prevalent in American culture in general, particularly that standardization, convenience, and efficiency were good things that should be aggressively worked toward. The converse was also true: since tastes and flavors were not standardized, the home economists usually ignored the question of just how a dish tasted, resulting in striking but questionable-tasting dishes like Perfection Salad, which held a lettuce salad suspended in transparent, unflavored gelatin. Again, the diminishing importance of the taste of food was not something that was specific to the home economists, as the food industry often paid more attention to the appearance and convenience of food than its taste. Since standardization, convenience, and efficiency were some of the dominant ideas of the time, the home economics movement easily increased in popularity. The food companies also picked up these same ideas, and they promoted many of their products using those themes.

It is impossible to write about the home economics movement without also writing about food companies, since, to a certain extent, the companies both absorbed the home economists and eclipsed them. The food companies absorbed the home economists by either outright hiring them, often just out of college, or, for more famous home economists, paying them to be consultants. The companies eclipsed the home economists by spending enormous amounts of money on advertising and promotions and by co-opting the home economists and their message. The co-opting is a bit difficult to analyze because of the complexity of establishing just what the home economics movement was by the 1920s or 1930s. Was the movement the leaders who had established home economics as a discipline in schools across the country a generation before? Was it the academics who continued to teach it? Or was it all the well-educated women who fanned out from colleges year after year, accepting jobs at appliance manufacturers, women's magazines, extension offices, and food companies? At some point any successful movement wins so many members, and becomes so diffuse, that it ceases to be meaningful.

At any rate, another way home economists affected American cooking was by creating recipes. Many, many recipes. The recipes appeared in women's magazines, in both regular columns and specific articles. They also appeared in cookbooks, although in the early twentieth century the number of cookbooks appearing every year was a fraction of that produced today. However, the number of cookbooks was increased by the new phenomena of food companies publishing their own cookbooks as a way to further sales of their products. Home economists, of course, were the ones who ultimately created new recipes or modified existing ones to include a particular food. For example, in 1916 the Postum Cereal Company published *Good Things to Eat from Wellville*, a cookbook that capitalized on a well-known health sanitarium located in the cereal capital of Battle Creek, Michigan. At that time the company offered three products, which were Postum (a dry, wheat-based mix that could be combined with water to make a drink), Grape-Nuts cereal, and Post-Toasties cereal. One of the three products appears in almost every recipe in the book. Most of the recipes were based on existing recipes that called for the addition of a Postum product, although the resulting dish could be a bit strange. The tomato soup recipe directs the cook to add Grape-Nuts to the hot, nearly finished soup, then simmer the soup for a few minutes and serve hot. A "Postum Icing for Cakes" includes two spoonfuls of dry Postum in the icing. Perhaps the most egregious example of just how far recipe writers went to incorporate a specific food product was a recipe for a Grape-Nuts sandwich, which called for a cup of Grape-Nuts, a cup of cream cheese, and a half cup of mayonnaise, all mixed together and spread between two slices of bread.[16]

The twentieth century produced more than its share of odd recipes. Some of this oddness is due to its distance in time from us—our grandparents and great-grandparents simply had different tastes than we do today, so what was normal for them seems strange to us. But some of this is also due to the sheer number of recipes that home economists were called upon to produce on a daily or weekly basis. The Postum cookbook has about 250 recipes spread across all the usual groupings of food, like salads, desserts, and meats and entrees. How does someone write 250 recipes, each of which includes a Postum product? Almost all recipes include only one Postum product, never two or three, pointing to the essential illogic of using the products in this way—they were all packaged foods, originally intended to be mixed with milk or water and eaten as is, never as ingredients in a homemade dish. So how does one create 250 recipes that use one of three Postum products? By either adding them to existing recipes, where the addition would ideally be as innocuous as possible, or creating a truly strange dish like a Grape-Nuts sandwich. If that was a recipe that ended up in the book, one wonders what kind of recipes were considered to be too unusual to be included.

One potential source of recipe ideas the author of the Postum cookbook ignored was foreign dishes. This is not particularly surprising, since mainstream American cookbooks of the early twentieth century largely ignored foreign food, in spite of the millions of immigrants who came to the United States in the late nineteenth and early twentieth centuries. Because foreign dishes use a variety of textures and flavors, some of those recipes might have been useful for a recipe writer trying to hide some crunchy Grape-Nuts within an entree.

In all fairness to the author of the book, at least one use of Post-Toasties (which are like corn flakes), described in the book can still be found in recipes today: using them in place of bread crumbs when making breaded and fried dishes, which results in a different, but still desirable, breading. Sometimes, in their search for something new, the home economists hit on something that was legitimately good and stood the test of time. The classic example of this phenomenon dates from the depths of the Great Depression, and it is a useful example of the interactions between trained home economists and food companies: the creation of the chocolate chip cookie.

The chocolate chip cookie was invented during the 1930s at the Toll House Inn in Whitman, Massachusetts. While the name of the inn, apart from it being a part of the name of the cookie recipe, is almost unknown today, at the time it was, if not nationally known, at least regionally well known. Kenneth and Ruth Wakefield had purchased the place in the 1920s and then built it into a successful restaurant and hotel. A few decades later Duncan Hines, who originally became famous by writing a restaurant guide for travelers, called the inn "one of the outstanding places in the country and . . . a special favorite of mine."[17]

There are several stories of the cookie's creation, mainly because the cookie has factored heavily in advertising from Nestlé in the decades since the creation. One version of the story, taken from Nestlé's website, describes the development as a lucky accident. Existing recipes for chocolate cookies required melted chocolate to be added to the mix, but Ruth Wakefield, who was in a hurry one day, simply added chopped-up bits of chocolate, apparently expecting the chocolate to melt while the cookies baked and then incorporate itself into the dough. Obviously, this did not happen—the chips softened but never really incorporated themselves into the dough, instead staying recognizable as bits of chocolate. The chocolate chip cookie, originally named after the Toll House, was born.[18]

This is a nice story, but it leaves out important pieces of information. Wakefield was a trained home economist who had been sent bars of chocolate specifically because Nestlé was looking for a new recipe to use in promoting its chocolate.[19] The invention of the cookie was not an accident, but rather the result of work by Wakefield in developing a recipe for Nestlé. The company, for its part, reciprocated by buying the recipe and incorporating the name of Wakefield's inn into both the name of the cookie and the name of the chocolate chip product.

The cookie that Wakefield developed does, in fact, appear to have been a brand new type of cookie. Adding bits of chocolate to a cookie recipe seems obvious in retrospect, but there do not seem to have been previous cookie recipes that required the cook to add bits of chocolate to cookie dough. Chocolate cookie recipes published before the 1930s always required the cook to add melted chocolate to the dough. The fact that Wakefield's new cookie used Nestlé's semisweet chocolate was no coincidence, since that chocolate was newly formulated. As a newsletter produced in 1941 by Nestlé's Semi-Sweet Chocolate Department put it, "In the past it was only possible to use the old fashioned bitter type of cooking chocolate. The process of preparing this chocolate for cooking or baking has always been associated with sticky fingers and messy pots and pans." The author went on to point out that "the new modern method of utilizing this chocolate is to add Semi-Sweet Chocolate in pieces. The success of this innovation is due to the fact that these small pieces of chocolate remain whole during the entire baking period."[20] Here, a technological innovation by Nestlé went hand in hand with creating a new type of cookie, courtesy of a woman trained in home economics.

One tenet of the home economics movement was the firm belief that cooking should be done in the home. While this was a continuation of an existing practice, this was not necessarily the way things needed to be. In fact, in the late nineteenth century there were women throughout the country who took an entirely different approach to professionalizing what happened in the home, working to make it so that they did not have to do many of the chores the home economists were so focused on.

In the late 1860s a woman with the very nineteenth-century-sounding name of Melusina Fay Peirce advanced an idea that, in the context of what was happening elsewhere in American society, must have sounded both radically new and blindingly obvious: that the most laborious housework—sewing clothes from bolts of cloth, laundering those clothes, and preparing food—should be moved out of the home and into a centralized location. This was not a market-based idea in which a sewing business would make the clothes, a laundry would clean the clothes, and a caterer would make the food. Rather, a single cooperative, owned by those who used its services, would supply all those needs. Peirce's idea was to be put into practice over and over again in a multitude of locations across America over the next few decades. It was an idea that was eminently practical and yet bound, again and again, to fail.

Peirce, the wife of a Harvard professor, introduced her idea in a series of articles in the *Atlantic Monthly* in 1868 and 1869. She had put a considerable amount of thought into just how what she called cooperative housekeeping might work, and the articles described not just the outline of the idea but also how it could function in reality.

As its named implied, the heart of cooperative housekeeping was the *cooperative*. The cooperative would have members who pooled their resources to get better prices for services or products than they would have on their own. Cooperatives were popular in the late 1800s. Farmers used them extensively, pooling (for example) each farmer's seed order into a single large order to get a better price on seed. Since cooperatives function to benefit their members, profits are usually paid back to the members.

Peirce's idea for a housekeeping cooperative would involve a few dozen families in a given neighborhood. The families needed to live relatively close to each other so that food, delivered via wagon, would arrive at least somewhat warm from the oven or stove. Under Peirce's original plan, each family would contribute $100 to the cooperative. This money would be used for the initial purchase or leasing of the facility and to outfit it with stoves, sewing machines, and other equipment needed for its tasks. Employees would be hired, and the cooperative would then supply its members with new clothes, laundry services, and hot food at retail prices. Members of the cooperative would earn dividends with each dollar they spent. [21]

There were several assumptions inherent in this plan, the first being just who would make up the cooperative's members. Lower-class women were precluded from household cooperatives because of the costs. There was the $100 fee to join the cooperative, a large sum of money in those days, but there were also ongoing costs involved with the cooperative: members were expected to purchase the cooperative's services *at retail cost*. Lower-class women (in fact, all women) could get those same services for free by simply doing the work themselves. At the other end of the spectrum, upper-class women did not need the cooperative's services because they already paid someone else to do the work for them.

Cooperative housekeeping drew its inspiration from what was happening in the world of business. In the early 1800s households were centers of production, but by the 1860s most of that production had moved to factories. Cooperative housekeeping was an attempt to move sewing, laundry, and cooking to, essentially, a mini-factory. Inherent in this move would be economies of scale. While it does take more time and energy to cook for a hundred people than for two people, it does not take fifty times more time and energy. Making twenty dresses at one time takes somewhat less time and energy than making twenty dresses over a long period of time. Presumably, members of the housekeeping cooperative would realize some cost savings.

They would also realize large amounts of time savings. Cooking and laundry did not just take some time for women to do; they took hours each week. As Peirce and other planners saw it, moving those tasks out of the house would free women for other activities that middle- and upper-class women were expected to pursue in the nineteenth century, like reading, writing, painting, or the arts in general. It would additionally give those who wanted it some professional managerial experience. The cooperative would naturally need people to manage the employees, and female members of the cooperative were logical choices to be those managers, since they would have previous experience in managing their own servants—the servants who were no longer needed.

Getting rid of those servants was a key to the real benefit of cooperative housekeeping. It is difficult to see it today because the vast majority of Americans do not have servants and so do not have a servant problem, but cooperative housekeeping was a way to kill two birds with one stone: it was a way to move a large chunk of work out of the house, and it was also a way to *get rid of servants in the house*. Once cooking, laundry, and sewing were removed from the house, only cleaning remained, a job that could be done by a servant hired for only a few hours each week.

Peirce's plan was attempted in different places over the next few decades, although none of them were successful long term. Part of the problem was that two legs of Peirce's three-part idea were knocked away by developments in the clothing and appliance industry. Ready-to-wear clothes, first introduced during the Civil War, reduced the number of women still making the entire family's clothes. Washing machines also made it easier to wash clothes at home, although, compared with today's machines, the process was still long and laborious and involved feeding clothes through a wringer. With these two parts gone, cooperative housekeeping was reduced to cooperative cooking.

Good Housekeeping reported, in 1901, on a cooperative kitchen set up in a suburb of Chicago. Ten families had joined together to start the kitchen, but there were problems from the beginning. They could not find a space to have the kitchen until one member "moved herself and her belongings upstairs and announced her lower floor for rent for the purpose of the association." They renovated the space, charging members $1 each for the expense. For tables and chairs, "It had been agreed that each family should furnish and eat from its own table, using its own chairs, table linen, silverware and dishes. Beyond this the family was to have no care save that of attending to the laundering of its own linen." A general manager, a cook, two serving women, and a dishwasher were hired for the operation, which was soon up and running.

The cooperative was "not a restaurant," the magazine reported. "That fact is made very plain. Each family is, however, allowed as many visitors as it wishes. The 'man of the house' may now bring home company to dinner without notice and without fear of the consequences of his act— even on wash day!" The ability to easily bring company home, of course, was one of the plusses of being a part of the cooperative. So was the fact that the woman of the house no longer had to cook, although the article was strangely silent on that point. Instead, the reporter put it in financial terms, what he referred to as "the most significant feature of the whole plan." Each meal cost the family an average of ten cents per meal per adult (children twelve and under were charged half price), and the meals were about the same as what a family of moderate means would prepare for themselves.

According to the reporter, the expenses were the main problem with the operation. Although members were charged ten cents per meal, the expenses came out to about eleven cents per meal, with the difference made up at the end of the month by members. Worse, the labor costs were unrealistic in the long term. Both the general manager and cook were experienced and from the neighborhood, and they had been unemployed when the kitchen started. If they moved on to better-paying jobs, the kitchen would likely have to increase the pay for those positions, which would increase the overall expenses for the cooperative. On the question of whether a cooperative such as that one could be replicated in other communities, the reporter put it all down to the passion of the members. "It is certain that the plan will utterly fail in any community," he wrote, "unless there exists among the members a spirit of keen, sympathetic and enthusiastic co-operation; such as we find in this instance."[22]

Ultimately, all of these cooperatives failed. As historian Faye E. Dudden has described, the cooperative housekeeping movement split into three camps. One group soldiered on, pressing for housework to be collectivized "as part of a socialist reordering of society in general or working to apply it to meet the pressing needs of working women." Another group went in a capitalist direction, attempting to do the housework as a for-profit business. A third group concentrated on the problem of hired help in the household, working as either home economists or sociologists, "developing programs to recruit and train working women to be more efficient domestic servants and good citizens."[23] At any rate, housework, including cooking, would continue to be performed in each household, individually, each housewife working by herself or with some hired help. All of this work meant lots of opportunity for any company that could step in with tools to make a housewife's life easier. The food industry was ready to take that opportunity.

In the last few decades of the nineteenth century, and the first few decades of the twentieth century, the food industry came into its own. By food industry, I mean all the different companies and individuals that make the products that fill supermarket shelves (including the owners of those supermarkets). These entities have a vested interest in home cooking, and during this period they worked as hard as possible to streamline cooking while increasing their own market share.

Many areas of the food industry came to resemble the industry of today. The growth of corporations in the 1870s and 1880s combined with a lack of government regulation to allow some individual food companies to not just grow but also dominate entire industries, in the process changing those industries forever. For example, before the 1870s the fresh beef industry functioned by moving live cattle to each city, where small operators slaughtered the animals and distributed the meat to consumers. Gustavus Swift, an immigrant with a considerable amount of experience in the meatpacking industry, watched the growth of railroads with interest. He realized that the central problem for meatpackers, when it came to long-distance distribution, was the quick deterioration of the meat, forcing meatpackers to kill the animals near where they wanted to sell the meat and giving them only a small window in which to sell all the meat. Swift developed an insulated railcar lined with sheets of ice that chilled the meat in transit. He then established a series of ice stations along a northern railroad route where the ice in the cars could be replenished. With this distribution network he was able to centralize his meatpacking operation in one place, Chicago, delivering chilled meat to East Coast cities like Boston and New York. By the 1880s meat prices in cities served by Swift had plummeted, and Swift was able to dominate the meatpacking industry for decades. (A government investigation in the late 1910s found that Swift had engaged in price fixing for thirty years.) The company was so dominant in meatpacking that the government forced it to agree not to expand into selling meat directly to consumers for fear that it could use its position in meatpacking to quickly dominate the grocery business as well.[24]

Gustavus Swift used refrigeration to revolutionize the meatpacking industry, while Clarence Birdseye used it to popularize frozen foods. Frozen foods had been around since the late 1800s but were not very popular. Freezers were so expensive that few grocers had them. The usual process for freezing foods was to freeze them slowly, which resulted in freezer burn and, when the food was reheated, mushy foods. Since freezing resulted in low-quality foods, low-quality foods were used for freezing, further reducing the reputation of frozen food.

Birdseye's contribution to the industry came about because of a job he took in Labrador, in northeastern Canada. People there routinely froze food by placing it outside, where the frigid temperatures quickly solidified it. Birdseye observed that there was no freezer burn with this food, and the texture of the reheated food was the same as it was before it was frozen. Clearly, the problem was not with freezing food—it was with the freezing process.

Returning to the United States, Birdseye built an automatic freezer that quickly froze food, and he started the General Seafoods Company, located in Gloucester, Massachusetts. The company did not really take off until a chance encounter with the daughter of the founder of the Postum Cereal Company, Marjorie Merriweather Post. While yachting she stopped near Gloucester and bought a frozen goose, produced by Birdseye's company, from a local store. She was so impressed with the quality of the goose that Postum eventually bought Birdseye's company, in the process creating the General Foods Company.[25]

Birdseye had solved the problem of the quality of frozen foods, but the real popularity of frozen foods would have to wait until after World War II, when freezers became cheap enough for grocers to routinely have a frozen foods section. In the early twentieth century, though, other convenience foods continued to develop. The quality of canned goods increased, and dry mixes appeared on store shelves. The new foods that appeared on American store shelves were not only packaged foods; new fruits and vegetables showed up as well. Produce was now routinely shipped across the country, which meant that the foods that underwent the trip had to be able to stand up to it. Iceberg lettuce was developed in 1903 as a product that could handle being jostled without being damaged, since existing varieties of lettuce were too fragile to make a long journey.

Avocados began appearing in produce sections. Unlike iceberg lettuce, the avocado was not only unfamiliar to most Americans but also different from anything they might have had experience with previously. The avocado is a fruit that is high in fat, soft when ripe, and not sweet, and it cannot be cooked in any way. As historian Jeffrey Charles has pointed out, the avocado took a twisting route to the American table. Some of the earliest growers, in early twentieth-century California, were people from back east who had bought California land with the intention of raising a cash crop. Brochures advertising land used avocados as an example of a crop that grew well in California.

As more and more people started growing avocados, selling the fruit became a problem. The earliest advertising pitched the avocado as a salad ingredient, which worked well because it has to be eaten raw and is a healthy addition to a salad. Sales exploded in the 1920s, moving from about 1,300 pounds sold exclusively to local markets to over a million pounds sold nationally by the end of the decade. Most people who bought avocados during that time bought it as a salad ingredient. Its most popular use today is in guacamole, a dish that did not gain mainstream popularity until the 1960s, with the rising popularity of Latin American foods.[26]

In the early twentieth century, new foods of various types appeared on store shelves, and existing foods took on a new appearance with the rise of individual packaging. Traditionally, most grocery items were sold in bulk, requiring a considerable amount of work by shopkeepers who had to, say, draw a pint of vinegar from a barrel for a customer. Bulk sales also resulted in quite a bit of waste—this is, after all, where the phrase *bottom of the barrel* came from, denoting items of exceptionally poor quality.

A classic example of how individual packaging transformed a product can be seen in crackers, specifically the "Uneeda" cracker, produced by the National Biscuit Company (better known as Nabisco). Before Nabisco transformed the market for crackers, crackers were sold, unpackaged and in bulk, by wholesalers to local stores, where new crackers were piled on top of old in the store's cracker barrel. In this process the brand name of the crackers was inconsequential, since there was only one cracker barrel in the store. Nabisco changed this process in three ways. First, it developed packaging for crackers that kept them relatively fresh and out of the cracker barrel. Since the crackers were now displayed on store shelves, in packaging, consumers could specifically select Nabisco's crackers. Second, the company created a marketing campaign that aggressively marketed the new Uneeda crackers to consumers—yes, to modern ears "Uneeda" is both trite and cloying, but at that time, when the concept of brand names was in its infancy, it seems to have been clever and memorable. Third, Nabisco hired salesmen to bypass the wholesalers and sell directly to local stores to ensure that its new product would be on store shelves. Uneeda crackers may have been more expensive than other crackers, but they were also fresher (good for the consumer) and, presumably, carried good profit margins (good for the grocer).[27] With these three innovations, Nabisco, which was already a market leader, was able to fend off competitors in a new, nationally oriented market.

In the late 1800s one new food looked forward, more than any other food of the period, to the future: breakfast cereal. It was one of the purest forms of convenience food available in that it required only that the user (cook is too technical a term) combine it with milk and, if desired, sugar. No heating or stirring was needed. It was a food that was recognized to exist in its near-final form. Even though cereal companies tried to get their products to be used in other dishes as an ingredient, that effort largely failed. Instead, cereal became associated in Americans' minds with one specific meal—as one food historian put it, the men behind the industry "almost single-handedly destroyed the traditional American breakfast."[28]

Breakfast cereals came out of the American tradition of eating grains like oatmeal for breakfast. By the late 1800s oatmeal had largely lost its association with the lower classes and was seen by many as having health benefits, and the connection to health is what helped breakfast cereals skyrocket to popularity.

The health connection came from Dr. John Harvey Kellogg's sanitarium in Battle Creek, Michigan. As Kellogg himself put it in a book on the sanitarium, the facility "combined the comforts of the home and the hotel with the medical advantages of the hospital and the added facilities and equipment requisite for the administration of baths of every description, electricity in its different forms, medical gymnastics, and other rational agencies, with careful regulation of diet."[29] Baths, electricity, "medical gymnastics," diet—the sanitarium covered all the bases for the well-to-do looking to improve their health, at a time when medical knowledge was still fairly primitive.

The San, as it was known, had a long history with what would become breakfast cereals. Ellen Gould White, the leader of the Seventh-Day Adventist Church, established the facility in the 1860s. She had previously visited a similar facility in New York State that served, and sold, a concoction made from whole wheat that had been baked twice and broken into pieces—this was called "granula." After Kellogg was hired to run the San, he, too, made granula from wheat, oats, and corn. When the owner of the New York facility sued the San for making granula, the name of Kellogg's food was changed, slightly, to "granola," giving us the name we have today.[30] Kellogg worked at creating other cereals as well, developing a process in which wheat paste was pressed between two rollers. The product was not quite right until his brother, who was working with him, processed a batch of wet wheat that had gone sour, resulting in crispy flakes when cooked.[31]

Kellogg's cereal was enormously popular, in part because of its connection to health but also because of aggressive advertising. By the early twentieth century advertisements for Kellogg's cereals regularly appeared in national magazines. The cereal was popular enough that it spawned many imitators, some of which set up shop in Battle Creek, near Kellogg's facility. Kellogg himself grumbled about what he called the "imitators and piratical schemers," writing, in a book about the San, how "by ingenious advertising, much after the method of medical quacks, some of these concerns have built up large business interests and have waxed rich by their ill-gotten gains. One party in particular has made some millions by the sale of a cheap mixture of bran and molasses."[32] That party was most likely Charles W. Post, a former patient of Kellogg's who went into the cereal business and became at least as successful as Kellogg himself. Post, who made much about his company's connections to Battle Creek (and, presumably, the San), irritated Kellogg so much that the doctor disowned Post's cereals by name, writing in his book that "the Battle Creek Sanitarium has never at any time had any connection whatever with the manufacture of [Post's] 'Postum,' 'Grape-Nuts,' . . . or any other of the numerous nostrums made or sold by parties advertising from Battle Creek."[33]

Advertising and a connection to health helped breakfast cereals become popular, but the cereals also caught on because they were so useful. Instead of having leftovers for breakfast (which meant, at the very least, preparing a fire for warming the food) or making something like pancakes and bacon from scratch, women could simply set out a bottle of milk and a box of cereal. Breakfast cereal quickly became a default food for breakfast, one that is so identified with breakfast that it is difficult to imagine having cereal for lunch or dinner.

Breakfast cereal was also groundbreaking in that it was a convenience food with no homemade equivalent. Condensed soups, baking mixes, and canned vegetables were merely factory-made versions of items that could be made at home; all the factories had done was move the food a little closer to being ready to serve. Breakfast cereals were based on hot cereals like oatmeal, but cooked oatmeal is not crunchy like cornflakes or Grape-Nuts, which were some of the earliest breakfast cereals. This, too, explains why breakfast cereals were so popular and why so many imitators quickly stepped in: because breakfast cereal was a brand-new type of food that had not existed previously. People like Kellogg and Post helped to create an entirely new category of food, one that still generates enormous income for its producers, takes up many feet of shelf space at every grocery store, and sits in the kitchen cabinets of the vast majority of Americans.

As food companies moved from being local to regional to national in scope, the disconnect that had developed between producers and consumers continued to widen. Particularly for urban Americans, the person who sold them their food was not the person who produced the food; they were only a middleman. Foods could and did have almost anything added to them without being labeled in any way, and in most places that was completely legal. The food industry of the time functioned in a completely different cultural landscape from today. Not only were there few laws devoted to food safety or purity, but the "buyer beware" attitude of most Americans also held that if someone bought a product that was impure, it was the consumer, not the producer, who was at fault. Home economists believed that housewives, each armed with a chemistry set to test the products they purchased, had the responsibility to urge companies to produce pure foods by only buying pure foods. They would vote with their feet.

Of course, this put a considerable burden of responsibility and work on the consumer, and, even if consumers did test everything, the approach would only go so far. It would not catch, for example, some of the problems with the meat industry Upton Sinclair wrote about in *The Jungle*. The book was based on research Sinclair did in the meatpacking districts of Chicago, and it exposed problems with the existing network of laws governing slaughterhouses. There were federal inspectors at slaughterhouses, but they only monitored meat that was intended to cross state lines—anything shipped within the state of Illinois was not inspected. Those animals could be, and frequently were, sick or otherwise diseased, slaughtered perhaps days before they would have died anyway. There were so few federal inspectors that meat intended for sale in other states was also questionable, since slaughterhouse staff simply waited until the federal inspectors went home to run the diseased cattle through. No home-based test would discover this sort of food problem.

Legislation to clean up the food industry was stalled in Congress when *The Jungle* became a sensation, and its popularity led to the passage of both the Pure Food and Drug Act of 1906 and the Federal Meat Inspection Act that same year. The Food and Drug Act was essentially a truth-in-advertising law, mandating that ingredients for most foods needed to be listed on the label. The Meat Inspection Act was aimed at strengthening slaughterhouse inspections.

Many food companies complained bitterly that the legislation was unnecessary, as the producers that put truly bad stuff in their products were outliers, but some companies used the new laws to their advantage. An example is Heinz, with its tomato ketchup. By the late 1800s ketchup producers routinely added benzoic acid as a preservative, and even though benzoic acid was not banned under the Pure Food and Drug Act, there was an ongoing public debate over whether it was safe. Critics claimed it caused stomach problems and sore throat, while supporters pointed out that it occurred naturally in cranberries and maintained that it was impossible to make ketchup without using benzoic acid, since the preservative kept the ketchup from fermenting in the bottle soon after being opened, particularly if it was left on the table or in a less-than-chilled icebox. The producers complained that they had no choice but to use the preservative.

In the midst of this debate, Heinz researchers found a way to produce ketchup without benzoic acid that did not ferment. They simply used older, established methods of preservation, and in doing so they permanently changed the taste of American ketchup: they doubled the amount of sugar and vinegar in ketchup, and also increased the amount of salt. This made Heinz ketchup much sweeter than that of its competitors, but Heinz could now claim that it was made without the controversial preservative. This it now did, both in labeling on ketchup bottles and in an advertising blitz that dwarfed any of its competitors. The new, benzoic acid–free ketchup gave Heinz a competitive advantage over the competition, and so, in conjunction with the change, Heinz increased the cost of its ketchup, up to about three times the price of its competitors.[34]

Other ketchups eventually followed Heinz's lead, dropping the benzoic acid while increasing the amount of sugar in their ketchup formulas. This is a rare example of a change in a processed product that also affected homemade versions of the same food. Even though very few people make their own ketchup these days, the recipes that are printed in cookbooks today reflect the change. To take two somewhat random examples of recipes, a ketchup recipe published in *Miss Parloa's New Cook Book*, from 1882, called for twelve tomatoes and two tablespoons of brown sugar. More than one hundred years later, an edition of *The Joy of Cooking* called for fourteen pounds of tomatoes (which, depending on the size of the tomatoes used in the 1882 recipe, might only be slightly more than called for in that recipe) and three-quarters of a cup of brown sugar, a sixfold increase in the amount of sweetener. In spite of that increase, the introduction to the *Joy of Cooking* recipe calls out commercial ketchup for being overly sweet.[35]

The movement toward individual packing for food products dovetailed nicely with this pure food movement. For example, as the makers of Cottolene, a butter or lard substitute made from cotton oil, proclaimed in a 1910 cookbook, their product was "packed only in sealed tins of special design, which are absolutely air-tight and protect the contents not only from all odors of coal-oil, codfish, etc., so common in the average grocery, but also from dust, dirt and other contaminations to which goods sold in bulk—such as lard—are frequently exposed."[36] The cookbook was not just a collection of recipes but also an advertising document that, in one way or another, explained all the reasons why a consumer should use Cottolene. The full title of the book is *Home Helps: A Pure Food Cookbook*, which played to those concerned about the dangers of eating impure foods. The book includes recipes from five well-known home economists whose names are prominently displayed on the cover, so it would attract women looking for recipes from known authorities. The volume also includes a page that lists testimonials from "Eminent Physicians" declaring, for example, that "nine-tenths of all human ailments are due primarily to indigestion or are aggravated because of it. The chief cause of indigestion is food prepared with lard."[37] Clearly, the marketers at Cottolene were working to sell their product through sales of that cookbook.

As new products appeared on store shelves, and as companies increased their geographical distribution, food companies increasingly turned to advertising to help them sell their products. In the days before psychology, much of the advertising was simple and straightforward, often a direct command to buy a certain product or a plain announcement of its availability. By the 1920s the most impressive magazine advertisements often featured color illustrations accompanied by text, sometimes paragraphs of it; one person who worked in the industry remembered it as "the days of the lush brush and the still more lush phrase."[38]

The marketing of products and brands extended to much more than simply placing advertisements in newspapers or women's magazines. As discussed above, companies often employed home economists to write cookbooks that could range in size from a pamphlet of a few pages to a book of well over a hundred pages, packed with recipes that promoted a particular brand. Consumers could write to the companies and request the books, and, along with those requests, consumers sometimes also sent cooking questions that would be answered by staff home economists at the food companies. These letters were an additional way to interact with consumers at a more personal level. In 1921, at the Washburn Crosby Company (which would later become General Mills), the head of the advertising department devised, almost by accident, another way for the company to interact with consumers. The male advertising department head was responsible for mailing responses to cooking questions from consumers, although the actual answers were written by the all-female home economics department. Since women, not men, were the ones who were supposed to know how to cook, he did not want to sign his own name to the letters. Instead, he came up with a woman's name. The first name was Betty, because it sounded wholesome, while the last name was Crocker, after a former director of the company. To sign the letters, the nonexistent Betty Crocker needed a signature, so, within the company, they held a contest, the winning signature coming from a secretary named Florence Lindeberg. In this way Betty Crocker was born, and a variation of that original signature is still used by General Mills today.[39]

Betty Crocker was certainly not the only food-related corporate character. Kellogg's had Kay Kellogg, Quaker Enriched Flour had Mary Alden, and Fleishmann's Yeast had Mary Lynn Woods. Some companies changed their minds about their character's name. Campbell's started with Anne Marshall and then switched to Carolyn Campbell, while Pillsbury started with Mary Ellis Ames and ended with Ann Pillsbury.[40] Even the government got into the act, creating Aunt Sammy as a radio character who spoke to women about cooking. Most of these characters appear to have been real to consumers as well. In 1949 General Mills commissioned a study of consumers to find who they thought was the most helpful home economics personality. The company was pleased to find that Betty Crocker was at the top of the list, with about 44 percent of women responding that she was the most helpful. Next was Aunt Jenny, who was the Spry Shortening corporate character, followed by Ann Batchelder, and then Ann Pillsbury. The results of this poll must have been at least somewhat galling to Ms. Batchelder, since she was a real person, the food editor at *Ladies' Home Journal*.[41]

Betty Crocker was created as a name to be signed to corporate letters, and she developed into a character housewives could relate to. Not all characters were intended to be relatable, and one character in particular, which still sits on grocery store shelves, shows another side to food company advertising in the late nineteenth and early twentieth centuries.

That character is Aunt Jemima, created to be the face of one product, Aunt Jemima self-rising pancake flour. The flour was created in St. Joseph, Missouri, in 1889, when a couple of businessmen who had bought a flour mill were looking for a new product to sell. They decided on self-rising flour for pancakes but knew that, to compete in the market, they needed a marketable name. While taking a walk through town, one of the men attended a traveling minstrel show. Minstrel shows were a popular entertainment of the time that featured white performers in blackface singing, dancing, telling jokes, and generally performing as racist caricatures of African Americans. A stock character in the shows was a mammy named Aunt Jemima (a mammy being a slave whose job was to take care of the master's children), and at that moment the corporate character of Aunt Jemima was born.[42]

The company that produced Aunt Jemima flour took the idea of the minstrel show mammy and used it in advertising, explicitly referring to her as being a slave before the Civil War. In fact, the company's advertising, widely used in the first part of the twentieth century, presented an elaborate story for Aunt Jemima that publicized her slavery. As the story went, she was the cook on the Louisiana plantation of Colonel Higbee. During the Civil War northern troops overran the plantation and threatened to rip off Colonel Higbee's mustache, but Aunt Jemima intervened, offering to serve her pancakes in return for saving the colonel's mustache. The pancakes were so delicious that the troops relented. After the war those same troops supposedly went South again, this time to get the recipe for Aunt Jemima's pancakes. In return for gold she handed over the recipe. This was the Aunt Jemima story. [43]

The flour was first produced at a single mill in St. Joseph, Missouri; by 1893 the company was doing well enough to have a display at the Chicago World's Fair where a black woman, dressed as Aunt Jemima, mixed and served the pancakes. Later advertising conflated the concocted story of Aunt Jemima with the black woman at the fair, presenting it as if Aunt Jemima herself were at the fair. [44]

Aunt Jemima advertising played on racial ideas, and these ideas are one version of a popular message from food companies: that their products were helpful and convenient to use (the classic book on Aunt Jemima is bluntly titled *Slave in a Box*). Cooking was known to be tiring work that had to be done several times a day, and companies often advertised their products as an aid to busy women. Using a former slave in advertising a product was an easy way for a company to communicate just how helpful the product could be. Of course, since the 1960s and the advent of the civil rights movement, the company that owns the Aunt Jemima trademark has rolled back the slave connection in the advertising. Today Aunt Jemima is notable as being one of the few African American food-related corporate characters, along with Uncle Ben and Rastus, the Cream of Wheat corporate character. Aunt Jemima's slave past is never mentioned today, as doing so would surely cause quite a bit of trouble for the company that owns the trademark.

Betty Crocker was a tremendous marketing tool for the Washburn Crosby company. She was a specific person the company could use in marketing materials, but, being imaginary, she did not suffer from the drawbacks that come along with being a real person, like personal scandals or aging. It is difficult to imagine it today, but huge numbers of Americans believed she was a real person, so much so that, when a rumor spread that she was getting married (and then, logically, quitting her job), the company had to publicly address the rumor. As Miss Crocker said on her radio show, "That was all a mistake. The girl who was married was a former member of our staff, but Betty Crocker is right here as usual."[45] However, sometimes the truth did come out. For years receptionists at Betty Crocker Kitchens, which offered free tours to visitors, kept tissues at their desks to offer guests who became overwhelmed when they found out the truth.[46]

For the first few years after her creation, Betty Crocker was simply the name signed to letters that went out to consumers. As time went on the home economists at the company used her name more and more until, in 1924, she made the jump to radio. Particularly after a radio show featuring Betty Crocker was broadcast nationally starting in 1926, it was on the radio that millions of listeners grew to know Betty. Radio was so important to spreading her fame that *Fortune* magazine, a few decades later, linked her to another famous radio voice. "The radio made Betty," the magazine declared in 1945. "It is fair to say that it did for her career in commerce what it did for Franklin D. Roosevelt's in politics."[47] Her show, produced by General Mills, was broadcast three times a week, and it would continue on radio for most of the next three decades (since it was much easier to find a voice that might sound like Betty than an actress who looked like her, she never moved to television). Mondays and Wednesdays on her radio show she discussed things like menus and meal preparation, while Fridays she hosted a popular cooking school.[48]

Betty Crocker was not the only cooking personality to appear on radio. The federal government produced *Housekeeper's Chat* in the late 1920s and early 1930s, hosted by the fictional Aunt Sammy. Unlike Betty Crocker's show, this was not broadcast nationally; rather, scripts were sent to individual stations so that local women, speaking with the local accent, could speak to women in a voice that might be more accessible than one from across the country. On the other side of the spectrum was the *National Radio Homemakers Hour*, nationally broadcast by CBS beginning in 1929. Radio then was like television today, with a multitude of programs that lasted anywhere from fifteen minutes to more than an hour and included sporting events, drama, comedies, soap operas, and live music. However, the radio cooking programs, and the first televised cooking programs broadcast in the 1950s, were primarily informational, not entertainment. The host patiently explained cooking techniques, listed menu items, and described recipes slowly, pausing so that listeners could write down ingredients and instructions. Cooking shows that entertained listeners, and viewers, would come in the second part of the twentieth century.

Grocery stores form a part of the food industry, and they also underwent changes in the early twentieth century. Turn-of-the-century grocery stores were different from today's stores in a number of key ways. Physically they were much smaller, selling a drastically reduced number of items (this was partially due to the smaller number of patrons but also because there were simply less food items for sale back then). Most items were located behind a counter or in a back room, not on the store floor, and sales clerks had to retrieve almost everything a customer wanted, giving them a considerable amount of power in pushing particular brands. Everything was sold in bulk, which required quite a bit of work from the clerks. If a customer wanted, say, a pint of molasses, the molasses would have to be dipped from a barrel into a container, everything wiped free of molasses drippings, and both the container and the barrel sealed. Because everything was sold in bulk, customers needed to be diligent in watching what was put in their basket; no one wanted, for example, the crackers from the bottom of the cracker barrel. Prices were not listed. Instead, after everything had been gathered for the customer, the clerk would calculate the total price, and then some haggling would ensue. Stores often extended credit to customers, which required extensive knowledge of the customer. This the clerk usually had, because customers tended to shop at the same location again and again.

As may be guessed, customers were sometimes frustrated by the experience of shopping at a local store. The male clerks could be aggravating to female shoppers. As one store manager put it, "A woman does not like to run a gauntlet of clerks looking her over when she enters a store. This is sometimes the case in stores where clerks are not busy and loll over the counter sizing up the ladies."[49] There was no anonymity with the experience, since the clerk knew exactly what was being purchased, and customers usually stuck with a particular store. As the son of a Chicago grocer remembered, "If my dad had 50 customers, that's all he had, 50. If he got 51 one day, it would be an odd thing. Somebody from the next block was passing by or got mad at his butcher that day."[50] The issue of pricing was also a sore point, since it was difficult for the customer to know if they were paying too much. One could use previous grocery visits as a guide to how much the bill should be, but the problem at the time was that, because large corporations such as Swift were bringing quite a bit of efficiency into food production, the price of some foods dropped over time.

This was the shopping environment that chain stores stepped into in the first few decades of the twentieth century. The chains, of course, started as individual stores, but as they grew they took a different approach to selling groceries that appealed to customers in at least two ways. First, prices were clearly marked on individual foods so the customer knew just how much each item cost. To keep prices low, the customer, not a clerk, selected items to put into her basket, resulting in less labor cost for the store but more work for the customer. For this system to work, all items had to be individually packaged, which food producers had been working on for a number of years. Since customers had physical access to everything in the store, some chains, like Piggly Wiggly, installed a turnstile at the front of the store to cut down on theft.

The second way chain stores appealed to customers was by being physically larger than a neighborhood grocery store. They offered more variety, and, because they served more customers, who in turn filled their own shopping baskets, the chains offered some anonymity to their customers.

Neighborhood grocery stores remained a common fixture in American life well into the twentieth century, but the chains expanded regionally. By the end of the 1920s Kroger had more than 5,000 stores, Safeway just over 2,000, and National Tea about 1,600. Each of these chains was dwarfed by the largest, A&P, which owned over 15,000 stores nationally.[51] Unlike local stores, the chains could not offer any sort of credit, since credit cards did not yet exist and the chains, because of their size, did not know customers well enough to know if they were a good credit risk. While this may have been frustrating to customers, since they always had to pay cash, it also meant that the chains lost no money to bad debts and could therefore keep their prices even lower than if they offered credit.

In the first years of the twentieth century, kitchens came into their own. A typical American kitchen in the late 1800s was, essentially, a workspace with a table, some shelves, and a stove or fireplace. In newer, larger houses the cooking workspace might consist of a kitchen with a stove and, in a separate room, a pantry, both situated at the back of the house in order to isolate the heat from the fire. In more rustic circumstances, the "kitchen" might be a table and fireplace at one side or corner of the only room of the house.

Originally there was not much specialized equipment made for kitchens. That changed in the first years of the twentieth century with the introduction of the Hoosier cabinet, made by the Hoosier Manufacturing Company of New Castle, Indiana. A Hoosier cabinet was a tall, freestanding cabinet made with an eye to packing in as many labor- and space-saving gadgets as possible (the general design was based on older baker's cabinets, but the Hoosier took the idea of compact usefulness to a new level). A porcelain counter extended out from the cabinet at about waist height where the cook could place mixing bowls or knead bread, the porcelain being much easier to clean, and therefore much more hygienic, than a wooden table. Several cabinets above the counter contained shelf space for dishes and utensils. Just below the cabinets, above the counter, were one or two hoppers for flour and sugar, the flour hopper having an attachment that sifted the flour as it was dropped into a measuring cup or container. A small rotating spice rack could be mounted between the two hoppers, placing a handful of spices within easy reach of the cook. Below the counter were drawers and another cabinet for storing large containers. The Hoosier cabinet was compact, well designed, extremely useful, and very, very popular.

Technological and cultural developments brought more specialized equipment into American kitchens. Iceboxes appeared, essentially insulated boxes with room for a large chunk of ice, delivered to the house by an iceman, and space around it for keeping foods cold. By the 1920s electricity and indoor plumbing became common, bringing sinks and some smaller electrical devices into the kitchen. Electric refrigerators appeared but were quite expensive at first, although electrical utilities loved them, since they were an appliance that was always on, drawing current both day and night. By the 1930s electric refrigerators were becoming far more common, and by 1940 about 44 percent of American households had one.[52]

Regardless of what was in them, American kitchens by the early 1930s were a collection of disparate elements. The icebox or refrigerator, sink, various cabinets and tables, and stove lined the room in something of a haphazard fashion, with a cabinet towering over a nearby sink, an icebox sitting by itself in a corner, and the clean horizontal lines of the modern kitchen nowhere to be found. The kitchen was ripe for a redesign, one that emphasized, above all, modernism and straight lines.

This shift in the look of American kitchens took place in the 1930s, during the Great Depression. As historian Leslie Land has described, the companies that designed and sold kitchen appliances faced two major problems in selling their wares at that point. First, few people had money to spend on new appliances. Second, the products they sold did not wear out very quickly. Stoves have few moving parts to break. Iceboxes and cabinets have none, unless you count door hinges and drawers.

In this difficult climate, appliance makers seem to have seized on promoting the idea that American kitchens were out of date, not because the appliances did not work right but because they did not *look* right. The look designers promoted was modernism, a design aesthetic that emphasized clean, straight lines and an aerodynamic, streamlined look.

The redesign of the American kitchen had a few major components. The long, elaborately carved legs of stoves and sinks of the era were antithetical to the modernist look, so the "bottom" of kitchen appliances (which was usually a false front made of a piece of flat metal) was dropped to the ground, held just off the floor by four stubby, nearly invisible legs. For sinks, this meant the addition of cabinets in the newly covered area below the sink. Ovens were reconfigured so that burners remained at waist height while the oven moved from a convenient waist height to the space below the burners, only inches off the floor, to the annoyance of cooks everywhere (ovens would briefly return to waist height in the mid-twentieth century, but that configuration quickly became passé). The new design, presenting a flat, vertical expanse of wood or metal from the countertop down to the floor, was easier to clean and cheaper to manufacture than the long legs of the old design.

As the bottoms of all appliances and cabinets in the kitchen dropped to the floor, kitchen countertops moved to a standard thirty-six inches above the ground. This standardization seems to have started in the plumbing industry. Before dishwashers were popularly available, everyone washed their own dishes, and the best height for the bottom of the sink, plumbers appear to have decided, was thirty-one inches from the floor. Most sinks were five inches deep, so the top of the sink was placed at thirty-six inches and, to keep everything looking clean and horizontal, the countertop was moved to the same height.

Historian Leslie Land has pointed out that, logically, h(⸰⸰ should have vigorously protested this bit of standardiza\ spent decades studying the optimal workspace height for (come to the conclusion that it varied by the cook's height. W the research showed that a thirty-six-inch-high workspace was not even the appropriate height for the average American woman—at the early twentieth-century average of five feet, three inches tall, thirty-two inches would have been more appropriate to fit the needs of the average woman. The problem for the home economists was that they had already been co-opted by the appliance companies. Any sizable manufacturer of stoves, iceboxes, refrigerators, or kitchen cabinets employed home economists, either on the staff or as consultants or contractors. The most famous of the home economists, those with cookbooks or magazine or newspaper columns to their names, usually had a tight relationship with food and appliance manufacturers, often penning cookbooks for the companies and lending their names to advertising. They were in no position to protest a movement that enabled appliance manufacturers to remake the American kitchen and, in the process, sell a lot of product. One might expect early feminists to have also protested the imposition of an impractical cabinet height on all housewives, but, like the women of Boston described at the beginning of this chapter, they were busy looking forward to a future where cooking would be done outside the home, making any discussion of kitchen cabinet height a moot point. [53]

Other changes involving cooking took place in American homes in the early twentieth century. Gas became more and more popular as a fuel not just for cooking but also for heating an entire house, and although it was much easier to use than coal or wood, some traditions were lost in the transition. *American Kitchen Magazine* carried a regular column on cooking with gas, and its October 1902 edition addressed how gas cooking might affect some Halloween traditions. Specifically, cooking some simple foods like potatoes, apples, or popcorn in the fireplace that warmed a room, rather than in the kitchen's cookstove, was popular when having guests in the fall and winter months (and yes, chestnuts were also on the list). The author of the "Gas Stove Department" column, whose job was obviously to promote gas cooking, took a somewhat defensive tone in her response to the demise of wood fireplaces or coal stoves in each room of the house. Potatoes took so long to roast that it was, in all, "questionable if our patience is equal" to making them, she wrote. If a party was "to be nfined to the parlor and library" (which certainly assumes a certain level of wealth), "apples may be roasted on the hearth before the gas log, and the pop-corn and chestnuts may be prepared beforehand." But the writer urged her reader to have a smaller gathering, which was "more in accord with the spirit of the night" and to gather not around the gas log in the library but around the gas stove in the kitchen. "The corn may be popped and eaten on the spot . . . [The] nuts can be made by putting the chestnuts on the iron cover over the flame. . . . Corn and apples may be roasted in the oven under the flame, and if the roasting is more prosaic than beside an outdoor bonfire, the accomplished result will be better eating." It should be noted that this was decades before the popularity of the "open concept" house where kitchen, dining, and living area are all opened into one large room, so gathering around the gas stove in the kitchen would mean occupying a relatively small room in the back of the house that was purposely kept separated from the rest of the structure— not an entirely pleasant place to host a party. [54]

Because of the need for nearby population, restaurants were an urban phenomenon. Although eating establishments were by no means a new development in America, in the late nineteenth century restaurants became somewhat more like they are today.

Society was changing, and the growth of restaurants was a response to some of those changes. Increasing demand for young women to work as clerks, secretaries, and other pink-collar jobs meant fewer women to work as hired cooks, and fewer cooks meant more demand for eating out from middle-class households. Couples who lived in small apartments with some disposable income, boarding-house residents tired of boarding-house food, and shoppers too distant from their houses to return for a quick meal all increased the demand for restaurants. Also during this time, the largest meal of the day, usually referred to as dinner, changed from being served at midday to being served in the evening, since working away from the house meant that men could no longer easily return home to eat a large meal in the middle of the day. This made the evening meal, which previously may have been leftovers or simple dishes, a more complex affair.

The problem was that there simply were not that many restaurants. Historian Andrew P. Haley has outlined a number of types of restaurants popular with middle-class consumers in the 1870s and 1880s in most large American cities. Lunchrooms were loud, bustling places with long á la carte menus and, true to their name, only open for the midday meal. Some restaurants offered table d'hôte dinners, a multicourse meal for a fixed price. The concept was somewhat similar to modern buffet restaurants in that it was an all-you-can-eat meal, but, instead of having all dishes available to patrons all the time, patrons received individual courses one at a time, with the understanding that they could order seconds of any dish they received. Since the selling point for these restaurants was more the quantity than the quality of food, these places did not have the highest reputations for those interested in good food. For male patrons there were beefsteak, or chophouse, restaurants that sold a cut of meat, usually with a potato and drink. These places were quick but focused exclusively on serving men. By the early twentieth century beefsteak restaurants were not considered proper places for women, even those who dined with their husbands. At the low end of the dining spectrum were what were called American restaurants, places that focused on the cheapest food possible, where critics constantly complained of chipped plates and low-grade food (then, as now, most of the restaurant business ran on extremely low margins). Then there were the intriguingly named coffee and cake saloons. These do not seem to have been too different from today's coffeehouses, places that offered cake and pastries, cold sandwiches, and coffee. Their drawing points were their hours (open early and closing late) and the fact that it was entirely proper for unescorted women to eat there. The drawback was their limited food selection.[55]

Toward the end of the nineteenth century a new type of restaurant began appearing in American cities. This type of restaurant was eminently respectable and might have become an option for middle-class families, but, instead, dining at one of these restaurants became a minefield for middle-class patrons. The problem was that the upper class began using restaurant dining as a way to define themselves in public.

The late 1800s was a time of intense business activity when new industries made many new millionaires, and a man could become a millionaire many times over. If the gulf between the rich and poor did not increase, it became quite obvious that those at the top had much more money than they ever had before. With so much potential movement into the upper class, that group needed some ways of determining just who was upper class, and restaurant going became one way to make that determination.

In the late 1800s the highest class of American restaurants were those that served French food. It was not so much that the food tasted the best—as Andrew P. Haley has pointed out, most accounts of meals at these restaurants barely mention the taste of the food—but the meals were elaborate and expensive, featuring eight or nine courses served on fine china, with complicated table decorations and menus festooned with ribbons and printed calligraphy.

The upper class loved the French restaurants, and the middle class tried to love them as well, for a certain period of time. The reason the upper class loved the French restaurants was the same reason the middle class came to despise them: while anyone could technically walk through the doors and order a meal, only the upper class could do this well and get good service.

The problem started when the patron walked through the door. He (unattended women were not welcome at upscale restaurants) and his party would be judged by the host as they entered and a determination would quickly be made as to whether the party would be seated near established upper-class diners, which held the promise of upwardly mobile social networking, or nearest the kitchen, known by all to be the worst table in the restaurant.

All of this being essentially an extended test to see who was of the upper crust and who was not, the menu was intentionally confusing. It was in French, a language not taught even in most colleges then. To make things worse, this was nonstandard French, a kind of pidgin derivative used by French chefs with unusual definitions for most words (many menus also included terms that had been developed in America and were unknown in French kitchens). Diners were expected to order a complete meal themselves, with some guidance from the waiter, who could of course withhold guidance from any diner who was not worthy of being at the restaurant to begin with.

Table settings included the panoply of utensils upper-class restaurants were famous for, and the rules for using these, outlined in many etiquette guides published in the late 1800s, could be frustratingly oblique—ice cream, for example, was to be eaten with a fork, not a spoon. The point of the etiquette guides was to teach people the rules for socially functioning in high society, and their popularity in the late 1800s shows that many people attempted to move into the highest levels of society. However, the guides were only of mixed value when it came to dining in restaurants. The guides had explicit instructions on which utensil to use during each course of a meal, but the concept of the restaurant—where one paid to eat in public—was too new an idea to make it into guides that were, by their nature, bound to tradition.

Even if a member of the middle class was able to be seated at a decent place in the restaurant, to understand the menu and order a quality meal, and to navigate the complex rules regarding which utensil was used for which part of the meal, there was still the matter of the bill. French restaurants were proper places, and while a married man could sit down to dinner with only his wife, a bachelor on a date was expected to bring chaperones and escorts to the point of needing a table for six rather than a table for two. The accountant, midlevel manager, or store clerk would be lucky to spend only a week's wages on the meal, but the bill could easily exceed that amount.

In the late nineteenth and early twentieth centuries the growing numbers, and increasing financial clout, of the middle class changed American restaurant dining, particularly as it pertained to families dining out. Excluded from the finest French restaurants, the middle class began frequenting ethnic restaurants in the creation of what would later be called "cosmopolitanism." This set of ideas upended the dining values of the upper class by promoting the idea that all kinds of ethnic foods, like Italian or Chinese, could be as good as French food. Even if a given middle-class family were unfamiliar with all the foods served at a Greek or Italian restaurant, the waitstaff and owner, anxious to appeal to a new set of patrons, were usually happy to explain the menu. [56]

Upper-class restaurants had a variety of responses to the growing clout of the middle class. Many of these restaurants were located in hotels that traditionally had charged a set fee for a room and three meals a day, thereby using hotel patrons to subsidize the restaurant. This arrangement was not quite as unfair as it might sound, though, because most of the patrons of these hotels were wealthy people who did not balk at the extra charge to their bills. As hotels expanded and grew to ten or fifteen stories high, though, the hotels had to appeal to a new set of patrons—businessmen—who did, indeed, balk at having to pay extra for meals they might not eat at a restaurant they might not have cared for. Competition forced the hotels to charge only for the room, which meant that the restaurant had to fend for itself.

Upscale restaurants were largely forced to change or go out of business, as New York City's Delmonico's (once seen as not just the best French restaurant in the country but simply the best restaurant) did in 1923. Those that adapted simplified their menus and provided English translations of the complicated French terms, or else moved to a mostly English menu, always keeping a few French words (the word *menu*, after all, comes from the French and is a replacement for the English but longer "bill of fare").

The restaurant industry grew with the middle class, and the industry in the early twentieth century experienced some growing pains when it came to the menu. As mentioned above, many restaurants had charged a single price for a meal of a set number of courses in which patrons could order as much as they wanted within a given course, something of a forerunner to today's all-you-can-eat restaurant. The problem with this approach was both the cost and the quantity of food—unless one wanted to consume a lot of food, the approach was expensive and wasteful. The alternative some restaurants came up with was to simply list all possible menu items and let diners order their meals entirely á la carte. This, however, was also problematic, since á la carte pricing worked better for those with small appetites than large. Ordering a few dishes resulted in a smaller bill, whereas ordering more—a full meal, dessert, and drinks— often resulted in a charge that exceeded what it would have been at a restaurant that charged a single price for multiple courses, leading to complaints from patrons.

It took World War I to resolve the issue. Americans were urged to conserve resources as much as possible to help with the fight, and the conservation extended to food. Restaurants simplified their menus. Rather than having a large number of options for á la carte dining, which increased the chance of wasting food (since a particular item may have been cooked but never ordered by a patron), restaurants began offering plate specials that consisted of an entree, vegetable, and starch, all served on one plate, for a single price. This pleased the patrons, since the price of that plate was usually reasonable, and it helped the restaurant by reducing the number of items on the menu.[57]

Between the end of the Civil War in 1865 and the end of World War II in 1945, many trends affected Americans' relationship with home cooking. Three events that changed both America and the world also had some effects on food and cooking in America.

Of the three events, World War I was the shortest. The United States formally entered the war in 1917, years after its beginning in Europe; sent no soldiers to Europe before the spring of 1918; and was only involved in a few battles before the end of the war in November 1918. Because the American government assumed the war would continue for years after our entry, some drastic measures were instituted, including food rationing, but, overall, the war did not have too great an effect on cooking.

The second event lasted the longest, as the Great Depression swallowed up most of the 1930s. The economy was in a shambles through most of the period—in 1933, the worst year of the Depression, a quarter of available workers were unemployed, and the unemployment rate would stay above 10 percent for the rest of the decade. The Depression's main impact on cooking was economic in that most Americans did not have enough money to visit restaurants regularly or to buy much processed food. Home cooking enabled families to stretch their money through substitutions in recipes, adding, for example, oatmeal to hamburger to extend the meat a little further. The Depression also had an impact on gender roles and relations. The types of jobs women typically performed, like nurse, teacher, secretary, or sales clerk, turned out to be the jobs that were still needed during an economic downturn, unlike male-oriented jobs such as factory worker or general laborer. Thus, by the end of the 1930s more women were working than at the beginning of the decade, and quite frequently their spouses were either unemployed or working only a few hours a week. In that situation, some men took up some of the slack in the kitchen.

And then there was World War II. Long-term rationing, which included food, influenced home cooking by spurring those with outdoor space to keep gardens. However, with millions of men at war and millions of women working outside the home, there was a greater need for both convenience foods and food prepared outside the home. Sales of cake mixes flourished partially because, at a time when both sugar and shortening were rationed, cake mixes were not, and also because cake mixes could be prepared quickly.[58] Restaurant usage surged for largely the same reasons: more money in workers' pockets, less time for those workers (large numbers of which were women), and the fact that restaurants meals were not rationed.

Although Americans did not realize it at the time, the end of World War II, in 1945, signaled the beginning of an economic boom that would carry well into the 1960s, lifting millions of Americans from the working class into the middle class. They had disposable income and frequently chose to spend that income on convenience foods, trading the time they gained for the money they spent. Convenience foods like cake mixes and instant coffee seemed like the foods of the future—until, suddenly, many people remembered that there was a different way to cook.

4

1945 TO THE EARLY 1970S

World War II ended in August 1945, with the surrender of Japan, months after Germany had surrendered. In the years after the war, food research that had been intended to help soldiers in far-flung locations helped American food companies introduce new types of processed foods. Frozen orange juice concentrate was developed using research on freeze drying, TV dinners were influenced by soldiers' C-rations, and the use of plastic containers was adopted from plastic research done by the military. In general, the trends that had existed back in the 1920s, before the shocks of the Great Depression and World War II, continued as they had before. Convenience foods were on the rise, grocery store shelves were stuffed with new products, and American consumers, their pockets filled with more spending money than ever before, often chose those new, more convenient foods over making foods from scratch. In the 1950s the dominant ideology about home cooking was that it was a good thing, that women should be cooking at home, but there was coming to be less and less of a reason to spend hours in the kitchen slaving over a hot stove when convenience foods were a perfectly acceptable alternative to cooking from scratch. American cooking seemed to be on the cusp of a new, easier era of home cooking, one dominated by partially prepared foods that came from food companies rather than raw ingredients that came from a farm.

And then, in the first few years of the 1960s, a new set of ideas came along that jostled for attention with the existing ideology. The ideology stressed cooking from scratch using the freshest ingredients possible, insisting that dishes made from convenience foods were nothing like foods made from scratch. Far from avoiding the effort inherent in scratch cooking, this ideology plainly stated that cooking from scratch involved real work, but the result was worth it in terms of better-tasting food.

These two sets of ideas regarding cooking are the two dominant ideologies of today, opposite poles of a cooking spectrum that still govern our ideas of cooking. When we plan what to eat, what recipe to make, and what to buy at the store, we are, consciously or unconsciously, responding to these two ideologies.

Ideologies are abstract ideas, though, and sometimes hard to wrap our minds around. To better understand these ideas, it can be helpful to look at specific people whose lives were influenced by these ideologies. With that in mind, I will be examining two women whose work in food largely embodied these two ideologies. The more famous of the two today is Julia Child, who spent much of her life advocating using the freshest ingredients to cook food from scratch. Less famous today, although famous in her time, is Clementine Paddleford, a food writer who worked tightly with food companies while producing newspaper articles read by millions across the country. There are a number of reasons why Paddleford is not better known today, but one of them is surely her embrace of a way of cooking that, while still very popular, is not the way Americans like to think they cook. Julia Child, whose fame rests on the idea of scratch cooking, represents what we think of when we think about cooking, while Clementine Paddleford, who had no problem with convenience foods and "shortcut cooking," represents how most of us cook on a daily basis.

In the summer of 1956, Clementine Paddleford took a trip out West. She was, at that point, one of the most popular food writers in America, with a daily column in the *New York Herald-Tribune* and a Sunday food column syndicated in millions of newspapers across the country. The purpose of the trip was to interview cooks for her columns and to get a feel for new cooking trends that had not yet made it to New York City, her home.

When she finished the trip, Paddleford wrote a detailed memo of her observations for coworkers at the *Herald-Tribune*, and the memo reads like a list of all the popular food trends of the few decades after World War II. She declared that barbecuing, the modern popularity of which started in the West in the 1930s, was "now a 'solid' in the way of entertaining. Almost every western home has an outdoor barbecue and usually a second built into the kitchen for cold weather use." Television parties, which had been popular a few years before, had declined as more and more families bought televisions, although they were still popular with teenagers who "gather in gangs around the television to enjoy favorite shows—of course demanding refreshments." A craze for flambéed drinks was at its height, and she reported ordering a drink in Boise that "came flaming, a sort of Martini made with lime juice and floating a half lime shell, green side turned in and this filled with dark rum, ignited!"

Dieting was also popular. "The meat dishes most popular are those prepared without sauces, salads with lemon juice only. No dessert to end dinner, or maybe just fruit and black coffee. Calorie talk is heard to the point of boredom east and west and in between. Results of the Rockefeller diet are on every tongue."

Paddleford was attuned to larger trends in American culture that affected the kitchen. The rising prosperity of most Americans led them to buy electrical appliances they might not have been able to afford during the Depression and could not buy because of rationing during World War II. She saw dishwashers and blenders in most of the homes she visited. She also saw some changing gender roles. "More and more I notice husband [sic] helping with daily home cooking, especially in the big cities, or in homes of working women." In smaller towns, though, the gender roles seemed to have reverted to what they were a generation before. There, fewer "women work than during the Depression and later war years. They run their homes, do their own work and save on maid and baby nurse fees."[1]

The changes Paddleford observed on her western trip provide a backdrop to what was happening in the world of American foods. Diets, television, a growing middle class that was able to purchase new kinds of kitchen appliances—America was changing. Clementine Paddleford was a keen observer of many of those changes, even though she missed one of the biggest transitions that would bring American foods into the future.

Clementine Paddleford's life was a study in contrasts. She was born in rural Kansas in 1900 but came to fame in Chicago and New York City. She wrote about food but did not have a home economics degree (her degree was in journalism). Married women with children were her typical audience, but she herself was a single woman with an adopted daughter.

Her job required her to make quick friends with interview subjects, but a bout with throat cancer in her thirties left her with a permanent hole in her throat (always covered with a black ribbon), and she was unable to talk in much more than a hoarse whisper. As a food writer, one would assume that food and cooking would be her passion, but she did not seem to have cared all that much about cooking.

Rather than cook herself, she used food, that most traditional of feminine subjects, as a way to be a professional writer. This seems to have been her dream even at an early age—as a teenager she rode her bicycle to the town train station before school to keep up on comings and goings, which she then wrote up for the local newspaper.[2] After getting her degree from Kansas State University, she moved to Chicago, where she worked for various publishers and generally enjoyed herself in a big city. There was a marriage and a quick divorce during this time, as well as the cancer, likely the result of a vigorous smoking habit. She moved her way up in her profession, finally landing in New York City writing about food for the *Herald-Tribune*, then a major newspaper. By 1953 she was making $30,000 a year at a time when a new house in the suburbs could be had for around $10,000.[3]

Clementine Paddleford became a popular writer because she was an engaging writer and a workhorse. She wrote in a breathless style that a coworker described as "unquestionably unique . . . she seems to abhor verbs. . . . For example, if she were describing herself, I have an idea the copy would read something like this: 'Gray of hair, and banged; blue, blue of eyes; warm of manner, and dedicated.'"[4] Her dedication came through in her work output. For most of the 1950s and 1960s she wrote a daily article in the *Herald-Tribune* and a weekly article syndicated in weekend newspapers across the country. She also wrote a column for *Gourmet* magazine describing new products and had the occasional article published in women's magazines like *Ladies' Home Journal*. Regarding her newspaper columns, the daily article was typical big-city food writing, describing a visit to a local restaurant, new trends in cooking, or simply padding an article out with marketing material from food manufacturers. It was the weekly column, titled "How America Eats" for most of its run, that captured her readers' attention.

Paddleford's strength as a journalist was her interviewing ability, and "How America Eats" played to that strength. Most weeks the column focused on a specific cook, and Paddleford ran the gamut of cooks from the famous to the ordinary. One week she might write about the foods Arturo Toscanini preferred (he liked rice soup with celery before performances), the next week could focus on a kitchen aboard a racing yacht, and the third week could be an interview with a housewife from Hoboken. Paddleford traveled widely in preparing her stories and had a considerable store of cooking knowledge.

Yet, as stated before, she does not seem to have cared all that much about cooking. In an unpublished autobiographical sketch she described weekends at a house in Connecticut, writing that "she cooks the easiest things going, grills everything possible over the open fire. Her pet peeve—those well meaning souls who talk recipes hour after hour."[5] In 1949 she printed a recipe for molasses cookies that accidentally omitted the molasses. "'THIS WEEK' [the syndicated Sunday newspaper section where her column appeared] has over a 10,000,000 circulation so you can imagine the mess I'm in," she wrote to the woman who gave her the recipe. She explained that the woman who normally tested recipes was on vacation while another assistant was out with pneumonia. "I didn't miss the 'lasses,'" wrote Paddleford, "a few ingredients mean little to me. What I watch for is if the copy reads pretty. If anyone had any doubts that the 'How America Eats' series wasn't being read—they can now change their minds."[6]

That Paddleford was more concerned with how her copy read than the actual recipe speaks volumes about her attitude toward food. She wanted to write a good story, and the quality of the food was a secondary concern. In that sense, her ideas about food were not too different from those of food companies. In the years after World War II they tended to be much more concerned with the convenience of food or its appearance rather than its taste. Largely, they were occupied with developing new processed foods, since these most affected their bottom line.

The few decades after World War II were something of a golden age of convenience foods. New foods like instant potatoes, frozen dinners, frozen juices, liquid diet drinks, dried milk, powdered coffee creamers, soft margarine, and nondairy creamers came on the market either during or just after World War II. Cake mixes, frozen vegetables, and instant coffee had been introduced before the war but took off during and afterward.[7]

Some product categories saw enormous change. Rising postwar wages meant more spending money for consumers, who rapidly exchanged iceboxes for refrigerators with freezers. This led to a dizzying number of frozen foods coming onto the market, some of which worked well, while others did not. Both frozen strawberries and frozen peas were early successes, while frozen milk never really caught on.[8] Frozen orange juice was an early success story, particularly for orange growers, who were able to sell even highly damaged oranges for processing. However, in 1963, other companies in the food industry bit back at the orange growers when General Foods released Awake, a frozen, synthetic orange drink that looked like orange juice but contained no actual fruit juice. It did have a lot of sweetener, though, and a lot of advertising to support it, and sales took off. Awake was so successful that orange growers pressured the Florida state legislature to retire an old law forbidding the addition of sweetening to orange juice. To compete with the new product, orange juice became sweeter and less healthy.[9]

Awake was a new product, which in and of itself drew some attention, but it also had a massive advertising budget estimated by one observer to be $5 million per year, half a million dollars more than the entire orange juice industry spent annually.[10] Advertising was important for the food industry, particularly when thousands of new products were being released every year. The fact that so much advertising was done by food companies had a distorting effect on the job done by food writers, Clementine Paddleford included, although in many ways she was something of a special case.

Food writing appeared in newspaper columns and in cookbooks, but one of the most popular places it appeared was in women's magazines. Although their readership has drastically declined today, during most of the twentieth century the largest women's magazines had readership measured in the millions, or tens of millions, and they usually had at least a few regular columns devoted to food. Part of this was because their readers, most of whom were housewives, were interested in the subject, but it was also because food companies provided a significant amount of advertising in the magazines—for example, in the 1920s about 20 percent of *Ladies' Home Journal*'s advertising revenue came from food companies.[11] These advertisements often came with strings attached, or at least an expectation that the advertised products receive some positive mentions on nonadvertising pages. While the magazine staff appreciated the revenue, the strings were not appreciated. In 1934 Paddleford submitted an idea for an article to *The American Home* magazine that took a historical look at Christmas meals. The magazine was enthusiastic about the article but not about the possibility of mentioning modern foods. In a response to the query, an editor wrote, "We give free publicity eleven months a year to callous, ungrateful food trusts—at Christmas, at least we are entitled to be pure of heart and duty-free to our dear advertising fraternity." The later rise of television in the 1950s and 1960s elicited panic at the women's magazines, as food companies had a new, direct link to consumers, and the magazines worked even harder to keep the food advertising coming.

Clementine Paddleford, though, does not seem to have had many negative feelings about the companies, or, if she did, she realized that dealing with their power, and perhaps using it, was part of being a food writer. The food companies worked to curry favor with her. When she published a cookbook based on her weekly "How America Eats" column, she received letters of congratulations from Nabisco, General Foods, and the McIlhenny family, producers of Tabasco sauce.

The food companies could be useful to Paddleford. They could, for example, give her article ideas. In the summer of 1956 she took her trip West, discussed above, when she interviewed cooks in five different states and ultimately generated twenty-seven articles from the trip. Before the trip she had gotten a number of leads on cooks to talk to, including a Denver woman suggested by some contacts at the food company Carnation. Paddleford visited the woman and ultimately wrote a story about her, but she admitted to others at her newspaper that the visit was a dud. "Just an average cook," Paddleford wrote in a memo about the trip, "but as I said, she is my 'carnation' tip and by golly I'll make this a sound story, but likely no[t] inspired except with imagination of which it will take plenty."[12]

That imagination came into play in a 1957 column Paddleford wrote about a meal eaten on the *Queen Elizabeth* while traveling across the Atlantic Ocean. She was served a majestic lemon soufflé that she described in her typically breathless writing style: "Such a beautiful soufflé! It came all a-trembling, rising high over the edge of its baking dish. Its golden crown wafted a lemony perfume." The waiter approached and cut into the soufflé, and then "the soufflé subsided with an indrawn sigh, almost imperceptible. The big moment was gone. My plate was served. I took the first bite and forever after will regret past extravagances with hosannas. I might have known I would meet up with perfection some day."[13] After this description Paddleford gave the recipe for the soufflé.

The story behind the soufflé was interesting and Paddleford's description of the dish enticing, but the problem is that it was entirely made up. Cindy Harris, coauthor of a biography of Paddleford and the original archivist of her papers, told me that Paddleford did not take any trips across the Atlantic around the time the article was printed. According to Harris, a red flag about the article is the fact that it is not focused on a particular cook, which usually means that Paddleford did not research the article herself. Rather, the article is based on a letter from a publicist from the California Lemon Products Industry News Bureau—note that the publicist did not represent the growers, but rather companies that made products from lemons, a good example of how farmers were moving farther and farther to the periphery of the food industry. The publicist's letter included a soufflé recipe that called for frozen lemon concentrate, and it included these lines: "While in New York and on the *Queen Elizabeth* to Europe, I fell in love with lemon soufflés. When I returned here, our home economist worked out the attached recipe for a Baked Lemonade soufflé."[14] Paddleford apparently took both the recipe and the idea of eating a lemon soufflé on the *Queen Elizabeth* and fabricated a story about herself eating the soufflé on the ship.

Clementine Paddleford seems to have had a soft spot for lemons, since a year later she wrote an article titled "Lemons for Zest!" Like the soufflé article, it was printed in her nationally syndicated column, but rather than describing a particular meal, Paddleford outlined a number of uses for lemon juice including flavoring breads and mixing it with melted butter as a sauce for vegetables. This article, too, was based on marketing material, this time from Sunkist. While Paddleford could not mention specific company names in her articles, Sunkist seems to have been quite happy with it, as the advertising executive who handled the Sunkist account sent a letter to Paddleford specifically thanking her for the article. As he wrote, "I imagine that Foote, Cone & Belding [the advertising firm that worked for Sunkist] wishes they could get as much sell concerning lemons into a 1/2 page as you were able to do in this article."[15]

"How America Eats" was the weekly, nationally syndicated column that made Paddleford famous, but by the mid-1960s Paddleford's approach to cooking was changing, along with that of much of America. "How America Eats" had focused on individual cooks who cooked from scratch, but in 1965 the name of the column changed to "Cook Young," something of a strange name change for a column written by a woman in her mid-sixties. In 1960 Paddleford had published *How America Eats*, a cookbook full of recipes that had been featured in her weekly column, and a new cookbook was planned for "Cook Young." Unlike *How America Eats*, though, this cookbook was not to be based on previously published recipes, nor would it focus on scratch cooking. Rather, it was to be based on reader-submitted recipes that emphasized what was often called "shortcut cooking."

As Paddleford put it in the introduction to the *Cook Young Cookbook*, "Cooking from 'scratch' is no longer the brag thing. Even Grandma and her league practice being instant gourmets." What was an instant gourmet? The emphasis was on the word *instant*, as Paddleford highlighted speed. "America's food cart has been hitched to a skyrocket. Never have so many people eaten so well with so little effort. Convenience foods are so diverse one couldn't cook through the list in years. Today a woman can count on two-thirds of her food coming out of cans and packages."[16]

The *Cook Young Cookbook* was something of a hybrid cookbook with one foot in the world of convenience foods (with its use of cans and mixes) and one foot in the world of scratch cooking (with its use of actual recipes and mixing bowls and ovens). It was not entirely unusual, as there were cookbooks before and since that time focused on this type of cooking. Poppy Cannon's *Can Opener Cookbook*, from 1951, is usually seen as, depending on one's point of view, either the high point or the low point of this type of cooking, as it was a very popular book that featured recipes where the cook spent more time using a can opener than a stirring spoon. This approach to cooking is something of a strange thing. The promise of convenience cooking is the *convenience*—one should not have to mess around with dirty dishes and hot ovens—so using packaged foods in this way seems odd. This sort of cooking is also hard to reproduce as the years go by, since the flavors of packaged foods like condensed soups and dried mixes have changed over time.

Clementine Paddleford introduced the idea for the *Cook Young Cookbook* in her nationally syndicated column, asking for recipes that used convenience foods in one way or another. She received a deluge of mail in return. Analysis of the thousands of letters she received provides some insights, not always positive, about American cooking in the 1960s.

Within a short time of the announcement of the book, she had received more than ten thousand submissions. An assistant went through roughly nine hundred of those and wrote a memo summarizing the types of material they were receiving from cooks across the country. About half the recipes were wrong for the book—they were recipes for cooking from scratch and used no convenience foods. The vast majority of the rest of the submissions were simply recipes copied from newspapers, magazines, or the back of boxes, and some of those recipes seemed to be very popular. There were about seventy-five submissions of a string bean recipe that used the same three branded ingredients. Duncan Hines cake mixes were the clear winner in the cake recipe category, but, as the assistant wrote, "on the merit of one ad only. The ladies have dubbed it the 'Jello Cake' and every woman in the country must have tried it." That recipe involved mixing "one package of Duncan Hines yellow cake mix, one package lemon flavored Jello, corn oil, eggs and water. After baking it is finished off with a fruit juice glaze. There is just enough work to make a woman feel self-satisfied. And she enjoys the business of stabbing the cake with a fork before pouring on the glaze. It's intriguing." Of the nine hundred recipes the assistant went through, only about one hundred fit the criteria for inclusion in the cookbook, but even those were merely variations on recipes that had appeared in advertisements for convenience foods. "The readers don't know they are all cooking the same things," the assistant commented, "but we know it!"

Part of the repetition in submissions came from the nature of the project. The recipes had to use some form of convenience food, which meant the recipes had to be relatively new, since most convenience foods had only been around for a few decades. And the main source of new recipes using convenience foods was, predictably, the food companies that produced the convenience foods—or, to be more specific, the home economists employed by those food companies. The recipes were printed on the back of food packages and in magazine advertisements, many of which were clipped by busy housewives looking for a quick meal idea. Sixty years after the beginning of the home economics movement, cooking had been simplified to the point that a cook only needed to know how to follow a recipe, not create a new one. "Today's busy women have neither the time nor the skill to develop their own recipes," the author of the *Cook Young* memo wrote, "but they are avidly interested in learning the new convenience cuisine. Our mail proves that their only source of information is the ad that can be torn out and filed."[17]

But did the housewives of the 1960s realize that all of their recipes came from food companies? A memo written a few months after the first memo, analyzing more of the submissions to the *Cook Young Cookbook*, sheds some light on just how housewives of the 1960s perceived the origin of the recipes they used. "When women mentioned the source of their recipes, many said 'don't remember,' 'probably a magazine,' 'a neighbor,' 'a newspaper column,' etc. and then often added 'changed it so much I now consider it mine,' even though the change might not have been more than using cream of celery soup instead of mushroom, sour cream instead of milk, dream whip instead of whipped cream, another flavor jello with another set of canned frozen fruits," the author wrote. "But it was still a box top recipe. Many, many women said they would like to do 'fancy' cooking but didn't have the time. So what they did instead was change the box recipe around a bit."[18]

The unnamed author of the memo went on to give a number of examples of slight changes that were submitted as original recipes, which included "substituting flavors of canned soups, or mixing various flavor cake mixes with various flavored jellos and instant puddings. [The women] like adding extra eggs to a cake mix, putting something additional into the canned chili and beans, biscuits and ready to bake pastries." However, the author noted that they sometimes went too far with substitutions, resulting in a "Pandora's box of concoctions." Campbell's had urged women to cook with canned soups, and Duncan Hines had suggested adding instant pudding or gelatin to cake mixes, but the author complained that "some women have gone so far as to mix pudding with gelatine, [*sic*] and leave out the cake."

The author finished the memo by writing, "American women may be unsophisticated cooks, but they are looking for ideas, and short cuts, and those ideas and short cuts seem to come right out of the ads, off the boxes, and from the can labels. They grow to love these recipes so that they will tell you with a straight face that it is their own, original idea—and they are delighted to share it with you."

The heart of any kind of cooking is a recipe, and the attitudes gleaned from submissions to the *Cook Young Cookbook* reveal several things about the state of American home cooking in the middle of the twentieth century. For one thing, housewives at that time seem to have seen recipes as providing a template for cooking that was not set in stone. Substitutions were permitted, within certain parameters. Not many cooks would substitute, say, cherry Jell-O for mushroom soup, but they could certainly switch strawberry Jell-O for cherry, or cream of celery soup for cream of mushroom soup. Even a single, minor substitution seems to have been enough for a cook to consider that she had drastically changed the resulting dish, to the point that she herself had created a new recipe.

The submissions also show that American cooks saw some convenience foods as being equivalent to ingredients rather than finished foods. Certainly, canned cream of mushroom soup could be served as a soup by itself, but it could also be mixed with other ingredients to make another dish entirely (and it should be noted that canned, condensed soup needed to have a liquid added to it to make it palatable as a soup). The organizers of the *Cook Young Cookbook* observed that some convenience foods had become pantry staples. Remarking on the number of casserole recipes that required canned soups, one of the memo writers commented that "American cooking would founder without Campbell's cream soups." She also noted, "Dehydrated onion and parsley are considered invaluable." Some older pantry staples were even now replaced with convenience foods. Recipes that in previous years would have called for whipped cream now required Dream Whip—as the memo writer put it, "Real whipped cream is now much frowned upon!"[19]

Home cooking was now both simpler and more complicated than it had been a generation or so before. There were new convenience foods, like condensed or instant soups, that could be added to other ingredients to quickly make dishes like casseroles. In some ways cooking became more complicated, though, with the question of just what cooking from scratch meant—was someone cooking from scratch if they added canned soups to other ingredients? The use of convenience foods affected the taste of foods. Processing foods changes the taste of the food, which is why processed foods have so much salt and sometimes so much sugar—the producer is trying to cover the processed taste. That taste, and the salt and sugar that came along with it, made its way into home-cooked foods.

In some ways the 1950s and 1960s were the apogee of processed foods, the time when it seemed that the steady introduction of new and improved convenience foods would eventually push fresh foods from the marketplace. This can be seen in the growth of supermarkets during this time, as stores grew larger and larger with shelves filled with more and more products. In the early twentieth century the average store stocked about five hundred items; by the 1960s a supermarket could stock more than six thousand items.[20] Many of these items, of course, were the same food in different flavors and from different companies, but the rate of introduction of new foods could be breathtaking. One grocery wholesaler offered its customers (grocery stores) 39 varieties of cake mixes in 1954 and 108 in 1964. Although this appears to be an increase of 69 mixes, between 1954 and 1964 the wholesaler actually added 207 cake mixes and dropped 138 items from its sales list.[21]

The seemingly inevitable rise of convenience foods can also be seen in the attitudes of professional food writer James Beard. Beard had gotten his start by catering parties in New York City before World War II, and by the 1950s he had several cookbooks to his name. Between 1952 and 1964 he corresponded with food writer Helen Evans Brown, and convenience foods came up several times in their letters. In 1953 he visited a restaurant trade show in Chicago and relayed to Brown what he saw, and what he did not see. "There were artificial onion soups, ice cream made from old rayon petticoats, barbecued sandwiches heated with a steam pipe in one second, cake mixes and pancake mixes by the ton," he wrote. "But as for anything to make food better or more truly flavorful, there was nothing. A sad commentary on the future of food in this country. If restaurateurs are intent on cutting quality and giving artificially puffed-up food, there is no chance for any of us to do missionary work."[22]

The "missionary work" Beard had in mind seems to have been in favor of using fresh ingredients in scratch cooking, but in his letters he often complained that he was getting no takers on that sort of cooking. Part of the problem was that he spent much of his time employed as a consultant to a multitude of food companies, most of which wanted to sell convenience food, not fresh food. Beard took the money, even if he sometimes did not believe in the products he was asked to help sell. He wrote a recipe booklet for Whirl, a butter substitute in a can, but told the company people frankly that, for some purposes, butter just worked better. "I cannot see myself selling [Whirl]," he wrote to Brown. "It looks like something for artificial insemination when it comes out of the can, and I am sure it is going to have that effect on most who see it."[23]

Beard also butted heads with the food company home economists who had final say on his recipes and who often substituted ingredients they believed were too complicated for the average housewife or used tools she would not have. One home economist substituted dried onion for the grated variety and dropped the rosemary from a recipe, arguing that most housewives would not have the pestle required to grind the herb (Beard groused to Brown that the rosemary could be used whole).[24] On another occasion a food company chef opined that a galantine, a traditional Polish meat dish of stuffed meat, was too difficult for the average housewife to make, since it took the chef four hours to make one himself. "I am sick of thinking the American housewife is dumb," Beard told the chef. "She can do anything if she wants to, and the reason she doesn't is because too many of you think everything has to be done for her . . . if you can read and know cooking there is nothing you can't achieve."[25] Helen Evans Brown agreed with his opinions of home economists and others who worked for the food companies. "Home economists!" she wrote in one letter. "Nothing I do is right any more . . . 'Lovely is not a word to apply to food.' 'Don't say stale bread, say day old bread' etc. See what I mean? I am so self-conscious about everything I write that I can't write."[26]

To some extent Beard made his peace with convenience foods, although he was not entirely happy with it. Responding to pressure to make his recipes simpler and easier, he admitted that "as much as I hate to say it, I am coming to the point of saying that we have to follow some of the trends and give quick-and-easies, and perhaps time each recipe and show shortcuts for most of them. . . . I'll hate us for taking the easy way out, but I know damned well we'll make money if we can make the easy things taste better than the others can, and I think that is probably our mission in life."[27] A few years later he even contemplated writing a book focusing exclusively on packaged mixes. "There are some good mixes on the market," he wrote to Brown. "I like the hot roll mix of Pillsbury and the buttermilk pancake mix of Duncan Hines, and their cake mixes aren't so bad either." He also reported finding some "lousy stuff as well. That vanillin [synthetic vanilla] is poison. I have managed to smother it in a couple of cases with rum and cognac."[28] He did eventually write the book that used packaged mixes, justifying it to Brown as an exercise to give cooks more familiarity with making baked goods the old-fashioned way. "I think the roll mixes have a tremendous value for people who would be afraid to attempt bread. They can get the feeling of yeast doughs from a mix and then go on to the recipe from scratch."[29]

The idea that convenience foods would take over the world was coming not only from food companies and food professionals but also from the government. In 1955 Beard heard about a conference of food editors where the overall message from the conference was "horrifying." "Soon," he wrote to Brown, "there will be no fresh foods on the market—just canned or frozen (this came from the lips of the Secretary of Agriculture)."[30]

Secretary of Agriculture Ezra Taft Benson was indeed a fan of processed foods. In the depths of the Cold War the United States worked hard to portray itself as a land of plenty, and one way to do that was through an abundance of food. America was well stocked with food to begin with, and increased food processing could help that even more, since fruits and vegetables frozen at the height of freshness could be frozen for months or even years, rather than allowed to rot because they could not be sold in time. Speaking at a 1954 event to commemorate the twenty-fifth anniversary of the frozen food industry, he reminded his audience that the government had, on many occasions, worked hand in hand with the frozen food industry. The USDA runs research stations across the country, each station conducting experiments fitted to local agriculture (so, for example, research done by the USDA in California in the middle of the century would be integral to California wines coming to international attention later in the century). Secretary Benson reported that USDA scientists had been researching frozen foods as early as 1904, and in the 1930s a regional lab had been set up with a specific role of working on research in frozen foods. Pointing to the frozen food industry's biggest success yet, he reminded his audience that the research done at the USDA station in Winter Haven, Florida, in 1944 had led to the development of the process for making frozen orange juice.[31]

In his address, Secretary Benson looked to the future. Farming usually exists in a state of either surplus or scarcity, and part of Benson's job was dealing with both extremes. When he spoke, there was a surplus of dairy products—in attempting to purchase its way out of the problem, the government then owned about 1.3 billion pounds of butter, cheese, and other dairy products ("If the American people were drinking as much milk as they were a few years ago there would be no surplus of dairy products," he complained). He hoped that advances in dehydrating milk might do for the dairy industry what frozen orange juice had done for the orange juice industry—that is, remove the fresh milk surplus by converting it into a commodity that could be stored and used later. His hopes would soon come true, as dried milk did help to revolutionize the dairy industry.

Some of his other hopes would require more time. News of the existence of the H-bomb, a more advanced type of nuclear weapon than the original atomic bomb, had recently broken, and although the threat of nuclear attack from the Soviet Union was very real, Secretary Benson looked to the positive possibilities from nuclear power. Nuclear energy had helped the USDA "speed up our knowledge of plant breeding [and] of fertilizer application," he reported, then asked, "Why can't it do much more? Can't we make the desert bloom through irrigation?" His idea was to use cheap atomic power to run desalination plants to supply fresh water to coastal cities, thereby allowing inland areas to keep their own fresh water for agriculture—a train of thought that clearly, in its mention of deserts and coasts, applied specifically to the always tricky water situation in California. With more water available, more crops could be grown, which would logically lead to more surpluses, but, again, he saw technology as a way out of the situation. "Why not new plants, new products to add to our standard of living—just as the rubber tree and the soybean have done? Aren't frozen foods new products? Plastics? Automobiles? Airplanes?"

By lumping frozen foods together with plastics, cars, and airplanes, Secretary Benson made it clear that frozen food, and food in general, was just another commodity to be produced and then consumed by the public. There was nothing special about food that made it different from coal, iron, or other resources, other than the pesky tendency of food growers to produce either too much or too little in a given year, and food processing was rapidly taking care of that problem. This showed that the food industry, along with all other industries in America, was changing with the times, adopting new technologies and inventions as they came along or were specifically developed to solve the problems of the food industry.

To anyone opposed to the changes in the food industry, Secretary Benson had only a few cutting, direct words: "Let's not be reactionary," he said. "The reactionaries are those with inflexible minds who always want the status quo. They are opposed to freedom to progress." Clearly, processed food was the future of not just the food industry but also American food in general.

Processed food was certainly making its way into the restaurant industry, which was at something of a low point in the first few decades after World War II. Sales were down from the wartime highs, particularly as family life increasingly centered on the home and women left their wartime jobs to be housewives and thus had more time for cooking. There were also issues with the quality of American restaurants. The problem was not that they were terrible; it was more that the best were simply not all that great.

Duncan Hines, long before he became a name on cake mix boxes, first became famous as a traveling salesman who kept lists of good hotels and restaurants he came across on his travels. Those lists eventually became guidebooks, sold at establishments he recommended. Hines's background was not in food, although he knew what he liked, and what he liked was a place that was clean and had good food. At that time, particularly in rural locales where health inspectors might never visit a restaurant, a guidebook listing recommended establishments was a near necessity for travelers. This situation would help the growth of places like Holiday Inn and McDonald's, places that were clean and standardized at locations across the country.

In some ways the state of American restaurants before and after World War II can be judged from the Duncan Hines guidebooks. They were not Michelin guides, and there was no actual rating system in the books, using something like stars or a letter ranking. The only real rating for a restaurant was whether it was listed, and a listing only meant that it was recommended. In reading the introduction to the 1961 edition, it appears that cleanliness was the most important factor in whether a restaurant appeared in the guide. The introduction is very specific in pointing out that establishments did not pay for the honor of being listed, and that there was no advertising in the book. The last part of the introduction is a section titled "Nothing Is More Important Than Cleanliness," and it advised travelers to be careful to only eat at places with clean kitchens. In this section the authors somewhat obliquely defined the kind of food they preferred by writing, "Satisfying food should have eye appeal, taste good and be good for you." However, the very next sentence came back to the issue of cleanliness and health: "Many laws have been passed in states all over the nation to safeguard the public's health," adding that "people eating out should give sufficient thought to the kitchen of a public eating place rather than be guided solely by chromium fronts and attractive interior decorations."[32]

This emphasis on cleanliness affected Americans' perceptions of what restaurant food should be. Anything that could be used to cover the taste of rotten or badly cooked food, like strong spices, was frowned upon, which meant that the most popular restaurant food was straightforward American meat-and-potatoes-type food. Most Americans had a traditional distrust of ethnic restaurants, so, when that distrust was coupled with a mania for cleanliness, the 1950s and early 1960s became a low point in the popularity of ethnic restaurants.

Fast food restaurants like McDonald's first became popular during this time by emphasizing quick service, low prices, and a restricted menu. Although the hamburger would come to dominate the fast food landscape, in the early twentieth century many people distrusted ground meat, and the meat and restaurant industry had worked to combat their suspicion. Because the customer could not witness the meat actually being ground up, and therefore almost anything could be in ground meat, the government passed a law that stated that meat marked "hamburger" could only be made from beef, not from other animals or other substances (of course, this only restricts the types of animals that can go into hamburger, not the parts of the animal that could be added). White Castle, the first hamburger chain, built its restaurants with the grill in clear view of the customer and used "white" in its name in an attempt to give it a sheen of cleanliness.[33]

Because the Duncan Hines guidebooks were the most popular restaurant guidebooks of the postwar era, restaurants had little impetus to raise their quality beyond what the books required. While the authors of the book may have emphasized food that had "eye appeal, taste[d] good and [was] good for you," these criteria were never defined. One of the reasons why Craig Claiborne, of the *New York Times*, became influential during the 1960s was because, as a restaurant reviewer, he was specific about what he liked and did not like, and he did not hesitate to give bad reviews to restaurants that fell below his expectations. Clementine Paddleford also reviewed restaurants, but, like many other food writers before Claiborne, she did not give bad reviews (as she explained, "I have to eat in restaurants").[34] By only holding restaurants to an expectation of cleanliness, reviewers like those from Duncan Hines allowed American restaurants to stay mediocre in the postwar years.

In spite of the popularity of convenience foods, there was still quite a bit of cooking from scratch being done in the years after World War II, as evidenced in an explosion in the number of cookbooks on the market (the rise in the number of cookbooks also points to growing prosperity for most Americans, with more disposable income to spend on cookbooks). In 1952 *Publisher's Weekly* included a roundup of new cookbooks, a list that looks strikingly modern in terms of its authors and subjects. The article was written by an employee at the Scribner Book Store in New York City who recalled that when she started in the late 1920s, just before the Great Depression, there were only three or four cookbooks in stock, while a more senior employee commented that when he started, in 1919, they only sold Fannie Farmer's cookbook. The article mentions, in one way or another, forty cookbooks coming out that spring.

Several cookbooks focused on French cooking. James Beard cowrote *Paris Cuisine*, which featured two hundred recipes from sixty famous Paris chefs. France was a destination for many American tourists, and the author of the article mentioned that, while the publisher did not indicate it, the book could function as a restaurant guide for tourists bound for Paris. Elizabeth David's *French Country Cooking* was being published for the American market after having originally been published in Britain. There was also a slim, sixty-page volume titled *What's Cooking in France*, written by the trio of Louisette Bertholle, Simone Beck, and Helmut Ripperger. Bertholle and Beck were amateur cooks living in France who had come up with the recipes, while Ripperger had written the rest of the book's text and selected the fifty recipes in the book from a longer list of recipes compiled by Bertholle and Beck. *What's Cooking in France* would not end up selling many copies, but the two women had plans for a much larger cookbook, and by the summer of 1952 they had more than six hundred pages of recipes. Ripperger had moved on to other projects by then, but Julia Child, living in France, soon took his place working on the cookbook that would make her famous.[35]

Other books looked at foreign dishes, although the number and variety of cultures was limited. In addition to a fourth cookbook on French cooking, two books featured Chinese dishes, while another, published by *Sunset* magazine, looked at the foods of a variety of cultures, organizing the recipes by type of dish rather than country of origin, resulting in "a sort of international hodge-podge effect."[36]

A number of cookbooks were devoted to cooking meals quickly or cheaply. *Magic Half Hour Dinners* sounds like a forerunner of Rachel Ray, with a menu and shopping list included for each meal and extensive use of both canned and frozen foods. *Quick and Easy Meals for Two* was for working wives, while the market for *The Busy Girl's Cook Book* was self-explanatory. *Solving the High Cost of Eating* was a large volume of 1,300 recipes "based on the very sound principle that packaged foods are more expensive than the ones you prepare yourself," the reviewer wrote, while noting that, after looking through the other books for busy cooks that used convenience foods, "I fear this is a lost cause."[37]

Finally, there were cookbooks that focused on particular types of meals or methods of food preparation. The blender had recently become a popular consumer item, and *Electric Blender Recipes* contained more than four hundred recipes for using the appliance, including many recipes that went beyond simply using it for drinks (the author of the review noted that she found "some of the cocktails, both alcoholic and nonalcoholic, quite frightening").[38] Two books were devoted to cooking primarily or entirely with vegetables, and a number of books were written specifically for those wishing to lose weight. Most of those authors approached weight loss from the standpoint of counting calories. *Eat and Grow Younger*, though, had a system that is not out of line with recent diet books; it "strongly advises a protein diet and recommends skim milk and natural foods such as honey and whole grain products."[39]

In general, the cookbooks produced in the mid-twentieth century are very similar to those produced today, and the differences are usually due to technology. The glossy, photo-filled modern cookbooks that are more like displayable coffee table books are absent, but the cookbooks of sixty years ago are much more like today's cookbooks than those of a hundred, or a hundred and fifty, years ago.

House styles changed in the middle of the century, and kitchens changed as well. During the 1930s and early 1940s not many houses were built, due to lack of money and, later, rationing of building materials. The war brought jobs, but the jobs often meant moving from one place to another, and when job seekers arrived in a place they often found that there was not much existing housing or that the only housing available was temporary, such as quick-built Quonset huts with tin walls and a curved metal roof. Two years after the war six million American families were living with either family or friends, and half a million lived in temporary housing. [40] Thus, after the war, when jobs stayed plentiful and wages stayed high, many American families looked to move into their own homes. Quite frequently, that home was a brand-new house in the suburbs.

Millions of suburban houses were constructed in the few decades after World War II. The low-slung ranch style house was popular, its living space all on one level, its interior floor only a step or two above the outside ground. In the midst of the baby boom the houses were often small, particularly when compared with houses built today, with less than a thousand square feet to share among two parents and a handful of children. Because of the small size, the houses often emphasized connections to the outdoors, with large picture windows and sliding glass doors leading to a patio in the back.

The floor plans in these new suburban houses were different from that of older homes, particularly when it came to the kitchen. Once the warmest room of the house, and consequently relegated to the back of the dwelling to more easily shunt off the heat to the outside, the kitchen in midcentury houses moved to the front and center of the structure. Modern stoves only warmed when they were engaged in cooking food, and they were insulated to hold in the heat, so excess heat was a minor problem, made even less of an issue after the widespread adoption of air conditioning in the 1960s and 1970s. In the family-oriented 1950s, kitchens were moved to the front of the house so Mom, working in the kitchen, could watch for the children coming home from school.

The idea behind turn-of-the-century homes was that each room had a distinct function, whether for dining, socializing, or preparing food. This had changed with the smaller postwar houses. As the *Better Homes & Gardens Decorating Book* from 1956 put it, "The hired girl, or the maid, has long since disappeared from most homes. Because of this, and also because of the cost of building, many houses have fewer rooms, serving more than one purpose—and engineered for the utmost in efficiency and easy care."[41] That book offered a variety of kitchen designs, including one with an open concept between the kitchen and family room, built with a curtain hanging from the ceiling that could be pulled to hide the kitchen, thus making "dining more pleasant for everyone."[42] The details of that particular layout are a good reminder of the smaller size of postwar houses, especially when compared to today's houses. At the end of the kitchen counter was a small desk "with handy telephone [that] does double duty as a serving table at mealtime." At the other end of the family room, opposite the kitchen, were two closet doors that hid a washer and dryer—laundry rooms were not yet standard, and many washers were on wheels, intended to be rolled into the kitchen when used and then hidden away.

The book illustrates some of the hallmarks of postwar kitchens such as the color schemes. While turn-of-the-century kitchens had been seas of white countertops, white appliances, white tile on the floor—all to better express the idea that the kitchen was clean and hygienic—postwar kitchens were "alive with color," as the authors of the book wrote. "Both major and minor appliances feature colors—pink, turquoise, yellow, brown, bright red, and special finishes of copper, silver, gold and brushed chrome are among the many choices now available."[43]

While separate dining rooms were still desirable for the occasional formal dinner, there was a definite movement to put at least some seating in the kitchen area. Some of this was because of the baby boom, as it was much easier for a woman to cook if she could keep an eye on her kids working at the table at the same time. With the baby boom came an increased feeling of the importance of family, and the kitchen, in some ways, seemed to be ground zero for the family. As the authors of the *Better Homes & Gardens Decorating Book* indicated, "The kitchen is a warm and wonderful place for the family to gather. Plan comfortable seating for part-time helpers and onlookers. Arrange a place for family meals. Plan enough counter space so children can make their own after-school snacks and not be underfoot."[44] However, many kitchens simply did not have room for much extra seating, which led to the popularity of the breakfast counter. This counter was a few inches below the standard counter height, intended to be used by people sitting in normal chairs, and it extended from the end of the kitchen countertop, often curving around a corner or doubling back on itself so that those sitting at the breakfast counter could easily face someone working in the kitchen. In this configuration, it was a home version of what someone could find at the diners and lunch counters across the country back then, with Mom substituting for the waitress or short-order cook.

The smaller kitchens also helped the popularity of a relatively new type of cooking in the years after World War II: the barbecue. As a social trend, barbecuing was an outlier, as it went against existing ideas about who should cook and where the cooking should happen.

The modern popularity of barbecue dates to the 1930s, when it was a cooking trend associated with the West. Previously barbecue had been seen as a southern thing, something that most northerners had never tasted and that was largely associated with large southern gatherings, particularly political rallies. But in the 1930s a craze for what might be called a western lifestyle came along, centered on California, where the weather was temperate enough to live outside, on the patio, for much of the year. Southern barbecue had focused on cooking meat for long hours at a low temperature, but with the new trend, barbecuing was the equivalent of grilling, cooking meat (or fruit, or vegetables) over an open fire for a short time.

With its connection to campfire cooking, barbecuing quickly became a masculine, not feminine, undertaking. This made it the rare cooking activity that men could do without fear of anyone questioning their masculinity (the other two activities in this camp were making weekend pancakes, usually by using a packaged mix, and drying, but not washing, the dishes). Although men were supposed to be the ones in charge of the grill, it should be noted that, traditionally, the man's role in barbecuing begins and ends at the grill, with the woman responsible for planning the rest of the meal, buying the groceries, making the side dishes, drinks, and dessert, and cleaning up afterward.

Barbecuing was also topsy-turvy in that it was often a purely outdoor activity in which the food was not only cooked outside but also consumed outside. Unlike most other foods, barbecued dishes like corn on the cob or hamburgers were intended to be eaten with the hands, often on disposable dishes. These aspects of barbecuing, and consuming a barbecued meal, helped with its popularity. The fact that barbecue could be eaten outside, informally, made it ideal for families with children. It was also ideal for parties, since the entire gathering could be taken outside of a small house.

In addition, barbecuing seemed to go against the postwar trend of buying and consuming more and more convenience foods. Cooking over an open fire seems to be the most primal activity possible, and so it is out of touch with an overall movement toward using more convenience foods. This is only true if one looks at whatever is being grilled over the fire. All the rest of the food served at a barbecue, like the side dishes, drinks, and dessert, could be (and often were) foods that were purchased, fully made, from grocery stores. In this way barbecuing was entirely in line with the overall trend in cooking through the mid-1960s.

In the mid- to late 1960s an opposing set of ideas came into view to push against the ideology set around convenience foods, one that stressed the primacy of cooking from scratch. That ideology has always been around, of course. For thousands of years scratch cooking was the only way of cooking a meal. By the 1950s and 1960s, though, convenience foods had made such inroads, and were so easy to use, that cooking from scratch was increasingly seen as an anachronism, akin to using horses to pull the family Dodge or a ringer and washboard to wash a family's clothes. This is not to say that no one was cooking from scratch by the 1960s. Clementine Paddleford, who saw no problem with using convenience foods in her articles or while cooking for herself, regularly featured scratch recipes in her columns, as did the women's magazines that relied heavily on advertising from food companies. It was more that scratch cooking had no single, important person singing its praises, and there was no mass movement that supported it.

That would change by the end of the 1960s. Scratch cooking would get its figurehead in Julia Child, and its movement in the counterculture that sprang up among many members of the baby boomer generation, then in their teens and twenties.

Julia Child promoted her ideas about scratch cooking from squarely within the realm of cooking. Her road to becoming a cook was long and twisted, and far different from the women who trained to become home economists, which resulted in Child having an approach to cooking that was extremely different from the average home economist.

Child's life was interesting long before she became a standard fixture on television. She was born Julia McWilliams in Pasadena, California, in 1912 to a well-to-do family. She did not learn much about cooking as a child, since the family had a cook, although her mother did handle the cooking on Thursday evenings (the cook's night off). Child's main interest in food was geared more toward consumption than production, and she later commented that she "had the appetite of a wolf."[45] Her first trip east was to attend Smith College, a traditional women's college, and after she graduated she lived in New York City for a few years, writing marketing copy for a local store.

Much of this was standard for a young woman of her time, and it has parallels to Clementine Paddleford's life. Both graduated from college, both spent time in the largest cities in America after college, and both worked careers that involved writing. A key difference in their lives was World War II: Paddleford was in her early forties and well established in a career when America joined the war, while Child was in her late twenties and not too attached to the work she was doing. Child signed up for government service in 1942, ending up with the OSS (the wartime forerunner of the CIA) in Washington, where she helped with various projects. One challenge for a military with members serving around the world, in jungles and deserts and on the high seas, is keeping stranded servicemen alive if disaster strikes. Child's group worked on solutions to potential problems. Sailors in a life raft needed water to survive—could that water come from fish the sailors might catch? Child was dispatched to the market to buy fish for the experiment. [46]

At first the OSS was mostly based in Washington, but as the war dragged on the head of the department sent his people out into the world. Child went to India to help with the war in Asia, and there she met Paul Child, who was also working for the U.S. government. They hit it off, despite their differences—he was worldly but introverted, she was outgoing and boisterous, and he was nearly ten years older than she. Together they were reassigned to China, and then they stayed together after the war, in the United States, getting married in the fall of 1946.

As was mentioned above, Julia Child's relationship with food by this point was more focused on consuming it than producing it. She liked to eat, enjoyed trying new foods, and, knowing that her husband was something of a gourmet, worked to learn more about cooking. This was, after all, the postwar period, when women (particularly married women with money) were expected to stay home and keep house. She had taken cooking courses just after the war, when she was apart from Paul and working to definitively "catch him" for marriage, and now she used a copy of *The Joy of Cooking* to learn more about cooking as a new housewife. This seems to have been a trying time. Describing making her first broiled chicken, she later said, "I put it in the oven for twenty minutes, went out, came back, and it was burned; I needed better directions."[47] Although Julia planned for a timely dinner, Paul sometimes had to wait until late in the evening before something edible emerged from the kitchen. This refusal to give up and to work until a job was done right would be a major component in the creation of the cookbook that made her famous (and would also keep Paul eating late dinners for years to come).

Paul took a job with the State Department with an assignment in Paris. After they were settled in, Julia, with a lifelong passion for learning everything she could on a given subject, signed up for classes at the Cordon Bleu cooking school. At this time the school was much less impressive than it is today. Then the school was run by the owner, who taught a dozen students how to be professional chefs (there was another class made up of housewives who wanted to learn how to cook French food—Child was originally in this class but quickly transferred to the professional class). Her fellow students were American veterans, their tuition paid by the government. The school had no modern appliances, which meant Child learned how to prepare everything using traditional, manual methods. To make ham mousse, they first pounded the ham in an enormous mortar (Child's size—she was six feet two inches tall—and strength came in handy here), then pushed the ham through a sieve and scraped the sieve clean. Much later she observed that, although the mousse was delicious, it took an hour and a half to make and could have been prepared in a few minutes with a food processor.

Child finished classes in six months and continued learning with a chef who had already been tutoring her. Still passionate about French cooking, she started a small cooking school with two French women, Louisette Bertholle and Simone Beck, the authors of *What's Cooking in France*, mentioned above. Together they taught students in Bertholle's recently renovated home kitchen. If the Cordon Bleu was Child's entry point to French cooking, her friendship with Bertholle and Beck was her entry point to the cookbook that would make her famous. The two women had already submitted the text for a new cookbook to a publisher in the United States, but, in its original state, the publisher had turned the manuscript down, with two suggestions: the women should get an American coauthor, and the recipes—appearing on six hundred typewritten pages—needed to be revised for American cooks. Child, with her knowledge of both American and French cooking and her indefatigable energy, appeared to be just the person Bertholle and Beck needed.

Work on the cookbook took the majority of the next decade, and Child and Beck did most of the work—although Bertholle is listed as a full author on the book, she did not have the time or inclination to put anything close to the amount of work her two coauthors invested in the endeavor. The book was to be for American cooks, who were mostly housewives, and it would present instructions for making French dishes in a clear, straightforward manner. It would be authoritative, which meant that the dishes should represent authentic versions of traditional French dishes. To find these, Child spoke to chefs around France and consulted books by accepted authorities on the topic, such as Georges Auguste Escoffier. The chefs were often more helpful than the books—as she read and compared instructions between books, Child realized that the recipes printed in classic French cookbooks were usually written in the kind of shorthand that appeared in American cookbooks of the early 1800s, suggestions written by (and for) professional cooks who already knew their way around French cooking. Plus, the authors often seemed to have just copied recipes from older books or from each other.

Although French cooking was perennially popular in America, there were no other cookbooks available that went as far as Child's book eventually would. Elizabeth David released *French Provincial Cooking* four years before Child's book came out, and although both books covered some of the same territory, David took a different approach to providing recipes. For example, she spent a few pages in her book on bouillabaisse, a traditional fish stew. She first presented some guidelines for making it, including the observations that the dish required olive oil and saffron and that the soup had to be set to a hard boil. She then provided a recipe, translated and copied directly from a French cookbook, which called for six types of fish, including some that are unusual in America. Following the recipe was about a page and a half, again copied and translated from another book, where a man described going fishing when he was ten years old and eating the catch, made up as a bouillabaisse. While all this might be interesting to those curious about French cooking, most American housewives who wanted to experiment with French cooking needed something much more direct, written specifically for them.[48]

Early in the writing process, Child, Beck, and Bertholle signed a contract with Houghton Mifflin for the book. Child and Beck worked on the manuscript relentlessly over the next few years, consulting each other in person while Paul Child was still assigned to Paris and keeping in contact via letters when the Childs spent a few years in Germany, and then when Paul was reassigned to Washington. In early 1957 Child and

Beck sat down to a meeting in New York City with Houghton Mifflin over what they had submitted so far—more than seven hundred pages that represented only the chapters on sauces and poultry. Hundreds, if not thousands, of pages still remained to be written, covering the rest of French cooking, an undertaking that would take several more years to research and write.

This was not the book Houghton Mifflin was looking for. Representatives from the publisher made it clear that they had no intention of publishing an encyclopedia of French cooking. The men involved in the meeting, in particular, were unhappy with the book's approach. As one participant in the meeting later remembered, the main complaint from the men was "Oh, Americans don't want to cook like that, they want something quick, made with a mix."[49]

At that point it was impossible to change the book's approach—the last thing the women wanted to write was a guide to French cooking with shortcuts—so they only had one way forward. "We'll just have to do it over," Child told Beck, and they rewrote the book over the course of the next two years. The resulting work was significantly shorter than what the authors had originally planned but still longer than the publisher wanted, so Houghton Mifflin ultimately passed on the book. The authors ended up at Knopf, a publisher with a reputation for taking manuscripts that required a minimum of editing. While the book was mostly in its final form, the editors at Knopf argued that the portion sizes were geared toward French, not American, eating patterns, particularly when it came to meat. In some recipes the book recommended about a third of a pound of meat per serving, which was low for American consumers raised with the expectation that meals would offer plenty of protein. Preparing the final draft, Child increased the meat portion to half a pound per person.

The book would appear in a market with few other serious French cookbooks. Over the course of the twentieth century, French cooking had fallen from its perch as the most respected type of cooking that denoted a patron as being in the upper class, but it was still respected by Americans in the middle of the century. Some of this was a holdover from its earlier status, and some of it also was the presumed complexity of cooking the French way. *Gourmet* magazine, first published in 1941, certainly admired French cooking and promoted it, although the magazine also advanced the idea of French cooking as being complicated and difficult by sometimes omitting directions when describing French recipes, with the reader apparently meant to understand that if they were unsure of just how to make the dish, they probably should not be cooking French food in the first place.

French dishes sometimes made their way to American tables in the 1950s and early 1960s, but usually in a simplified form. For example, food historian Mary Drake McFeely has traced the path of one popular dish, boeuf bourguignon, from the pages of *Gourmet* in the 1940s to women's magazines and popular cookbooks in the 1950s. When the dish first appeared in *Gourmet* in 1942, it called for both stewing meat and veal knuckle (if available), vegetables, red wine, madeira (if possible), and brandy. The instructions for making the dish were vague. The stewing meat should be browned in butter "until the meat is 'closed,'" although the author did not define what he meant by "closed." The next line of instructions had the cook remove the meat from the casserole dish, add a tablespoon of flour, and "make a *roux brun*," which, again, is not defined. Later, the recipe called for the optional veal knuckle with no indication of how the knuckle should be prepared before it is added. [50] These are the sorts of instructions for a cook who has some familiarity with boeuf bourguignon, not for a novice, like the vast majority of American cooks. Versions of the dish, however, became popular in America during the 1950s, particularly since, as McFeely pointed out, it was something that could be made ahead of time and would supply food for a crowd, the 1950s being the heyday for the cocktail party. In 1951, boeuf bourguignon appeared in a revised version of the Fannie Farmer cookbook, where it was essentially an Irish stew with some alcohol thrown in. [51]

Mastering the Art of French Cooking, as Child and Beck's book was ultimately named, appeared at an opportune time. Millions of American men had some familiarity with French cooking, having served in Europe during World War II two decades previously. Rising incomes in the years after the war allowed many Americans to visit Europe on vacation, and by the 1960s regular air service operated between America and Europe, making it even easier to get to Europe (not to mention faster).

Americans' growing familiarity with France likely helped sales of *Mastering the Art of French Cooking*, but so did the extent to which the book so thoroughly cut against the grain of the overall trend in American cooking. This was evident in the first line of the foreword: "This is a book for the servantless American cook who can be unconcerned on occasion with budgets, waistlines, time schedules, children's meals, the parent-chauffeur-den-mother syndrome, or anything else which might interfere with the enjoyment of producing something wonderful to eat."[52] Children, time, and money—these were the concerns of midcentury Americans, but they were also concerns that often resulted in cooking that was far from the best.

French cooking was complicated; the authors of *Mastering the Art of French Cooking* were clear about this fact. Their example in the foreword was a lamb *navarin*, or stew. "A perfect navarin of lamb, for instance, requires a number of operations including brownings, simmerings, strainings, skimmings, and flavorings," they wrote. "Each of the several steps in the process, though simple to accomplish, plays a critical role, and if any is eliminated or combined with another, the texture and taste of the navarin will suffer." From this single example they went on to generalize about problems with attempting to replicate French cooking by using shortcuts: "One of the main reasons that pseudo-French cooking, with which we are all too familiar, falls far below good French cooking is just this matter of elimination of steps, combination of processes, or skimping on ingredients such as butter, cream—and time. 'Too much trouble,' 'Too expensive,' or 'Who will know the difference' are death knells for good food."[53] The version of boeuf bourguignon that appeared in *Mastering the Art of French Cooking* required the cook to separately sauté beef, bacon, and vegetables in a casserole dish, to brown the beef and bacon in a hot oven for a few minutes, and then to cook everything in the oven, with the meat barely covered in beef stock and wine, the liquid scarcely simmering, for three to four hours.[54]

The reality of traditional French cooking, with its multitude of steps for each dish, is reflected in the layout of the book's recipes. Most cookbooks list the ingredients for a recipe first and then outline the steps in making the dish. Fewer cookbooks, including *The Joy of Cooking*, list the ingredients within the recipe, as they are called for in the cooking process. Each recipe page of *Mastering the Art of French Cooking* lists the ingredients on the left side of the page and the steps using those ingredients on the right side of the page, with a horizontal line marking a break before the next step in making the dish. With this format a cook can easily see just how many steps are involved in making a complicated dish and, while making the recipe, where she is within the overall recipe.

Although most readers likely did not realize it, *Mastering the Art of French Cooking* did make two important accommodations to busy American cooks, adjustments that were common in American cookbooks but not their French counterparts. First, the authors made sure to note what steps in a recipe could be done ahead of time. For example, the recipe for Braised Stuffed Beef Rolls is more than two pages long, but the next to last step notes that the rolls could be prepared up to that point and then refrigerated. The last step simply has the cook simmer the rolls in sauce for a few minutes before serving. This sort of consideration for stopping and starting the cooking process was absent from traditional French cookbooks because those books were largely written by professional cooks for other professionals, not for housewives who might not have the time to cook a dish immediately before serving it.

The second innovation in *Mastering the Art of French Cooking* was that, although the recipes were firmly grounded in traditional French cooking, the authors, particularly Child, incorporated the latest cooking technology in the instructions for making the dishes. Some of the technological adoption was necessary for writing a cookbook for Americans. In order to cook like most Americans, Child had bought an electric stove while living in Europe (where electric stoves were unusual), although she did not enjoy using the stove—like many people, she preferred to cook with gas. Some of the adoption of new technology was also to help the book stand out against other books of French cooking, although this was not too difficult. The French chefs who might have written a cookbook for the American market were often committed to making dishes the traditional way without using new kitchen appliances. They also had the difficulty of hearing about, and obtaining, those new appliances that were usually introduced in America before they made their way to Europe. For example, although the electric blender was first sold in America in the 1930s, the appliance was still unusual in France twenty years later. Child realized the usefulness of the blender in cooking and worked to incorporate it into the cookbook while also intentionally not introducing the machine to the French cooking school leaders who might be thinking about writing their own cookbooks.[55]

Making these changes—notes on when a cook could stop while making a dish and the incorporation of new kitchen appliances—to traditional French recipes helps to explain why Child and her coauthors spent so many years working on the book. Although the book's foreword did not indicate it, allowances were made for "shortcut cooking," but the short-cuts were ones the authors believed would not affect the final dish (for example, some recipes allow the use of canned broth). At the same time, though, the book was radically different from most other cookbooks on the market in that it did not apply the kinds of shortcuts that were popular in postwar cooking. There were no mixes or condensed soups listed as ingredients, and very long cooking times are often called for.

It should be noted that although Julia Child would later become a television personality and famous cook, before the book came out she had no connection to the American food industry. She did not work for food publications like *Gourmet* or the women's magazines, she had no friend-ships with well-known chefs, and she was not a consultant to a food company. She certainly knew the names of people like James Beard and she read *Gourmet*, but the circles the Childs traveled in were either diplo-matic in Washington, D.C., because of Paul's State Department jobs, or diplomatic and cultural in Paris, where Julia met many French chefs as the result of her research on the book. The bulk of her training in cooking happened in France, at the Cordon Bleu or as a personal student of a chef, and that training was geared toward being a professional cook. She was not trained as a home economist in America and so had no assumptions of what was proper for American housewives to cook, either in terms of nutrition or in the amount of time it should take to cook a meal. Child came at the cookbook from the point of view of someone who knew how to cook French food, who was passionate about French food, and who believed that American cooks could make and would be interested in French food, given a well-written cookbook. *Mastering the Art of French Cooking* was to be that book.

For Child's career, though, the book was only half the equation—what really brought her fame was her television show, *The French Chef.* The show would never have existed without the book, since she was doing publicity for the book when the opportunity for the show came along. WGBH, a Boston public television station, produced a book-review pro-gram she appeared on. Rather than simply talk about the book, she re-quested that a hot plate be ready for her appearance and brought every-thing to make an omelet on air. This was unusual—most guests simply sat in a chair and talked about their book. The appearance was a success, so much so that the station produced a few sample cooking shows featuring

Child. These, too, were successful, and by early 1963 WGBH was broadcasting *The French Chef* as an ongoing program.

Julia Child's show was unlike anything else on television. It was certainly not the first cooking show on television, nor the first that featured a serious cook. James Beard had hosted a show in the 1940s, but it fizzled, since his engaging personality did not come through on camera. European-born, Cordon Bleu–trained Dione Lucas had a popular program in the late 1940s and 1950s, and she was every inch the serious professional. During one episode she was mortified when a soufflé collapsed as she unwrapped it, although she then received quite a bit of mail from viewers who felt for her (the incident showed that she was not, in fact, perfect).[56] Lucas was undoubtedly a good cook and teacher, but her personality was anything but warm and engaging.

For Julia Child a collapsing soufflé was just another day on the set and a way to show viewers that, although things might go wrong while cooking, there were also ways to salvage the situation. During her first year of broadcasting she produced one show devoted to potato dishes, which included a recipe for potato pancakes. While preparing to flip the pancake she advised viewers, "When you flip anything you just have to have the courage of your conviction." She flipped the pancake, but part of it missed the pan, breaking the pancake. "When I flipped it, I didn't have the courage to do it the way I should have," she explained. "You can always pick it up." She then went on to observe, "If you're alone in the kitchen, who is going to see?"[57] Child's ability to make mistakes on air but still continue with the show was endearing to viewers, particularly those anxious about preparing a complex French recipe that might not turn out completely correct.

The kind of cooking that filled *Mastering the Art of French Cooking* and that appeared on Child's cooking shows was worlds away from the simplified cooking advocated by many home economists and by the convenience food industry. In fact, it was just the sort of complicated, labor-intensive cooking the convenience food industry pushed against—for decades, the industry had presented itself as the solution to that cooking problem. Instead of spending time combining the ingredients for a cake, a cook could just open a cake mix; instead of baking bread, she could just buy packaged, sliced bread at the store; instead of grinding coffee beans and operating a coffeemaker, she could just pour instant coffee granules into boiling water. It is difficult to imagine now, but to Americans born in the late 1800s, these sorts of developments must have looked like miracles.

To those born later, however, this was just how life worked. Baby boomers, those born in the years during and after World War II, had always lived in a world of cake mixes and canned foods, and quality frozen foods had appeared so early in their lives as to have always been there. It was this group that comprised a second front in the promotion of the idea that cooking from scratch was not just what someone with no access to convenience food did, and that scratch cooking was, simply, a better way of cooking.

These were members of the counterculture, the hippies and young people in general who sought an alternative to the "straight" life of their parents and of the suburbs that so many of them came from. They listened to rock and roll, dabbled in Eastern religions, protested the Vietnam War, smoked pot and tried LSD, spent time in a commune, and went to and maybe finished college. Certainly, everyone's experiences were different, and not that many people actually visited Haight-Ashbury during the Summer of Love or attended Woodstock, but the general idea of experimentation was a defining characteristic of the baby boomer generation. This experimentation extended to food, and continued in several directions.

There was a strong strain of vegetarianism. Some of this was due to circumstance, as meat tends to cost more than alternatives like rice and beans, and budgets for many young people were tight. But there could be a political side to vegetarianism as well. Francis Moore Lappé's *Diet for a Small Planet* came out in 1971, at a time when there was a rising sense of alarm over what appeared to be an impending food shortage. The problem was that the worldwide population was growing so quickly that it would soon outstrip global food production, forcing a global crisis that would likely occur before the end of the century. This was not a new idea, and it had actually been predicted to happen at some point by an English writer named Thomas Malthus back in 1798. He had calculated that population grows exponentially while food production merely grows arithmetically, meaning that population growth will always defeat food production because of simple math.

Lappé's solution was vegetarianism, and it was also based on simple math. Americans consumed more beef than any other type of meat. As she explained it, to produce a single pound of beef a rancher has to feed the animal twenty-one pounds of grain. If the animal were taken out of the equation, twenty-one pounds of grain would be opened up for consumers to eat instead of the animal, an enormous increase in available food. However, the amount of food could be increased even further if, instead of grain, other, more productive crops were grown on the land previously used exclusively for growing food for beef cattle and raising the cattle. Thus, vegetarianism was the solution to the coming food crisis, a way to feed the billions of people on the planet.

The strength of Lappé's argument was its straightforwardness. The book quickly became a bestseller. It certainly did not hurt that, rather than being published by one of the small, underground publishers of the time with a history of printing vegetarian or counterculture books, she went with a division of Random House. Lappé's solution to the problem of the coming food crisis was also attractive in its simplicity. Making a vegetarian casserole did not just feed oneself and one's family but also, by avoiding meat, helped to feed people in other parts of the world. Besides, Malthusian math, in which population always eventually exceeds the food supply, clearly showed that it would soon be impossible to keep eating meat. Changing to a vegetarian diet was just getting a jump on what everyone would soon be doing.

Of course, not everyone today is vegetarian, and meat is widely available. While there may be a global food crisis at some point in the future, it did not (and probably will not) happen because of overpopulation. The problem with Malthusian math is that it assumes that the food supply is directly related to farm acreage—without increasing the available acreage, one cannot increase the food supply, and farm acreage can only be expanded at a certain rate, slower than population growth. But during the 1970s the amount of food produced per acre grew drastically in a way that Malthusian math did not foresee. By increasing the reliance on technology, particularly fertilizers and pesticides, and developing new ways to break food down into its component parts, farmers were able to increase how much food they produced on an acre of land while food processors were able to increase what they could do with a given amount of food. Yes, there are still people starving in the world, but this is because of distribution problems, not production problems.

The embrace of vegetarianism by at least some in the counterculture was made easier by the movement's interest in ethnic foods, particularly those of the non-Western variety. Some of this was because of an overall interest in non-Western cultures, and some was because, if one was rebelling against the "white bread" ways of one's parents by not shopping at the supermarket, ethnic grocery stores were usually the only game in town. The foods of many cultures are meatless to begin with—a plus for vegetarians—and many international dishes could be made quite inexpensively. Somewhat surprisingly, French cooking became popular among the counterculture, but in a form very different from what had ruled the finest restaurants in America at the turn of the century. The French cooking favored by the counterculture was usually simple, regional, peasant cooking that eschewed fancy, rich sauces—a style of cooking practiced by, among others, Alice Waters, who opened Chez Panisse in Berkeley, California, in 1971. As historian Warren J. Belasco has pointed out, though, the rich sauces and use of butter, cream, and eggs that French cooking is often known for were popular with counterculture cooks simply because they could be used to spice up an otherwise low-fat, low-calorie vegetarian dish. [58]

Conceptually, the counterculture's approach to food (what Belasco calls the "countercuisine") involved subverting a host of ideas involved in mainstream cooking. With good reason, food companies had been obsessed for decades with the idea of cleanliness, of making and presenting to the consumer a product that was germ- and bacteria-free. The counterculture, then, became interested in food that was alive in some way, such as bread, beer, and yogurt. Food processing companies researched new ways to take ingredients apart at the molecular level and rebuild them into a food so that, for example, breakfast cereal contained vitamins not because of an ingredient in the cereal itself but because they were sprayed on at the end of the manufacturing process. The counterculture advocated using natural ingredients, often bought in bulk, when cooking, avoiding as many processed foods as possible.

The counterculture had started in cities like Berkeley in the late 1960s, but by the early 1970s it was making its way to the countryside. Increasingly restrictive and hostile cities helped make the decision for those in the counterculture to move, as did the attractiveness of completely controlling one's life on a piece of land. Some of this control extended to food, and the ability to support oneself on just the fruit of the land.

The counterculture rejected processed foods in general, so growing one's own food seemed to be a wonderful opportunity to get in touch with where things came from. The problem was that most of the young people who moved to the country had never lived in the country before, let alone grown their own food, and there was often an extremely steep learning curve. *Organic Gardening and Farming* magazine was the go-to guide for learning about growing one's own food, particularly since, along with most modern technology, the counterculture rejected the chemical fertilizers and pesticides traditional farmers were becoming more and more dependent on.

There were other guides for those seeking to make their own way. For example, *Carla Emery's Old Fashioned Recipe Book* offered guidance on all aspects of living in the country. Emery, who was born in Los Angeles but spent her childhood on a ranch in Montana, decided to write the book after her grandmother gave her a few years' worth of back issues of *Organic Gardening* (which shows that it was not just young people who were attracted to the organic farming movement). The magazine was clearly geared toward those moving to the country, and Emery thought she could write and sell a book that would function as a complete guide for those who did not know much about country living. As she writes in her book, having never written "anything longer than a poem," she assembled a table of contents, placed an ad in three different magazines offering the book for sale for $3.50, and figured that she could write the book in two to three months. Two months later, when the ad came out, hundreds of people sent checks for the book; four years later, when the book was finally completed, she sent off mimeographed copies of her self-published book (she had kept in touch with those who had paid for the book).[59] That, in a nutshell, is a pretty good example of the headstrong ethic of the day.

Emery offered mimeographed copies of the book for years before a mainstream publisher picked it up. The book did indeed have guidance on all aspects of country living, mostly as it applied to food, with sections on topics ranging from food preservation to raising cattle to "home industries" like quilting or soap making. In its coverage, and its assumption that readers would be involved with aspects of their own food production, the book is strikingly similar to books written a hundred years earlier, although it actually goes beyond books from the 1800s in terms of its coverage. Emery's book, for example, has a few pages on making vinegar and explains that different kinds of vinegars are made from different ingredients, like white vinegar from grain or malt vinegar from barley, and then she goes on to instruct the reader in just how to make those vinegars. *The Housekeeper's Encyclopedia*, published in 1861, discusses the best vinegar for pickling and advises the reader to just buy "pure distilled high wine vinegar" from a maker of vinegar—there are no instructions on how to make vinegar.[60] By 1861, although a majority of Americans still lived in the countryside, an increasing number of them were buying many items, like vinegar, from a nearby store. In this, the impetus to move to a piece of land in the late 1960s and 1970s and make everything one needed was much more of a personal choice than that lifestyle had been a hundred years before—except for Americans who either lived on the frontier or were too poor to afford it—because by the 1860s buying something was often a better option than making it.

In the mass-market, nonmimeographed version of the book, the cover of *Carla Emery's Old Fashioned Recipe Book* directly addressed just how much of a throwback to old times the book was. The cover illustration shows a mother and three children working in the kitchen. One child carries a basket of vegetables, perhaps potatoes; a second child peels a potato, the long peel falling into a trash bowl; and a third child, carrying a teddy bear, looks up at the mother, who is lowering sealed Mason jars into a big black kettle on the stove. The stove she works at is no modern, streamlined electric or gas model but a large cast iron cookstove, the kind any cook of the late nineteenth century would have been proud to own.

This points to a sore point for many women who moved to the countryside, whether they moved as part of a single family or participated in a large commune, where many people worked together for the good of the group: traditional gender roles made the move as well. Just like in the nineteenth century, men worked outside the house, engaged in farming or tending large animals, while women worked inside or near the house, taking care of the children, cleaning, and cooking. The continuation of rigid gender roles was not a problem that was particular to the back-to-the-land movement; in many, if not most, groups in the counterculture, women were usually relegated to cooking and cleaning, if there were any of that work to be done, and they often resented it. As the inclusion of instructions for making vinegar in Carla Emery's book indicates, though, those who moved to the countryside often set themselves up for quite a bit of work, based on the idea that they should support themselves as much as possible with the fruits of their own labors. In this the amount of work each gender should do had become wildly out of balance since the nineteenth century. Women might be washing cloth diapers and making chicken soup from scratch, starting with the "first kill the bird" step, while men could certainly use tractors and pickup trucks to finish their jobs more quickly and easily.

By the mid-1970s the idea that convenience foods were at least equal to, if not better than, fresh foods was under serious attack. Julia Child, among others, led the attack from the gourmet side of things, showing American cooks, both in her cookbooks and through her television shows, that they *could* cook a complicated French dish if only they had time, a good teacher, and quality, fresh ingredients. The counterculture launched its own assault from a different direction, often criticizing convenience foods on the basis of health and doing what was good for planet Earth. While the counterculture started at the fringes of society, many of its ideas would be picked up by the mainstream, and, as it aged, the generation the counterculture came from would become one with a considerable amount of disposable wealth, ensuring that many of its ideas would be picked up by businesses ready to cater to it. Even today the two main ideologies of the 1960s, that which espouses processed convenience food and that which promotes fresh, unprocessed foods, are the two main sets of ideas that dominate how we think about food.

As we move into examining the past fifty years in the next chapter, we can see that the ideas surrounding processed foods—that they are quick and easy to use, although they might cost a little more—have not changed much since the 1960s, but the other ideology, promoted by people like Julia Child, has grown and matured, becoming as much a part of our food culture as processed foods are.

5

THE EARLY 1970S THROUGH TODAY

And so we come to the most recent period, when home cooking appears to be in decline. We go to restaurants, we have food delivered, we buy a snack at the convenience store, we do almost anything to avoid cooking at home—what happened?

The past half-century happened. During those five decades American food changed tremendously. We are more educated about food than we have ever been before, more ready to try new things, we have the cheapest food in the world, and we have an extremely mechanized and efficient system for food distribution. We are also more obese than we have ever been. All of this happened in the past fifty years.

What I will do in this chapter is look at the major changes that have occurred in American cooking over the past few decades, including the rise of celebrity chefs and an explosion of food programs on television. While doing that I will also look at many of the same topics that have been covered in every chapter so far, including the state of American kitchens and changes in the restaurant industry. One good place to start with all of this is where many of us end up at the end of a busy day: watching television.

In the aftermath of Julia Child, other cooking shows premiered on American televisions. There was, for example, Graham Kerr's *Galloping Gourmet*, where each program began with the tall and acrobatic Kerr leaping a chair while holding a full glass of wine in one hand. In many ways Kerr was the antithesis of Child. He grew up cooking—his parents had owned hotels in England, and he had spent time working in hotel kitchens. He saw himself primarily as an entertainer and oriented his show in that direction, having the first studio audience for a syndicated cooking program as well as a hidden camera that filmed audience reactions. Comedians such as Lucille Ball and Danny Kaye supposedly loved him, while those in the cooking and food business, such as Dione Lucas, James Beard, and Craig Claiborne, did not. While it was popular, Kerr's show was only on for a few years, regularly broadcasting from 1969 to 1971, when the show shut down after Kerr and his wife (who produced the program) were hurt in an auto accident.

In the 1970s and 1980s cooking programs went in two directions, split between commercial and noncommercial television. On commercial television, before the advent of the Food Network, cooking shows as discrete half-hour programs faded away. Viewers could still see cooks cook, but only in short segments usually produced by a local TV channel, and that would probably be slotted into the evening newscast. Nationally, an example of this was Chef Tell, a German cook whose name was actually Friedman Paul Erhardt, who had a regular ninety-second cooking segment on *PM Magazine*, a syndicated news and entertainment program.

If one wanted to watch a half-hour cooking program during those years, the place to do so was not commercial television but PBS, which broadcast a myriad of shows catering to all types of tastes. There were a series of programs featuring Julia Child, including *Julia Child & Company* and *Dinner at Julia's*; *Yan Can Cook*, which focused on Chinese cuisine, hosted by Martin Yan; Jeff Smith's *The Frugal Gourmet*; Justin Wilson's series of shows on Cajun cooking; and many other programs. The shows were on PBS rather than commercial television because PBS uses a different revenue structure: rather than making money on straight advertising (which requires high viewership for all programs), PBS makes money from viewer memberships and from underwriting from companies. Thus, even though a show like *The Frugal Gourmet* might not draw as many viewers as another program could, if the PBS members appreciate the show, then it can be considered a success. That there were so many shows also comes from the distributed structure of PBS, where an individual station might produce a program that could be picked up by other stations nationally (this can have its downside—the first thirteen episodes of Julia Child's *The French Chef* do not exist anymore, as the original videotapes were gradually worn out by different PBS stations showing the episodes over and over).[1] While PBS broadcast hours of cooking shows on the weekends, the network seems to have been leery of letting the shows expand to other parts of the network's schedule. When the producer of some of Child's shows suggested that the network might want to broadcast cooking shows during the week, the network's response was that they were "the network of *Nova* and *The News Hour*. *Sesame Street*. We are not interested in spending any more time in the kitchen than we already do."[2]

There were more cooking shows than ever before, and people watched those shows, but were all those viewers actually cooking? Probably not. In 1989 the *New York Times* published an article whose title at least partially answered that question. In "A New Spectator Sport: Looking, Not Cooking," journalist Trish Hall examined the potential effect of all those cooking shows. Hall spoke with a number of professionals in the food industry. The producer of *Madeleine Cooks*, a PBS cooking show, opined that the popularity of the food programs was simply voyeurism: "I think people watch cooking shows almost like they watch a ballet or a football game. . . . People like looking at food." The host of a food-oriented radio show in Los Angeles believed that the programs had a considerable effect, but on restaurant dining, not home cooking. "When they've seen Julia Child do paella, they feel more comfortable when they go to a restaurant," he said. "They know what's in it. It helps them know how to order." Hall also spoke with someone at Prentice Hall Press, which published cookbooks, who believed the popularity of the shows signaled a major change in attitudes toward food. "If you're going to buy a book to cook from, you buy 'The Fanny Farmer Cookbook' or 'The Joy of Cooking,'" she said. "Cookbooks are life-style books at this point."[3]

PBS aired many cooking shows over the years, but presenting two hours of cooking programs on a Saturday afternoon, as many PBS stations did, was a far cry from airing nothing but food-related shows twenty-four hours a day, seven days a week. That development, the creation of the Food Network, would have to wait until the early 1990s.

That a cable channel devoted solely to food might not be such a good idea is a difficult concept to grasp today, since there are a few channels devoted solely to that, including the Food Network and its sister network the Cooking Channel. Allen Salkin, author of *From Scratch: Inside the Food Network*, makes the argument that the creation of the Food Network relied on other developments, similar to how the popularity of rock and roll in the 1950s and 1960s relied on developments in the radio and television industries and the baby boom. The development of the Food Network relied, obviously, on the development of the cable TV industry, especially the expansion of cable TV from a few high-profile channels like HBO and ESPN to the plethora of options we have today. It also relied on the existing PBS cooking shows to create a base of potential viewers, a base that was a curious cross-section of the population. Joe Langhorn, the person who came up with the idea for the Food Network after being tasked by his boss with creating proposals for a variety of channels, was at first cool on his own idea until he mentioned it to his female barber and his male drinking buddy, both of whom said they watched cooking shows (his buddy could even quote Cajun cook Justin Wilson's catchphrases).[4] And the development of the Food Network relied on legal quirks of the cable TV industry, including a ruling that cable companies had to reimburse local TV stations for carrying their signals. Many of the early investors in the Food Network were station owners who, rather than taking money from the cable companies, had those companies carry the Food Network, thereby getting the new channel into more homes more quickly.

The Food Network was created during the rush to get as many channels on the air as possible. The group that created it was made up of businesspeople, not foodies. Reese Schonfeld, the first head of the network, got the job because he had spearheaded the creation of CNN. He never cooked, and he and his wife had even gone so far as to remove the kitchen from their Manhattan apartment, since they always either dined out or delivered in (they did still have a coffeemaker). Heidi Diamond, a later Food Network executive who had previously been at Nickelodeon, had likewise ripped out the kitchen from her apartment to make more closet space.[5]

In spite of this lack of food knowledge among executives, in the early years the Food Network did have a nucleus of managers with a considerable store of food knowledge, and talent without that knowledge was often paired with others who knew about food. As the network grew in subscribers and went through a few changes of ownership, though, personality came to trump cooking experience, particularly after mid-2001. Chefs such as Emeril Lagasse, Bobby Flay, and Mario Batali were on before the shift, as was Alton Brown, who had been a cinematographer before he switched careers and went to cooking school—he shot R.E.M.'s "The One I Love" video, for example. After 2001 many of the Food

Network's biggest stars had, arguably, more personality but less formal food experience. Rachel Ray did not have any formal training in cooking, having grown up working in restaurants. Paula Deen had started a catering business, the Bag Lady, that delivered lunchtime meals to Savannah, Georgia, businesses, and she eventually opened the Lady & Sons restaurant in Savannah.

Perhaps the most extreme example of personality over food experience is Sandra Lee, who came to food by way of other businesses, including curtains, scrapbooks, and gardening (she was on QVC long before she was on the Food Network). She took a two-week course at a cooking school in Ottawa, Canada, but decided that the cooking techniques she learned were too complicated, prompting her to develop the "semi-home-made" style of cooking she became known for. This relies heavily on using convenience foods to make a meal, an approach that sometimes gets closer to assembling a dish than cooking it. For example, a recipe for vanilla cream pie, from her 2002 *Semi-Homemade Cooking* cookbook, uses store-bought vanilla pudding and nondairy whipped topping, along with bananas, sugar, butter, and vanilla extract. Instead of a store-bought pie crust, the recipe calls for a ten-inch flour tortilla to be used as the crust. Why a tortilla instead of a pie shell? Because a second source of revenue from the book, in addition to book sales, appears to be product placement. Lee specifies a brand name for the tortilla, the same brand name mentioned in an earlier recipe for black bean quesadillas. Of the seven ingredients in the vanilla cream pie recipe, only one, the bananas, does not have a brand name attached. [6]

As the Food Network matured, it moved into other programming. It kept some of the traditional cooking shows—known in the industry as "dump and stir" shows—and added additional types of programs such as cooking competitions. While the Food Network had aired *Ready . . . Set . . . Cook!*, its version of a British cooking competition show, in the first few years of the channel's existence, competitions really heated up after the network began airing the Japanese import *Iron Chef* in 1999 (an American version of the show, naturally, began airing a few years later). Cooking competition shows became so popular that another channel, Bravo, produced its own competition called *Top Chef*, while the Food Network produced competitions focused on cooking particular foods, like cupcakes.

In a 2009 *New York Times Magazine* article, Michael Pollan pondered the popularity of the Food Network and cooking competition shows in particular. In the context of a continual decline in home cooking, the popularity of cooking shows seems confusing—why are people so interested in watching other people do something they themselves do not do? In some ways Pollan's question misses the point of television viewing, as, for example, professional football is by far the most popular televised sport while only a tiny fraction of viewers play football themselves. But Pollan does make some good observations about cooking competition shows. The point of the shows, with their time limits and restrictions and requirements on ingredients (such as *Iron Chef*'s demand that participants make an entire meal that features one unusual ingredient), is certainly not to teach viewers about cooking. As one of Pollan's friends asks, do people learn how to play basketball by watching NBA games? Pollan concludes that cooking competitions teach viewers two things. They teach viewers about "culinary fashion"—essentially, what to order at restaurants without being afraid. And they teach viewers "how to taste and how to talk about food." This lesson particularly comes through in the interactions and proclamations at the judges' table. Taken together, the takeaway lessons for viewers are not related to cooking—that is, producing food—but instead talking knowledgeably about food and judging it—that is, consuming food.

Cooking shows, whether of the "dump and stir" variety or cooking competitions, have contributed to Americans' overall knowledge of food. The programs not only show viewers how to use ingredients they might not be familiar with and how to make a dish they have never seen but also teach viewers how to judge the difference between good and bad foods. This ability to discern is a new phenomenon; before the 1980s or so, there simply was not much written about judging food or how that might be done beyond examining hygiene or appearance. Americans, as a whole, are also much more adventurous in their food tastes today, which is likely another effect of cooking shows, since if a viewer sees a particular, intriguing dish made on TV, they are more likely to order it in a restaurant or try to make it themselves.

One hallmark of current American food culture is the celebrity status of professional chefs. They appear on television, they write cookbooks, they are interviewed by food magazines like *Bon Appétit*, and their restaurants are visited by food bloggers. They help define what dishes and cuisines are popular. With the present prominence of celebrity chefs it is difficult to imagine that, before the 1980s, and certainly before the 1970s, working in a restaurant was the bluest of blue-collar jobs and certainly not a steppingstone to stardom.

Before the 1970s most of the best-known cooking personalities were fictional, like Betty Crocker; women who had come up through the ranks of home economics, like Fannie Farmer; or people with a connection to cooking who had never been chefs, like James Beard, who got his start in catering, or Julia Child, with her cookbook and television show. Well-known chefs were few and far between, and most of them were more well known among professional cooks than the general public, people like Charles Ranhofer, who worked at Delmonico's restaurant in New York City in the mid-1800s, or French chefs like Georges Auguste Escoffier. One exception to that rule was European chef Dione Lucas, who had a televised cooking show in the 1940s. Beyond that, the famous cooking personalities before the 1970s tended not to come from the restaurant world.

Much of this was because of the state of American restaurants. Chefs become celebrities today because they provide new twists on existing ideas, like melding together cuisines or updating an almost-forgotten dish so that it is new and exciting. These were the last things restaurant goers seem to have wanted in the middle of the twentieth century. Most Americans were not at all adventurous in their eating, and so fusion, or updating, was usually out of the question. Mostly, American diners wanted something safe and certain when they went out to eat.

But some of the lack of inspiration coming from American restaurants was also because of a lack of knowledge, on the part of both the diner and the chef. There have long been two ways to become a chef. One can work one's way up, starting as a busboy or dishwasher, slowly learning the ropes over time until one is a chef. A chef-in-training might learn under someone with an instinct for cooking, or he or she (usually he) might learn under someone with no flair for cooking whatsoever, only an eye for following a written recipe and somehow making it through the lunch rush. It is a scattershot approach. The other route to becoming a chef is cooking school. In the 1950s and 1960s American cooking schools usually focused on quantity over quality, teaching students how to prepare and serve dozens, or hundreds, of meals in an hour or two. Obviously, convenience foods played into this approach, and the schools showed students how frozen and dehydrated foods could help them do their jobs. The mindset was that cooking was just a job one did, like plumbing or accounting, not an outlet for creativity.

This attitude began to change in the late 1960s and 1970s with the baby boom generation of cooks. As with so many other things, this generation was not satisfied with what it found when it got to the working world, and some of these cooks set about changing what it meant to be a cook. For many chefs in this generation the change started with a trip to Europe, particularly France. Alice Waters, for example, spent time in France while in college at Berkeley, and the experience had a profound effect on her cooking.

The shift in attitudes was not just marked by cooks from that generation; it was also a change in attitude toward food and cooking among Americans in general, and the change percolated into restaurant kitchens across the country, even affecting chefs who had never thought about traveling to Europe. Bob Lape was a news reporter at an ABC affiliate in New York City who witnessed the change. Lape filmed a weekly segment called "Eyewitness Gourmet" that was aired as the last segment on the local evening news. The segment, only a few minutes long, was filmed at a different restaurant each week, where Lape spoke with the restaurant's chef about a particular dish and then tried the food, on camera. "Eyewitness Gourmet" was quite popular. ABC affiliate stations across the country quickly picked it up, and Lape eventually filmed over a thousand segments. Lape, a seasoned TV reporter, was surprised by the popularity of "Eyewitness Gourmet," especially in terms of the letters from viewers that came in—he estimated that the station received between a million and a half and two million recipe requests while the segment aired. [7] Just the fact that a segment such as this appeared on evening newscasts across America, where a reporter simply visited a restaurant, talked with a chef about the food, and sampled the food, indicated that attitudes toward food were changing.

In the course of doing "Eyewitness Gourmet," Lape noted that the chefs' ability to talk with him about their work changed. "When I started interviewing these guys and getting them to talk on camera, in those days you would find very few chefs who could do the explanation part," he said. "But as years passed the more television generation American chefs that you ran into, the better they were at explanation if not inspiration." [8]

As time went on, the ability to explain what they were doing, not just in terms of how they were cooking a particular food but also in how to explain an overall philosophy of cooking, would become a hallmark of the celebrity chef.

But chefs had a long way to go. During the 1980s a number of chefs became well known to the point that they were almost household names, people such as Mark Miller, Paul Prudhomme, and Wolfgang Puck, but they were not superstars. They may have been paid well for cooking at an event, but they still flew coach to get there and were put up in a cheap hotel during the event. By the end of the 1980s the era of the famous chef seemed to have faded away.

Two things were lacking for chefs to really become superstars: they needed lots of television coverage to become, in some way, a part of peoples' daily lives, and they needed agents to help them with connections and business deals they could not work out on their own. They would get both of these things, almost simultaneously, in the 1990s.

Television coverage came with the Food Network, which had an insatiable appetite for on-air talent. During the first few years of its existence, it had a strict no-rerun policy for shows it produced. Even though it usually repeated the same program within a twenty-four-hour period, once that twenty-four-hour period had elapsed, the channel would not show that particular program again (an early head of the network had come from the world of cable news, where reruns simply don't work). To find talent, the network had a cooking show named *Chef du Jour* where different chefs came in and filmed five episodes back to back that would air over the course of a week. The show functioned as both a test bed for prospective talent and something to put on air. The original shows that appeared on the first few years of the Food Network were usually low-budget affairs with poor production values, and *Chef du Jour* was no exception, as the producer made it clear to chefs that once the show began taping, he would not stop no matter what happened. When Mario Batali did the show, he shredded his knuckles on a cheese grater and then, to hide the blood, put his hand into a bowl of tomatoes, the acid of which burned like fire. Coming back from a commercial break, he kept that hand wrapped in a towel and hidden behind a bowl, pressing into the countertop to stop the bleeding.[9]

Most famous cooks, or those who would later become famous, spent at least some time on the Food Network simply because it had so many openings for talent. Julia Child was there from the beginning mainly because, as the most famous chef alive, the creators of the channel decided they could not announce the creation of the network without her involvement (however, she could not cook on the channel because she already had contracts with both PBS and *Good Morning America*). Mario Batali came to the network's notice because of his restaurant Pó, and he made a positive impression on network talent scouts when they visited his restaurant. Bobby Flay, who had two restaurants to his name and had appeared on *Live with Regis and Kathie Lee*, was invited onto a Food Network talk show hosted by Robin Leach (who had become famous with *Lifestyles of the Rich and Famous*) and ended up marrying Leach's co-host. Emeril Lagasse, who, unlike Batali and Flay, lived in New Orleans instead of New York City, had come to the attention of the network because of some appearances on a cooking show on the Nashville Network, another cable channel.

Regardless of how they came to the network's attention, appearing on the Food Network was both a huge opportunity and an incredible amount of work. To keep expenses low the network, in the early years, filmed its programs as quickly as possible. Emeril Lagasse's first show was *How to Boil Water*, which focused on basic cooking for men. Filming was done at a studio in Nashville, Tennessee. Every few months Lagasse flew into town for eight days, during which they would film sixty-five episodes at the rate of about eight per day, giving the network three months of shows. While Lagasse survived on caffeine, others associated with the production of Food Network programs seem to have needed a bit more stimulation. Lagasse's trademark catchphrases like "Bam!" and "Kick it up a notch!" were originally intended to wake up the camera operators, who, moonlighting from other jobs, were nodding off in the studio.[10]

With more television exposure, chefs started to get agents to represent them. One early agent who focused on chefs was Shep Gordon, who had specialized in musicians such as Alice Cooper and Luther Vandross and actors such as Michael Douglas. From Gordon's point of view, chefs were as creative as rock stars and actors, but they were neither paid nor treated like stars. In 1993 he added a group of thirty-seven chefs to his existing client list, including some of the most famous chefs of the day, such as Paul Prudhomme, Wolfgang Puck, and Mark Miller. In return for 10–15 percent of what they made from appearances and endorsements, Gordon's agency lined up appearances for clients and generally helped them decide which deals were best for them. A *New York Times* article about the signing of the chefs illustrated the problem chefs faced when the reporter spoke with a Florida resort executive who booked chefs for a yearly crab festival at the resort. While the property charged guests $50–$125 to attend the festival, the chefs received no pay to cook at three events other than transportation, lodging, and, as the executive put it, "a chance to have a good time in the sun." Regarding the possibility of paying the chefs, the executive said that the resort "would not be interested if we had to pay them in addition to that. Besides, there are enough other chefs out there who would do it without being paid. It's good advertising for their restaurants."[11]

As author Allen Salkin has pointed out, big endorsement deals for chefs only became possible because of exposure on venues like the Food Network. A similar thing had happened in the sports industry when the television networks started carrying sporting events in the 1960s; only then, with mass exposure, could athletes start making endorsement deals. In this Shep Gordon's client list was ideal for the Food Network. Gordon was based in Hollywood and mostly represented West Coast chefs, while the New York City–based Food Network had easy access to any chef in the city—as Bobby Flay once said, in the early days "the main requirement to be on [the] Food Network was being able to get there by subway."[12] One of Gordon's favorite lines was "You don't get rich from working. You get rich from going to your mailbox." That is, the real money was not in cooking, acting, or making music but in collecting royalties from licensing deals (it should be noted that this is the same man who made Alice Cooper rich by, in part, putting him on lunch boxes).[13] Endorsement deals and royalties came from the increased exposure, and sometimes other deals that did not always end well. Emeril Lagasse had a line of cooking spices that sold well, but he also starred on *Emeril*, a sitcom that ran for eleven episodes on NBC in the fall of 2001 before it was dropped.

One outcome of the chef-as-celebrity phenomenon was a change in the nature of cookbooks. They were still collections of recipes, but for celebrity chefs they also worked as promotional material, often written in a way as to let the reader feel closer to the chef. Older cookbooks were seldom used in this way. The only knowledge about the author's personality that a reader could get from something like *The Joy of Cooking* or Fannie Farmer's cookbooks might come obliquely from the organization of the book or the author's relatively straightforward, no-nonsense approach to cooking. With celebrity chefs, the author's personality is often front and center and is a drawing point for readers.

Mario Batali's 1998 cookbook *Simple Italian Food: Recipes from My Two Villages* is an example of this type of cookbook. In the introduction Batali describes his journey as a chef, a journey that matches the archetype of the modern American chef. He started as a cook on the West Coast, working at several locations with the Four Seasons Hotel Company. That job tended to focus on cooking large amounts of food quickly rather than making a smaller amount of higher-quality food. As he writes in the introduction to the cookbook, he decided to move to Italy to "submerge myself into Italian life and to refine my cooking and language skills."[14] He worked to find an apprenticeship, sending out letters to Italian chefs and receiving only one positive reply, which he accepted. He spent three years in Italy, working at a restaurant and learning a new approach to restaurant cooking that stressed the importance of quality, locally grown ingredients, and simple cooking. As he puts it in the introduction, "Simplicity and purity reign over all."[15] He returned to America after his time in Italy, eventually opening a number of highly acclaimed restaurants in New York City.

The introduction to the book describes not just his journey but also his philosophy of cooking. This is a part of being a celebrity chef: they do not simply present recipes but also let their readers know their approach to cooking. Batali's philosophy of cooking is fairly close to that of most other celebrity chefs, particularly those influenced by European cooking. "Today I would describe my cooking style as filled with Italian spirit and exuberance but equally Italian and American in its flavors," he writes. "It's based more on superior ingredients than it is on fancy techniques, which is why most of these recipes are very easy to re-create in a home kitchen, just as they would be made by good home cooks in Toscana, Piemonte, or Venezia."[16]

Jamie's Kitchen, a cookbook by British celebrity chef Jamie Oliver, tells a different story but also works to make the chef's personality shine through in the book. At the start of the book's introduction, Oliver mentions the recent birth of his daughter and then shifts to talking about an idea he had been mulling over for years: "to train a team of unemployed kids with an interest and passion for food and to open a new first-class restaurant in London to be run by them."[17] The opening of the restaurant does not seem to have happened, and although there is a photo of Oliver with a group of teenagers, the text explains that the group is in training as chefs, and there is no mention of a plan of opening a restaurant with that specific group of people.

Mostly, the cookbook presents Oliver, both in the photos and in the text, as a chum and cooking resource. "I'd like you to have a go on your own and think of me as a mate who's on hand to give you a bit of extra guidance," he writes at the end of the introduction. "I want to give your cooking a kickstart, so be creative, give it your best shot and, as always, have a laugh."[18] Pictures throughout the book show him in faded denim jeans and a T-shirt walking through London streets with food from a grocery store, horsing around in a coat with kitchen utensils attached to it, or smiling casually at the camera, all clearly with the intention of promoting his particular public persona.

Since the 1970s Americans, as a group, have acquired more and more food knowledge. The "dump and stir" cooking shows showed them how to make dishes they had never heard of before, and the cooking competitions gave them the tools to describe and judge food. Cooks like Julia Child and the counterculture of the 1960s and 1970s pushed back against processed foods, arguing that fresh foods tasted better than processed foods and were morally superior. In the context of all of this it was natural for Americans to start thinking a lot more about the foods they were eating, not just abstractly in terms of food systems but in a much more specific way: What is this Big Mac made from? Where did this carrot come from? Can I really trust this salad? What effects, exactly, does eating processed food have on my life?

Attempts to get answers to questions like these highlight some problems with the American food industry. Because the industry is set up to be as efficient as possible, it can also be maddeningly opaque in terms of where our food comes from, whereas this was not always the case. An example can be seen in wheat. For most of the nineteenth century farmers bagged the wheat they harvested and then sold the bags of wheat to granaries and processors. The bags were usually marked with the farmer's name, and farmers worked to grow the best wheat they could, since they would be paid by the quality of the wheat they bagged. In this system it was easy to find out where a particular batch of wheat came from. In the late nineteenth century the entire process changed as wheat moved from being sold by the bag to being sold by the ton, in bulk. Farmers no longer bagged their wheat but instead sold it by the loose truckload. Wheat was standardized into several different grades, and farmers were paid by whatever grade their wheat fell into. Because wheat was no longer bagged, it was impossible to tell where a particular batch of wheat came from, and impossible to trace it back to its source. This resulted in cheaper wheat, since bagging requires a lot of labor, but it also resulted in disconnect between the farmer and the consumer. [19]

The modern realization of this disconnect has led to a few developments. Many consumers and farmers have attempted to reestablish this connection by frequenting farmers' markets or by setting up CSAs. With farmers' markets, area farmers bring produce to a certain location on a particular day to sell directly to consumers, although different farmers' markets have different rules on just who can sell. Some markets have strict rules that might allow only farmers from a certain radius to sell produce they grew themselves, while other markets allow anyone to sell, even wholesalers who purchased their produce on the open market rather than growing it themselves. In a CSA (which stands for community-supported agriculture), a farmer offers memberships or shares where consumers receive a portion of whatever the farmer harvests. The consumer gets food directly from the farmer, although they cannot choose what food that is, and the farmer gets assured sales, since the memberships or shares are sold before the harvest comes in. Both farmers' markets and CSAs are examples of a trend of preferring to buy from local vendors.

Another larger trend in American culture that has affected cooking is what has been called DIY culture. DIY stands for "do it yourself," and those involved with the culture like to learn how to do many of the tasks Americans have either given up or moved away from, including things like making cloth from raw wool or creating robots from electrical parts. The connection to food is often seen in the more technical side of making foods, rather than simply cooking. Examples include making beer or wine, bread, sausage, and cheese, foods that require special equipment, time, and patience to make.

In some ways this DIY culture has intersected with the popularity of artisanal foods. If the 1950s was the heyday of processed foods that came from large corporations, the 2000s can be seen as a heyday of small-batch, crafted foods that come from smaller companies or from individuals. These foods are usually more expensive because of their rarity, but, because of the presumed time and attention put into their production, they are usually assumed to either taste better than mass-marketed equivalents or provide tastes for which there is no mass-market equivalent. An example that became mass market itself is Ben and Jerry's, a Vermont ice cream company that became known for offering high-quality ice cream that was originally hard to obtain. In 2000 the Anglo-Dutch company Unilever purchased Ben and Jerry's, and its ice cream is today widely available in grocery stores. Ben and Jerry's is an outlier of the phenomenon, though, since the point of small-batch, artisanal foods is that they are not mass-produced. Another example is mezcal, a type of liquor made from agave, of which tequila is the best-known example. However, there are many other types of mezcal, and there are still people in Mexico who make small batches of it with the intention of both drinking it and selling it locally. American liquor distributors are becoming interested in developing the market in America, especially because this is just the sort of artisanal food that is likely to catch on in America (making hard liquor without a license is illegal, and the law is strictly enforced in America; otherwise it would likely be a popular activity for DIYers). [20]

Americans kitchens have changed over the past half-century. The role of the kitchen has changed as well. In the 1950s a kitchen was primarily a workspace, but today, particularly when Americans spend less and less time actually cooking, the kitchen has multiple functions. In a kitchen design book published by *House Beautiful* magazine in 2007, author Emma Callery wrote, "The modern kitchen is the social (some would say emotional) hub for the family, often where children play or do their homework and their parents catch up on what's happening, click out a few orders online and maybe finish some office work." She added that the kitchen is not just a hub for the family—"it is often where guests congregate, making it something of a showroom, too, especially on the weekend." [21]

This added functionality—that of a social center—has been possible because the average house size has grown considerably over the past several decades. For example, Levittown, New York, was a suburb of over seventeen thousand homes built after World War II. The most popular house style in Levittown was the Cape Cod style, which had 750 square feet of living space. [22] The average size of a new house completed in 2015 was over 2,400 square feet. [23] While new houses have more rooms than postwar houses, some of that growth has also gone into the kitchen, allowing developments like the kitchen island, a concept that did not exist in the 1950s. This additional space has allowed more seating in the average kitchen, although a suggestion from the *House Beautiful* book is still a bit unusual: "One way of making the kitchen truly inviting is to have a comfortable sofa in addition to the usual kitchen chairs—assuming you have the space, of course."[24] Televisions have made their way into many kitchens, allowing both cooks and those eating in the kitchen to watch while they work. The rise of kitchen islands has allowed a relocation of the kitchen sink, which the author of the *House Beautiful* book points out has everything to do with the social nature of the kitchen. As she writes, "Sinks were once positioned under a window so that mothers could enjoy the view into the yard and keep an eye on the children playing. Now sinks often face into the central space so that whoever is washing up can see and communicate with the other people in the room, and maintain a sentry's view of the children in the room."[25]

As the amount of work most people put into cooking has declined, the approach to designing kitchens has also changed. Fifty years ago the kitchen was primarily a workspace because, apart from people living in the heart of the largest cities, there simply were no good options for dining elsewhere. With cooking, particularly cooking from scratch, being more and more optional today, kitchen designs reflect that reality. The author of the *House Beautiful* book asked readers to first think about how they plan to use their kitchen, and then design from that point. "Are you a one-, two-, or even three-sink household? If the only prep you do for a meal is to tear off the packaging on a pre-cooked meal, or freshen up on the way out to a restaurant, you have different needs than someone who prepares fresh food every night, glass of wine in hand and cool music in the background."[26] The author clearly ties kitchen design to lifestyle decisions in ways that writers fifty years before did not do. Certainly, in the mid-twentieth century those planning on building or remodeling a kitchen had many decisions to make ranging from just how large the kitchen should be to what its layout should look like, but there was always the assumption that the kitchen functioned primarily as a workspace. Today, that is no longer true.

A kitchen today can also function as a way for a family to show off its wealth. Unlike the kitchens of a hundred years ago, kitchens in recently built homes are no longer hidden in the back of the house. Rather, with the rise of the open-concept floor plan, kitchens are open to the main living space in the house, making them extremely visible. Even if they are barely used, modern kitchens include a variety of large appliances such as a refrigerator, stove, and dishwasher, all of which can be opportunities for conspicuous consumption. The other furnishings of a kitchen, like the countertops and cabinets, can also be outfitted with expensive materials to impress visitors. This ability to show off a family's wealth is peculiar to the kitchen; there is no other public space in a home that by default contains so many appliances that can be used in this way.

As our kitchens have changed, so, too, have some of the options for what we make in those kitchens. In the mid-2000s a new trend in cooking came along: storefronts where consumers assemble a set of meals that can be frozen and then cooked days, or even weeks, later. As reported in the *New York Times*, at one Seattle-based chain clients go online to put together a list of between six and twelve dishes and reserve a time to assemble the food. When they arrive all ingredients are available prechopped and ready to be measured and put together. For twelve dishes, each of which serves six people, the cost was $216, which sounds pricey but comes to only $3 a serving. Clients interviewed in the article spoke about both the savings in time, since they did not have to shop for or prepare the ingredients, and the savings in money, with a lack of wasted food. For $30–$50 more, clients could skip the assembly and simply pick up the finished dishes. [27] This option seems to have been much more popular for time-strapped cooks; while a Fort Worth–based chain mentioned in the article still has clients come in and assemble dinners, the Seattle chain has dropped the assembly entirely and only offers pick up or delivery of the already frozen dinners.

There are also meal kit delivery services, like Blue Apron and Hello Fresh, which will ship a recipe and all necessary ingredients for the dish to your doorstep. These types of services started in 2012, and by 2016 they were a $400 million business with more than one hundred different companies shipping meal kits. [28] There are a number of things about the kits that make them attractive. Obviously, they reduce much of the complexity involved with cooking, since the customer does not need to shop for the ingredients, and, given that the companies only ship what is required for the recipe, there is no waste. They also allow customers to experiment with cooking new dishes and using ingredients they may never have used before. The meal kits are more expensive than purchasing the ingredients at the store, although the issue is somewhat complicated by the fact that a kit might include an exotic ingredient that is not commonly available. In terms of cost, *Consumer Reports* investigated five kit delivery services in 2016. Purple Carrot, a service that specializes in vegan dishes, offered one kit that cost $11.33 per serving, which included ingredients that cost $3.46 per serving from a grocery store. At the other end of the spectrum, Green Chef sold a kit that cost $13.49 per serving, which included ingredients that cost $10.94 per serving from a grocery store.[29]

One of the attractions of the meal kits is that, although the consumer does not select the recipe or shop for the ingredients, he or she still does the cooking. The *New York Times*, though, raised the question of whether the consumer is, in fact, cooking if they use a meal delivery kit service. A reporter asked several prominent food authors whether preparing a dish from a company like Blue Apron qualified as cooking. Michael Pollan said it was, and that a positive attribute of the kits is that they can be a learning experience for someone wanting to learn how to cook. Mark Bittman, who used to write for the *New York Times* before going to the vegan kit delivery service Purple Carrot, also said that they could be a gateway to independent cooking. Of course, these responses focus on the potential of the meal delivery kits rather than responding directly to the question of whether using the kits is cooking. Cookbook author Andrea Nguyen, who has provided recipes to one of the services, did not see it as cooking, since she believes that shopping is an important part of the cooking process. Culinary historian Laura Shapiro disliked the artificial nature of the entire enterprise, instead emphasizing the importance of food-related family traditions: "I can't imagine we are going to look back and say, 'Oh remember that Blue Apron Burmese curry we used to have on Thursdays?' It's not the same. It's not ours. It doesn't have our family sentiments behind it."[30]

Home cooking is still done today, although cooking from scratch is becoming a rarer and rarer thing. Convenience foods such as canned soups have become fully integrated into methods of cooking, being used as both dishes in and of themselves and ingredients in other dishes.

Americans are much more open to new tastes and styles of cooking than they were fifty or a hundred years ago, and this is reflected in our knowledge of ethnic cooking. A hundred years ago Italian cooking began and ended with macaroni, which was perceived as a food eaten by immigrants who had not yet transitioned to American cooking. These days Italian food is perceived by many Americans not as a simple, monolithic cuisine but as a collection of regional cuisines, including that of places such as Tuscany or the Piedmont area. Fruits and vegetables that were completely unknown in American grocery stores, like mangos, bok choy, and kale, are now available year round in the produce sections of most grocery stores. These developments have occurred because of our expanded knowledge of food and cooking, and they have resulted in Americans cooking a larger variety of dishes than ever before.

For those who do cook, there are newer appliances to help them with their work. The Cuisinart food processor, introduced in 1973, reduced the time and effort involved in chopping large amounts of food to almost nothing. The appliance was created by an American but was based on a French invention that was much larger and more expensive, and which was aimed at the restaurant, not home, market. The first Cuisinarts sold for $160, quite a bit of money in the early 1970s. The product languished until good reviews appeared in *Gourmet* and the *New York Times*.[31] After that, Cuisinarts sold well.

By the end of the decade anyone who wanted to cook gourmet food, and who had the money, owned a Cuisinart. It enabled the user to chop food into unimaginably small pieces and, therefore, to make dishes previously out of the range of most home cooks (at least those who did not want to spend hours chopping). Because people could now do it easily, they did it. A lot. Bee Wilson has pointed out that, as purees and mousses appeared on more and more restaurant menus, courtesy of the Cuisinart in the kitchen, there was a push in the other direction, toward rustic food marked by large, unevenly cut chunks of potatoes, carrots, or whatever was in the dish. Unlike the mousses, where it might be impossible to tell all the individual ingredients in a dish, the ingredients of the rustic food were obvious to anyone who ate them.[32]

Another appliance that came to popularity during the 1970s and, particularly, the 1980s, was the microwave. This tool came from defense-related research on radar, and there are a host of stories as to just how Percy Spencer, working for the Raytheon Company, realized that radar waves could cook food. One story has him noticing that a chocolate bar had melted while in a lab coat pocket, while another has an egg exploding nearby. At any rate, he and his team of workers recognized that anything exposed to the waves would be heated. The resulting oven was released in the 1950s, but it was not until the late 1960s, when the price of an oven dropped below $500, that they began selling in any numbers, and not until the 1970s that sales really took off.[33]

Unlike the Cuisinart, a microwave is today considered a standard cooking appliance. There are some things it does extremely well, like heating frozen foods or cooking fish, but there are also some things it cannot do, like roasting (although some microwaves were sold with a heating element so they could cook like an electric oven). When microwaves first became popular, though, many people assumed that the appliances could cook almost anything and might soon replace standard gas or electric ovens. There were microwave cookbooks such as Barbara Kafka's *Microwave Gourmet*, the title of which certainly made it seem like a microwave was a high-class cooking tool like a Cuisinart. There was even a cooking show devoted to microwave cooking, *Microwaves Are for Cooking*, on PBS. There was also an avalanche of food products made specifically for the microwave. In 1987 nearly eight hundred microwavable products were introduced; by the end of that decade 80 percent of American households had a microwave.[34]

Microwave Gourmet is something of a strange book to leaf through. The heyday of the microwave was decades ago; since then other kitchen appliances (such as the bread machine and yogurt maker) have seen their popularity wax and wane. *Microwave Gourmet* is very much a product of its time, with the heady enthusiasm for the new product that can do almost anything. The book's author, Barbara Kafka, is deeply committed to the idea of using the microwave for nearly all cooking, although in the introduction to the book she admits that she is a relatively recent convert to using the appliance extensively. She provides a list of foods that can quickly and easily be made in the microwave including vegetables, fish, risotto, and broth. But this being a general-purpose cookbook, many other standard recipes are listed as well. She includes a pot roast recipe that has the cook microwave two-and-a-quarter pounds of brisket for an hour, wrapped in plastic wrap with vegetables and broth. A butterscotch pudding recipe, which calls for four egg yolks, has the cook microwave various ingredients for a total of fifteen minutes, stopping and starting three times to add more ingredients. Kafka even includes a tempura recipe (surprising because tempura is deep-fried). Introducing the recipe, she announces that it is not just possible to deep fry in the microwave but also easy. The recipe has the cook microwave the oil in a nonplastic container for fifteen minutes to get the oil hot before dropping four to six pieces of battered vegetables or fish into the oil and microwaving the container another minute, until the battered pieces are golden brown. Once those pieces are removed from the oil, the container should be microwaved five minutes, and then the process can be repeated with another group of vegetables or fish.[35]

The tempura recipe illustrates a problem with time- and labor-saving devices like the microwave: sometimes they do not save any time at all. Between waiting fifteen minutes for the oil to initially heat up and waiting another five minutes between batches of tempura, using the microwave for deep-frying takes about as long as it does to fry on the stovetop.

This paradox, where new technological devices that should save us time do not, has been noted by researchers who study how Americans spend their time. One study, from 1965, found that Americans spent about as much time doing household chores in the 1960s as they had spent in the 1920s, before appliances like vacuum cleaners and washing machines were widespread (some studies even found that Americans spent more time in the 1960s than they had forty years previously).[36] The 1965 study, performed again in 1975, found no connection between ownership of labor-saving devices and doing less work. As the authors of the study wrote, "People with dishwashers spent 1 minute *more* time doing housework, those with washing machines spent 4 minutes *more*, and those with vacuum cleaners spent 1 minute less. . . . Similar insignificant results were found when the appliances were matched to the housework task—for example, dishwashers with meal cleanup"[37] (italics in original).

Those authors advance an explanation for why technology often does not save us any time, and they use the microwave as a central example. All a microwave does is heat food, but "heating the meal . . . is only part of the task; to the extent that the table must be set, beverages poured, and side dishes prepared, the potential time savings get lost in the process."[38] If the food can be heated a little faster, then maybe there is extra time for making the table look a little more inviting, or for preparing another dish for the meal. This, essentially, is Parkinson's Law, which says that a task will expand to fill the amount of time we allot to it. If we think it will take roughly fifteen minutes to prepare a meal, then it will take about that amount of time, and any extra time means that we can add something else to the meal.

So how long, on average, do Americans spend cooking, eating, and cleaning up after meals? Not much time at all. The Bureau of Labor Statistics does an annual study where participants track everything they do over a twenty-four-hour period and then report that to researchers. In 2015 we spent about six minutes per day shopping for groceries, thirty-six minutes cooking and cleaning up, and an hour and ten minutes eating. The numbers are slightly different for men and women. Men spent four minutes grocery shopping, twenty-one minutes cooking and cleaning up, and about an hour and fifteen minutes eating, while women spent eight minutes shopping, fifty minutes cooking and cleaning up, and an hour and seven minutes eating. Women spent more time shopping, cooking, and cleaning up, while men spent more time eating. [39]

Those numbers do not tell the whole story, though. An important component of time is our perception of it, and our perception of how we use our time is more than a little skewed. In particular, we are very bad at estimating how much free time we have.

Back in 1991 Juliet Schor, a Harvard economist, published a book titled *The Overworked American: The Unexpected Decline of Leisure*. Using data from a range of sources, Schor showed what many Americans had suspected: that we were working (that is, working for pay) more than we used to. Much, much more. Over a thirty-year period, between the 1950s and 1980s, Americans had added an entire month's worth of paid work to our year. We did this by working overtime, taking second jobs, and not using the vacation time we had. It was no wonder that so many Americans felt so frazzled so much of the time, and no wonder that home cooking was being replaced by restaurant meals or convenience foods. We simply don't have the time for that sort of cooking any more.

But hold on. In the aftermath of the publication of that book, which received a significant amount of publicity, other researchers who specialized in time studies reported that their own research, some of which was used by Schor, did not back up that conclusion. In *Time for Life*, a book written as a response to Schor, researchers John P. Robinson and Geoffrey Godbey reported that their research (which used time diaries, similar to the Bureau of Labor Statistics research discussed above) showed that Americans were actually working much less than we used to. Robinson and Godbey had done three separate studies, in 1965, 1975, and 1985. They found that, between 1965 and 1985, employed women worked about six hours less per week (from nearly thirty-seven hours per week in

1965 to about thirty-one in 1985), while employed men worked six and a half hours less per week (from forty-six and a half hours per week in 1965 to just under forty hours per week in 1985).[40] Not only did they find that we were working less, we were also spending less time overall doing household chores. During the same period women cut out eight and a half hours of housework per week, going from almost twenty-seven hours spent on the task to about eighteen and a half hours. Some of this decrease was because men actually increased their share of the housework, moving from only spending about four and a half hours per week on housework in 1965 to about nine and a half hours in 1985 (the increase is just about equal to how much less time men were spending working for pay).[41]

The problem with Schor's *The Overworked American* was the methodology used in her calculations: she mixed and matched a number of time studies in a way that led to an incorrect conclusion. At the same time, though, her conclusion, that we have less free time than ever, clearly felt right to many people. Why is this?

Robinson and Godbey spend a considerable amount of space in their book looking at this very question: Why, if we have lots of free time, do we feel so rushed? Feeling so rushed causes us to make decisions we otherwise might not; in the context of the book you are reading, feeling rushed might cause us to pick up dinner from a restaurant or grab a frozen pizza instead of making a meal from scratch when we actually might have the time to make that meal from scratch.

The two researchers offer a couple of insights into our feeling of overwork. One issue is that Americans are terrible at estimating how much time we spend doing things. Robinson and Godbey mention a few studies, done on large groups of people, where participants estimated that they have between seventeen and nineteen hours of leisure time per week. Other studies asked participants how much television they watched, and respondents estimated that they watched about three hours per day. The problem, of course, is that the two estimates do not match: together, respondents estimated that they fit twenty-one hours of television viewing per week into only about eighteen hours of leisure time.[42]

One thing that confuses our perception of time is a practice called time deepening, which is a way to make our leisure time more productive. That we might want to make our nonproductive time more productive is a hint of where the practice might have come from. One economist believes it came about as people became more productive at their work; as one part of their life became more productive, they wanted the rest of their life to also be more productive (think of it as the "work hard, play hard" approach). People affected by this worked to either do things faster or, alternatively, throw material goods into the mix as well. Activities that were slower were abandoned (Robinson and Godbey list "contemplation, singing, dancing, writing poetry" as examples) in favor of faster activities (like "driving a car for pleasure, shopping, tourism").[43] Multitasking is a method of time deepening, too, as we can surf the Internet while watching TV, performing two leisure activities at the same time. Added to this is a particular quirk of human nature: those who sign up for some things sign up for lots of things. People involved in a club like Rotary are more likely to be involved in another club as well; those who use their free time to play a sport are likely to play several different sports. This tendency even had to be adjusted in Robinson and Godbey's data. Participants in their study, which was completely voluntary, had to track every activity they did in a twenty-four-hour period and how long and when they did each thing. The researchers assumed that very busy people would not want the additional work of tracking and reporting what they did, but it turned out that the opposite was true: very busy people were more likely to agree to participate than people who were less busy, as if the busy people simply saw the work involved with the study as another thing to add to their already long list of things to do.

In the fight between the feeling that we have less time than ever and the reality that we are working less than those a generation before us, the feeling of being rushed usually wins out. We go out for lunch rather than spend the time to make something to take to work; we grab a frozen dinner instead of planning, and making, a meal from scratch. The food industry has spent quite a bit of time and money making sure that they have something ready for us to eat quickly, no matter what we want.

The food industry as a whole has changed over the past fifty years. Some of this change has happened behind the scenes, hidden away from consumers, while some of the change has happened so slowly that it is difficult to realize anything actually changed, unless one looks back over a period of decades rather than years. Consumers have changed as well; for one thing, we're larger, on average, than we were fifty years ago.

Is there a connection between changes in the food industry and America's weight gain? A group of economists worked to find out, publishing a study titled, simply, "Why Have Americans Become More Obese?" Their conclusion was that yes, there is a connection between what has happened in the food industry and American waistlines. Specifically, the food industry, which has spent so much time working on processed foods, has made it so easy for Americans to eat those foods that we have been consuming more and more food.

How large are we? The study looks at the body mass index, or BMI, a number calculated using a person's height and weight. A BMI in the low teens means the person is severely underweight while a number in the mid-forties is about as large as someone can go and still be, well, alive. People with a BMI of thirty and above are classified as obese. In the early 1970s roughly 16 percent of Americans were obese; by the late 1980s and early 1990s that number had nearly doubled to 30 percent (the study focuses on the 1980s because that is when most of the weight gain of the past few decades occurred). As the authors of the study noted, the change occurred not simply because the average person was heavier but also because there were many more people with very high BMIs that skewed the average slightly higher. Interestingly, those people who are often thought to ingest almost nothing but convenience foods—single men— had the lowest obesity rate among the different classifications of genders and marital status, with only 18 percent obesity by the late 1980s and early 1990s. Those in the most obese group were married, unemployed women, at 36 percent.

While the climbing obesity rate is alarming, the authors of the study point out that the shift means that the average individual gained only about ten to twelve pounds. There are two ways Americans could have gained weight: they either ate more or exercised less (or had some combination of these). To gain the weight and keep it on, the average individual would only have to eat an additional 100–150 calories per day, which is not difficult to do. As the authors write, that would equate, per day, to "three Oreo cookies or one can of Pepsi."[44] Or Americans could have exercised less, as that many calories equates to walking about a mile and a half.

By looking at surveys of food intake, produced by the Department of Agriculture, the study's authors found that, between the mid-1970s and the mid-1990s, Americans were eating more. In particular, they were snacking more, getting between 160 (for women) and 241 (for men) extra calories per day from snacks. Other meals roughly balanced out. Over the two-decade period both men and women ate slightly less for dinner and slightly more for breakfast and lunch (the authors point out that those shifts, particularly in eating slightly less for dinner, cuts out increased restaurant portion sizes as being a culprit in the weight gain).

The fact that Americans were eating more snacks implicates the convenience food industry, since candy bars, sodas, chips, and the myriad other foods stocked by almost any convenience store are what Americans usually go for when they want a snack. The study's authors point out that, since the 1960s, the food industry has made great strides in solving the problems involved with making food at a factory and shipping it across the country for consumption weeks or months later. With modern packaging and distribution channels, the industry can control the atmosphere, temperature, and moisture of the food that it produces; it can keep microorganisms from growing on that food; and it can preserve the flavor of that food while it is in transit and while it sits on store shelves.

The authors of the study are economists, and they pay particularly close attention to the efficiencies that have been built into the processed food industry since the 1950s. One of their main examples is the French fry. Americans have always eaten lots of potatoes, but before the middle of the twentieth century we usually enjoyed our potatoes either baked or mashed. Since then, though, the French fry has become the most popular form of potato. This is somewhat strange, though, as Americans do not have a history of eating French fries. Cookbooks from the nineteenth or early twentieth centuries do not include recipes for making French fries. Likewise, it is difficult to find a recipe for French fries in a cookbook published today. Why is that? Because making French fries at home is difficult. The potatoes have to be peeled and then cut in a certain way, and then they have to be carefully lowered into the hot grease—carefully, because the water content of the potato means the grease will likely splatter the moment the vegetable hits that grease. No one makes French fries from scratch because it is easier to buy a bag of frozen fries at the grocery store or to get them at a restaurant.

The French fry is an example of the efficiency of the processed food industry. Think of other convenience foods that, while possible to make at home, no one ever does make at home, foods like potato chips or cream-filled pastries such as Twinkies or Ho Hos. Again, they are physically possible to make but time and labor intensive, items that are inexpensive enough that anyone who wants one simply buys one at the grocery store or the local convenience store.

The authors of this report conclude that Americans have gained weight largely because it is so easy to eat fattening, highly processed foods. Convenience stores are packed with high-calorie snacks that seem to cry out for us to buy them, so much that not having a candy bar or soda every so often is moving against the grain of American culture. This is not to say that many people do not eat those convenience foods—some abstain because the foods are unhealthy while others do it because they simply cannot eat them. Many people are on diets that have no place for those foods.

The growth of special diets over the past few decades has pushed many people into home cooking, although the food industry, seeing an opportunity, has responded by creating some products that are geared toward special diets. These diets include those that are for religious reasons, those for losing weight, and those that are in response to a particular health problem, often food allergies.

Diets based on religious restrictions are nothing new. Many religions have food restrictions, some of which are permanent (such as restrictions against pork for Jews and Muslims) and some of which are temporary (like a ban on eating meat on Fridays during Lent for Catholics). Since these restrictions have been around so long, and affect so many people, the food industry has responded to the restrictions. For example, many foods are marked, after being certified, as being kosher or pareve for Jewish consumers. Restaurants advertise sales on fish entrees on Fridays during Lent.

Dieting for weight loss is also not new, although the obesity epidemic is a fairly new phenomenon, coming on strong only since the 1970s. Specific diet plans tend to fall in to one of two camps. They either recommend eating or avoiding particular types of food or specify precisely what should be eaten at each meal. For example, high-protein, low-carbohydrate plans like the Atkins Diet are in the first camp, giving general recommendations for what to eat but allowing dieters to eat anything within those guidelines. The Scarsdale Diet, popular in the 1970s, was a fourteen-day diet with a specific list of what should be eaten at each meal.

Generally, the stricter the diet, the more difficult it is to either eat out or use convenience foods. Because of how specific it is, the Scarsdale

Diet usually guarantees that dieters will be eating homemade foods for the two weeks they are on the program. The popularity of the diet also affects food choices. Since the Atkins Diet is so popular, it is possible to find foods at the grocery store that specifically have the Atkins seal of approval on the package.

If someone wants to lose weight, though, there are certainly convenience foods that can help with this. Diet shakes are one option, with brand names like SlimFast and Atkins; the dieter simply replaces two meals per day with two shakes and then eats the third meal as they normally would. That idea is taken to its logical conclusion with programs like Nutrisystem, a meal plan in which all food is shipped directly to the dieter from the company and the dieter eats nothing outside of what is shipped. This, of course, is the ultimate dream of much of the food industry, where a consumer eats only the food that is shipped directly to them. However, this is an extremely niche product that shows no sign of becoming the default way of obtaining food in the future.

And then there are food allergies. Diagnoses of food allergies have exploded in America over the past few decades, apparently for a few different reasons. Celiac disease, an allergy to gluten (which is in wheat), is an example of a food allergy that appears to have more sufferers than twenty or thirty years ago. However, the increase is actually because the disease is better diagnosed today. During much of the twentieth century European researchers were at the forefront of celiac research, far outpacing American researchers, to the point that Americans more or less gave up on researching the disease. Since Americans were not researching the disease, news of developments in diagnosis and treatment was not spread to American doctors, with the result that American doctors usually did not know the disease even existed. Until the past few decades the disease was usually diagnosed as something else.[45]

Peanut allergy, though, does appear to be something that more people suffer from than ever before, and the cause of this is still under investigation. In fact, the cause is so baffling that some recommendations from experts appear to have actually increased the outbreak. In 1998, after a study showed that avoiding potential allergens helped to reduce food allergies in children, the United Kingdom's Department of Health issued guidelines recommending that children avoid the most common food allergens, including peanuts. Logically, this makes sense—maybe repeated exposure to a particular food makes children allergic. In the years after the new recommendations the rate of peanut allergies increased drastically in the United Kingdom. Other researchers noted that children in Israel had much lower occurrences of food allergies, including peanut allergy. One difference between British and Israeli children is that a common snack food for children in Israel is made from peanuts—so perhaps exposing children to common allergens is actually a good thing. Researchers are still working on it. [46]

Again, the food industry has responded to the growing numbers of people with food allergies, although that response can sometimes only go so far. The issue is that sufferers of some food allergies exist along a continuum. For example, if those who have the most extreme versions of celiac disease consume any amount of gluten, no matter how small, they will immediately have a reaction that can include anaphylaxis, in which their tongue might swell up and they become lightheaded, or they may have severe digestive problems. For this group, having an entree marked "gluten-free" at a restaurant is still a problem because of contamination— if the gluten-free dish is prepared in the same kitchen where other dishes are prepared, the gluten-free dish can become contaminated with minute amounts of gluten. Other sufferers could have much less severe responses and might be able to tolerate small amounts of gluten, meaning that they can eat a gluten-free dish at a restaurant.

The food industry's response to celiac disease was intensified in the early to mid-2010s as being gluten-free became something of a fad, and many people without celiac disease went gluten-free because of perceived health benefits. As Harry Balzer, a vice president at NPD Group, a market research company, said in 2014, "About 30 percent of the public says it would like to cut back on the amount of gluten it's eating, and if you find 30 percent of the public doing anything, you'll find a lot of marketers right there, too." [47] Grocery stores began segregating gluten-free products into a separate section, a result of both the popularity of gluten-free foods and the growing number of foods marked as being gluten-free. Those foods became so mainstream that some websites that specialized in selling gluten-free foods shut down. For example, General Mills started a website in 2010 called glutenfreely.com that sold gluten-free products. It closed the site just three years later because those products had become widely available in most stores. That food allergies are an opportunity for grocery stores can be seen in the fact that, while the average consumer spends $33 on a trip to the grocery store, a gluten-free customer spends about $100.[48]

Americans spend more money eating at restaurants than we did in years past. The U.S. Department of Agriculture tracks a number of different statistics related to food, including what percentage of our incomes we spend on food we eat at home versus the percentage spent on eating away from home. They have yearly data dating back to 1959, and the percentages do not change that much from year to year. When one looks at the data over time, though, a clear trend comes out: we are spending more money eating out than we used to, and the dollar amounts are almost equal. In 1960 some 15 percent of our income went to the food we ate at home compared with only 3.5 percent eaten away from home. By 2014 we spent just 6 percent on at-home food and 5.4 percent on food eaten away from home. Some of that change is because food is cheaper than it used to be while labor costs are higher, somewhat skewing the numbers in favor of eating out. But there is undoubtedly a shift toward eating out. Of course, just because we are spending almost as much on eating out as we are on eating at home does not mean we spend half the time eating out. One consumer research company reported, back in 2005, that Americans spend an average of about $8 per person eating out compared with just over $2 per person in food costs when we eat at home.

In the past fifty years restaurants have become ubiquitous in American society. The industry is very segmented, with types of restaurants that cater to almost any situation. Fast food places serve food that is inexpensive and quickly served. Casual dining places like Applebee's or Chili's have wait staff, a larger selection of food, and are more expensive. Fast casual restaurants like Chipotle attempt to bridge the gap between fast food and casual dining by offering a smaller menu, higher-quality foods, quick preparation, and moderate prices. There are chains that focus on ethnic foods, American foods, pizza, barbecue, and everything in between. This sort of segmentation did not exist fifty years ago, and it offers an almost endless amount of choice for diners.

The industry also offers more choice in dining at home. While "carry out" has always been an option at restaurants, many chains have promoted taking food away by marking parking spaces near the restaurant as being specifically for patrons waiting for carry-out food. Other restaurants, particularly pizza places, will deliver food to patrons, while in many cities there are services that will deliver food from restaurants that do not deliver themselves.

Because of the segmentation of the industry and the intense competition between businesses, restaurants are often quick to adapt to new trends. With the increase in food allergies, many restaurants have created special menus that either are tailored for a particular type of allergy, like celiac disease, or list all allergens in each dish on the menu. The popularity of some diet plans, like low-carbohydrate diets, have spurred some restaurants to add dishes that are made to be compatible with that diet (and are noted as such on the menu). As this book is being written, in 2016, Panera Bread is heavily marketing the concept of clean food, which the chain defines as being without "artificial preservatives, sweeteners, flavors or colors from artificial sources," and transitioning all of its food to be "clean." This, the chain likely believes, will appeal to potential patrons who are concerned with artificial additives.

All in all, the restaurant industry has worked to make restaurant food as accessible as possible. It has tried to overcome potential obstacles patrons might have to eating at a restaurant, like food allergies, reduced time, a desire to eat higher-quality food, and a lack of much money. In this it has been at least moderately successful, as the amount of money Americans spend at restaurants is almost as much as we spend at the grocery store.

Like it has touched everything else, the Internet has affected food and cooking. Its ultimate effects are hard to discern at this point, though.

One way it has affected home cooking is by shifting the balance in recipe production. Previously there were two main sources of recipes: food companies that used their recipes to promote their products, and food writers who were a part of traditional media and who wrote cookbooks and in newspapers and magazines. Using the Internet as, essentially, a publishing platform, anyone can easily publish a recipe in a place where many people can see it (whether those people actually do see it, and make the dish, is another issue entirely). Often, these recipes are for a particular niche audience, such as those suffering from food allergies or people with specific diet plans, and because cookbooks and magazines often underserve those niches, those recipes have a better chance of becoming popular.

The Internet functions as a way of accessing media, and this has also changed cooking. Websites like YouTube have thousands of hours of cooking videos on all possible subjects. The recipes from food companies that used to run primarily in magazine advertisements are now accessible on their websites. Archived cooking shows are easily available on streaming services. Through the Internet we have access to more cooking information than any other culture has in the past.

The Internet makes it easy to create, find, and join groups, some of which have a cooking component. For example, those suffering from specific food allergies can easily find groups of people online who also have those allergies and who post recipes and advice for others. Another example is people who enjoy a particular type of cooking, like barbecue or making beer, who, again, post recipes and advice. In this way they can advance the body of knowledge available to people with their same interests, even for those with very niche interests.

The Internet has also enabled particular types of businesses to flourish, or at least exist. Around the turn of the twenty-first century a very popular Internet business was one that delivered groceries, allowing customers to select the foods they wanted from a long list and have those items delivered to their doorstep. As it turned out, these were more popular with investors than consumers, and the grocery delivery business became one part of the Internet bubble that burst in 2001. As of this writing, the meal delivery kits business may also be in a sort of bubble, and this is another food-related business model that could not exist without the Internet.

American cooking has changed tremendously in the past fifty years, although much of this change has been a shift away from cooking from scratch. We are much more knowledgeable about food than people were in the 1960s and have access to more food knowledge and information courtesy of the Internet. At the same time, the restaurant industry has grown considerably, and the convenience food industry has made it very easy to buy whatever snack item we might want. What all of this might mean for the future of cooking is the subject of the next, and final, chapter.

6

THE FUTURE OF HOME COOKING

Reay Tannahill's *Food in History* is one of the classic texts for food historians. Published in 1973, long before the current avalanche of food-related work, Tannahill traces the history of eating from misty prehistoric times all the way through the 1970s, and at the end she offers some observations on what the future of food might look like. After spending several hundred pages outlining the history of foods like bread and beer, both of which have been made for thousands of years and are still very popular today, her vision of the future is a little shocking. What might the future entail? Factories. Not something like factory farming, where thousands of chickens are raised in tight coops, but actual factories. "Protein, carbohydrates, vitamins and fats can all be created in the laboratory out of a wide variety of materials," she writes, using soybeans as an example of source material, although there are many others. "Protein can also be extracted from fuel oil, and it is confidently predicted that natural gas will prove an equally valuable source."

She then describes just how such a factory, set up "to serve perhaps fifty thousand people," might operate. Tanks filled with water and "microscopic plants" would be exposed to sunlight that would cause the plants to grow rapidly. Some of the resulting biomass would be fed to cattle, pigs, and chickens "to provide red meat for gourmets and eggs for everyone." Some would be made into ingredients like flour. And some— well, this is where Tannahill's vision of the food of the future becomes particularly dystopian. The book was written at the height of the fear that the growing global population would soon push our food systems into complete collapse, so Tannahill's vision of the future is one where real animals barely exist. Some of the plant material would be used to make dairy products, but without the use of an actual cow. Instead, the plant mass would be "processed through laboratory-grown milk-producing glands, to give milk for drinking or for conversion into butter and cheese." And for nongourmet red meat, part of the plant mass would be spun into something approaching meat: "long wrist-thick tubes of 'fillet steak,' for example, ready for automatic slicing into tournedos-sized portions." The system would not be able to provide fruits and vegetables, so, she conceded, they "would probably continue to come from private gardens and specialist growers."[1]

Luckily, this particular vision of the future never came to pass. Tannahill was actually right about some aspects of what she describes, since a shockingly large proportion of processed food is *highly* processed, in factories, using methods that are close to what she describes. But the overall vision of people worldwide eating almost nothing but food produced in factories is far from the mark (most dystopian predictions of this sort have the super-rich eating fresh foods while the poor eat factory-made foods, while the reality today is that Americans are the ones who eat the highest percentage of food produced in factories while some of the poorest people in the world, who also grow or catch their own food, are the ones eating fresh foods).

This has not stopped people from at least attempting to get to this future, where all food comes directly from a factory. For example, there is Soylent, a product engineered to be the only thing you have to eat (yes, it takes its name from *Soylent Green*, the 1973 Charlton Heston film set in a future where most of the population consumes only soylent green, a food that is made—spoiler alert!—from people). Soylent, the modern product, is not made from people, but rather from soy protein, oils, and a laundry list of vitamins, minerals, and additives. As of this writing, it is available in liquid form (with a coffee variation), as a bar, and as a powder, all made so that you can survive on just Soylent. The cost is not too outrageous, as the powder costs about $8 per day, and, since it supplies all the nutrition a human body needs, it is just about the most efficient food product in existence. There is no cooking on the consumer's part (they even throw in a free pitcher and scoop with the first order). Is this the food of the future?

Of course not. Soylent may supply the calories and nutrition a body needs, but it is also largely tasteless and consuming it is, frankly, boring. Humans eat because we need calories and nutrition but also because it causes some pretty good sensations. We like flavors and textures, as the most successful chefs and food companies know extremely well.

If food that looks and tastes like it came from a factory is not the future, what about the opposite? What about a return to home cooking?

There are undeniable health benefits that come from cooking at home. Not from simply microwaving a pizza, but actually cooking from scratch, at home. Part of the benefit is the lack of processed foods—cooking from scratch using almost any recipe will involve at least some fresh ingredients, even if canned foods or dry mixes are involved.

There is also a belief held by many people that cooking our own food gives us something, and by not cooking our food we have lost it. What "it" might be is usually hard to define. Michael Pollan falls into this camp, and he is definitely not alone. There is sometimes a certain stridency in this argument, such as that seen in the title of Ann Vileisis's *Kitchen Literacy: How We Lost Knowledge of Where Food Comes From and Why We Need to Get It Back*. The argument often relies on the idea that there is something special about cooking, something that makes it different from everything else we do as humans. Writing in the *New York Times* in 2009, Pollan explained that "cooking—unlike sewing or darning socks—is an activity that strikes a deep emotional chord in us, one that might even go to the heart of our identity as human beings."[2] Richard Wrangham's *Catching Fire*, which theorizes that the ability to cook food is what shifted us along the evolutionary chain toward becoming human, is usually used as an example of the deep connection between cooking and humanity, as is the basic fact that we were cooking long before we figured out how to grow plants from seeds or domesticated animals. Thus, the argument goes, cooking will always be with us, and by not cooking on a daily basis we have lost something—maybe a part of our humanity?

There are some significant problems with this argument, beginning with its vagueness. When what we may have lost is never really defined, it is difficult to argue that we still have it. The argument also ignores a large part of the historical record. As a group, humans have been cooking for thousands of years, but large numbers of humans within that group never cooked. In American culture men have not usually been the ones working in the kitchen. If the argument is that, by not cooking, we have lost something, the same argument should be applied to all those people who never picked up a pan in their lives. Did they lose something through their inaction, and did the women who cooked gain something by spending all those hours in the kitchen?

The argument also conveniently ignores what, historically, has been the fundamental problem with cooking: Who is going to be stuck doing it? Certainly, many people enjoy cooking, but many also dislike it, and it is easy to enjoy something you do not have to do day after day, week in and week out. Women have traditionally been the cooks in American households, and it is easy to forget that one of the reasons convenience foods caught on so quickly is because many cooks wanted something to make their jobs easier. If there is going to be a mass return to cooking, the question of just whose job that will be needs to be addressed.

Finally, the argument places an enormous amount of importance on food and cooking relative to all other objects and activities humans partake of. Why is cooking so much more important than, say, sewing? Could the argument be made that, in giving up making our own cloth and sewing our own clothes, we gave up something to the factories? What makes the food we eat so much more important than the clothes we wear? To take the question in another direction, along with sewing and cooking, another responsibility women commonly had in the nineteenth century was helping sick and infirm family members. If we, as a culture, went back to considering it our responsibility to visit and help the elderly and those with long-term illnesses in the hospital, might that be a step in the right direction? More than, say, cooking our own meals?

Pollan himself sometimes does not seem very hopeful about the future of cooking. In the same article that was quoted above, he asks a consumer researcher just what it would take for Americans to go back to cooking their own foods. "Not going to happen," the researcher says. "Why? Because we're basically cheap and lazy. And besides, the skills are already lost. Who is going to teach the next generation to cook? I don't see it." Pollan continues to prod the researcher, asking just what might get Americans to eat healthier. The researcher finally says, "You want Americans to eat less? I have the diet for you. It's short, and it's simple. Here's my diet plan: *Cook it yourself.* That's it. Eat anything you want— just as long as you're willing to cook it yourself"[3] (italics in the original).

My prediction on the future of cooking is this: the future will not be a whole lot different from the present, and as things change, they will change slowly. Evolution, not revolution.

There are a number of trends that favor Americans drifting further and further from home cooking. There is an ever-shrinking amount of time we have to cook. Even if we don't spend more time at a job than we did decades ago, many of us are more overcommitted than ever. Restaurants and grocery stores offer many more alternatives to cooking than existed in years past, and these alternatives show no sign of going away. There is also no longer a strong ideology that ties women to cooking from scratch. Yes, in many households women still do the bulk of the cooking, but these days most people believe it is perfectly fine for those women to use convenience foods or, if the money is available, to just pick something up on the way home from work.

At the same time, there are also a number of trends that favor at least a continuation of home cooking, if not a swing back in that direction.

There are many more potential cooks. I am not talking here about the growing population of America, but rather about a new gender actually being involved in cooking. In the majority of this book the word *cook* has worked interchangeably with the word *woman*—until the past few decades, women were the default cooks in all American families. Today, particularly with younger people, that is changing. An entire generation has grown up watching men like Mario Batali and Emeril Lagasse cook on television. While these men are professional chefs, they were also on cooking shows that presented the message that "you, the viewer, can make exactly what I am making, if only you follow what I am doing." In 2008, during the financial crisis, the *New York Times* published an article on an increase in home cooking. Yes, some of that was because money was tight for so many families. But an industry analyst from a company that monitors consumer habits also noted that cooking was losing its gender identification. As the analyst observed, "Men are preparing more dinner on a nightly basis than ever in the history of this country."[4]

There is more cooking information available to the average person than ever before. In 1800 the only source for cooking information, apart from friends and relatives, was a cookbook, and there were not many cookbooks in circulation. During the 1800s women's magazines became popular, and they also offered cooking information. Then radio came along in the 1920s, television in the 1950s, and the Internet in the 1990s.

Today, anyone with a computer is only seconds away from a recipe for boeuf bourguignon and a video on how to make it. If one subscribes to the correct streaming video service, one can even watch Julia Child make the dish on one of her cooking shows. All of this information means that it is easier than ever to learn how to cook, to learn new techniques and cook new dishes, and to find out about ingredients one might never have encountered before. Cooking may be more of an optional activity than in years past, but if one chooses that option, it is certainly easy to learn.

Along with that, Americans have more access to ingredients than anyone before us, and it is easier to cook than ever before. For most fruits and vegetables seasonality is a thing of the past, and for items that still have a certain season (like corn on the cob or blueberries), that season has been extended by moving crops in from Canada, Mexico, or South America. We also have the most inexpensive food in the world. The U.S. Department of Agriculture produces a chart comparing the percentage of our income that we Americans spend on food with the same information for eighty-five other countries. We are at the top of the list, spending only 6.4 percent of our incomes on food.[5] Some of that is because processed foods are inexpensive, and some is because we have much higher incomes than many other countries. But still, we have access to some inexpensive food. When it comes to cooking we have more utensils and appliances to assist us than ever before. Food processors, blenders, mixers, and other tools drastically cut the time and effort involved with making many recipes. Large appliances such as refrigerators, stoves, ovens, and dishwashers make food preparation and cleanup a breeze. It has never been easier to cook than it is today.

There are a host of corporations with a vested interest in the continuation of cooking. Manufacturers such as Viking, GE, LG, Samsung, and Whirlpool want to sell you kitchen appliances, and that cannot happen if the kitchen does not exist. Similarly, food companies such as General Foods, Nestlé, and Tyson, as well as stores that feature groceries such as Kroger, Whole Foods, and Walmart, want some level of cooking to continue. Certainly, the highest sales margins are usually on processed foods, so that is what food sellers would like for consumers to buy, but they do still sell items such as fresh produce and meat.

And there is the place where all the cooking happens: the kitchen. In spite of a long decline in home cooking, the kitchen does not appear to be in danger of going away any time soon. Watch almost any home improvement show today, and you will see that the two most popular ideas for renovating a house are to tear down dividing walls to get to an open concept layout and to renovate the kitchen, preferably with granite countertops, stainless steel appliances, and an island. The kitchen island is the key kitchen development of the late twentieth and early twenty-first centuries. It has only happened because the kitchen has grown over the past few decades, not shrunk—if, with the decline in cooking, the kitchen was becoming a less and less important space, shouldn't it have shrunk? Instead, American kitchens have moved from a hidden space at the back of the house, as they were in the early twentieth century, to become larger and more prominent. Obviously, some of this is conspicuous consumption, a way to publicly show off expensive countertops and high-end appliances. But something else is happening. Kitchen islands are popular both because they offer more countertop space, which is good for cooking, and because they offer more social space. The default island design is such that one side of the counter is flush with the cabinets below, where the cook can stand and prepare food, while the other side has an overhang, where people can sit and talk with the cook, or talk with each other. During the course of the twentieth century the kitchen moved from being a workspace to a combination work and social space, the only place in the house like that. The other prominent public room in the house, which might be called the family room, changed during the century as television became more and more important. That room was reworked so that it is not as social as it once was; now all furniture in that room faces a wall with a television hanging on it. The room is not set up for movement, or even talking. It is designed for sitting and watching.

I believe that the social aspect of cooking will ensure its continuation. When someone like Michael Pollan writes about the deep need we have for cooking, I believe he is close but not quite right: the deep part of cooking is not the act of cooking but the act of eating together. Cooking has only ever been done by a part of society (usually women), but eating involves everyone. This is why, in the course of this book, I have not spent too much time focusing on just what cooking is and what it is not. Any type of cooking is just a means to an end; as any good cook knows, the important part of cooking is the eating.

NOTES

1. COOKING IN 1800

1. Richard Wrangham, *Catching Fire: How Cooking Made Us Human* (New York: Basic Books, 2009), 2.

2. Kenneth T. Jackson, *Crabgrass Frontier: The Suburbanization of the United States* (New York: Oxford University Press, 1985), 280.

3. Quoted in Nancy Carlisle and Melinda Talbot Nasardinov with Jennifer Pustz, *America's Kitchens* (Boston: Historic New England, 2008), 30.

4. Harold L. Peterson, *Americans at Home: From the Colonists to the Late Victorians* (New York: Charles Scribner's Sons, 1971), plate 48, *Mount Family Kitchen* by William Sidney Mount, pencil, 1830–40, Suffolk Museum & Carriage House, Stony Brook, Long Island.

5. Patrick Shirreff, *A Tour Through North America* (Edinburgh: Oliver and Boyd, 1835), 221.

6. Carlisle and Nasardinov with Pustz, *America's Kitchens*, 38.

7. An English Gentleman, *An Excursion Through the United States and Canada During the Years 1822–23* (London: Baldwin, Cradock, and Joy, 1824), 146.

8. Geoffrey Crayon, Esq. (Washington Irving), *The Sketch-Book of Geoffrey Crayon, Esq.* (Paris: Baudry's European Library, 1846), 322–23.

9. "Book for Receipts" Recipe Book, Ms2008-024-Special Collections, Virginia Polytechnic Institute and State University.

10. Mrs. J. C. Croly, *Jennie June's American Cookery Book* (New York: The American News Company, 1870), 149.

11. Mrs. E. F. Haskell, *The Housekeeper's Encyclopedia* (New York: D. Appleton and Company, 1861), 230.

12. William Bircher, *A Drummer-Boy's Diary* (St. Paul, MN: St. Paul Book and Stationery Co., 1889), 125.

13. Mary Randolph, *The Virginia Housewife* (Columbia: University of South Carolina Press, 1984), xiii–xvii.

14. Amelia Simmons, *American Cookery* (Hartford, CT: Simeon Butler, 1798), 36.

15. Simmons, *American Cookery*, 20, 23.

16. Carlisle and Nasardinov with Pustz, *America's Kitchens*, 55.

17. Simmons, *American Cookery*, 23.

18. Jack Larkin, *The Reshaping of Everyday Life 1790–1840* (New York: HarperPerennial, 1989), 33–34.

19. Paton Yoder, *Taverns and Travelers: Inns of the Early Midwest* (Bloomington: Indiana University Press, 1969), 69–70.

20. Herman Melville, *Moby-Dick, Billy Budd, and Other Writings* (New York: The Library of America, 2000), 93–94.

21. "Table 3. Population of the 33 Urban Places: 1800," U.S. Bureau of the Census, https://www.census.gov/population/www/documentation/twps0027/tab03.txt, accessed December 14, 2015.

2. THE EARLY TO LATE 1800S

1. Catharine E. Beecher and Harriet Beecher Stowe, *The American Woman's Home* (New York: J. B. Ford and Company, 1869), 74.

2. Ruth Schwartz Cowan, *More Work for Mother: The Ironies of Household Technology from the Open Hearth to the Microwave* (New York: Basic Books, 1983), 98.

3. Harold L. Peterson, *Americans at Home: From the Colonists to the Late Victorians* (New York: Charles Scribner's Sons, 1971), plate 86.

4. Ellen H. Richards, "The Eight Hour Day in Housekeeping," *The American Cooking Magazine*, April 1902, 21.

5. Peterson, *Americans at Home*, plate 117.

6. Peterson, *Americans at Home*, plate 118.

7. Nancy Carlisle and Melinda Talbot Nasardinov with Jennifer Pustz, *America's Kitchens* (Boston: Historic New England, 2008), 68.

8. Mark Twain, *A Tramp Abroad* (New York: Oxford University Press, 1996), 574–75.

9. These examples were taken from Seed Savers, a group that sells heirloom vegetables, specifically the Yellow Moon and Stars watermelon, Chocolate Beauty pepper, and Mandan Bride corn. See http://www.seedsavers.org/.

10. Thomas F. De Voe, *The Market Assistant* (New York: Hurd and Houghton, 1867), 9.

11. Fredrick Accum, *A Treatise on Adulteration of Food, and Culinary Poisons* (London: Longman, 1820), 290–91.

12. Accum, *A Treatise on Adulteration of Food, and Culinary Poisons*, 256.

13. Bee Wilson, *Consider the Fork: A History of How We Cook and Eat* (New York: Basic Books, 2012), 222.

14. Sue Shephard, *Pickled, Potted and Canned: How the Art and Science of Food Preserving Changed the World* (New York: Simon & Schuster, 2000), 242, 245.

15. Shephard, *Pickled, Potted and Canned*, 150–51.

16. Wilson, *Consider the Fork*, 155.

17. Mrs. E. F. Haskell, *The Housekeeper's Encyclopedia* (New York: D. Appleton and Company, 1861), 235.

18. John D. Billings, *Hardtack and Coffee* (Boston: George M. Smith & Co., 1888), 138.

19. Billings, *Hardtack and Coffee*, 139.

20. De Voe, *The Market Assistant*, 21.

21. De Voe, *The Market Assistant*, 21.

22. Beecher and Stowe, *The American Woman's Home*, 59.

23. Beecher and Stowe, *The American Woman's Home*, 157, 342.

24. Beecher and Stowe, *The American Woman's Home*, 194.

25. Beecher and Stowe, *The American Woman's Home*, 119.

26. Beecher and Stowe, *The American Woman's Home*, 125.

27. Beecher and Stowe, *The American Woman's Home*, 143.

28. Beecher and Stowe, *The American Woman's Home*, 293.

29. Beecher and Stowe, *The American Woman's Home*, 466.

30. Hon. E. Stanley, *Journal of a Tour in America* (London: Privately Printed, 1930), 64.

31. J. Richard Beste, *The Wabash* (Freeport, NY: Books for Libraries Press, 1970), 70.

32. Beste, *The Wabash*, 183.

33. Andrew P. Haley, *Turning the Tables: Restaurants and the Rise of the American Middle Class, 1880–1920* (Chapel Hill: University of North Carolina Press, 2011), 122.

34. Haley, *Turning the Tables*, 49.

35. Haley, *Turning the Tables*, 172.

3. THE LATE 1800S THROUGH 1945

1. "The Relative Cost of Home-Cooked and Purchased Food," *Massachusetts Labor Bulletin* 19 (August 1901): 96.

2. "The Relative Cost of Home-Cooked and Purchased Food," 94–95.

3. "The Relative Cost of Home-Cooked and Purchased Food," 80.

4. "The Relative Cost of Home-Cooked and Purchased Food," 87.

5. "The Relative Cost of Home-Cooked and Purchased Food," 87.

6. Elizabeth E. Lea, *Domestic Cookery* (Baltimore: Cushings and Bailey, 1869), 229.

7. William Woys Weaver, *A Quaker Woman's Cookbook: The Domestic Cookery of Elizabeth Ellicott Lea* (Philadelphia: University of Pennsylvania Press, 1982), xxxiii.

8. Madge E. Pickard and R. Carlyle Buley, *The Midwest Pioneer: His Ills, Cures & Doctors* (New York: Henry Schuman, 1946), 43.

9. *Good Housekeeping*, January 1901, 85, 83, 77, 81.

10. Laura Shapiro, *Perfection Salad: Women and Cooking at the Turn of the Century* (New York: Farrar, Straus and Giroux, 1986), 37–38.

11. A. Nichola, "Easy Means of Relieving Pain," *Good Housekeeping*, March 1901, 216.

12. Shapiro, *Perfection Salad*, 176.

13. Shapiro, *Perfection Salad*, 140.

14. Shapiro, *Perfection Salad*, 178–84.

15. Shapiro, *Perfection Salad*, 185.

16. *Good Things to Eat from Wellville* (Battle Creek, MI: Postum Cereal Company, 1916), 12, 30, 24.

17. Duncan Hines, *Adventures in Good Eating* (Ithaca, NY: Duncan Hines Institute, 1957), 168.

18. "The Nestlé Toll House Cookies Story," https://www.verybestbaking.com/articles/nestle-toll-house-story, accessed September 13, 2016.

19. Bruce Weinstein and Mark Scarbrough, *The Ultimate Chocolate Cookie Book* (New York: William Morrow, 2004), 4.

20. *What's New in Home Economics*, September 1941, 151. A copy of this is in file 25, box 229, Clementine Paddleford Collection, University Archives and Manuscripts, Richard L. D. and Marjorie J. Morse Department of Special Collections, Kansas State University, Manhattan, Kansas (hereafter referred to as "Paddleford Collection").

21. Faye E. Dudden, *Serving Women: Household Service in Nineteenth-Century America* (Middletown, CT: Wesleyan University Press, 1983), 185–86.

22. Milton B. Marks, "The Longwood Co-Operative Kitchen," *Good Housekeeping*, February 1901, 101–3.

23. Dudden, *Serving Women*, 190.

24. Roger Horowitz, *Putting Meat on the American Table: Taste, Technology, Transformation* (Baltimore: Johns Hopkins University Press, 2006), 30–31.

25. Sue Shephard, *Pickled, Potted and Canned: How the Art and Science of Food Preserving Changed the World* (New York: Simon & Schuster, 2000), 303–8.

26. Jeffrey Charles, "Searching for Gold in Guacamole: California Growers Market the Avocado, 1910–1994," in *Food Nations: Selling Taste in Consumer Societies*, ed. Warren Belasco and Philip Scranton (New York: Routledge, 2002), 132–50.

27. Harvey A. Levenstein, *Revolution at the Table: The Transformation of the American Diet* (New York: Oxford University Press, 1988), 35–36.

28. Levenstein, *Revolution at the Table*, 33.

29. J. H. Kellogg, MD, *Battle Creek Sanitarium System: History, Organization, Methods* (Battle Creek, MI: Gage Publishing Co., 1908), 11.

30. Elizabeth Riely, "Sylvester Graham and the Origins of the Breakfast Food Industry," in *Oxford Symposium on Food & Cookery 1989: Staple Foods* (London: Prospect Books, 1990), 200.

31. Mary Ellen Snodgrass, *Encyclopedia of Kitchen History* (New York: Fitzroy Dearborn, 2004), s.v. "Cereals."

32. Kellogg, *Battle Creek Sanitarium System*, 205.

33. Kellogg, *Battle Creek Sanitarium System*, 206.

34. Bee Wilson, *Swindled: The Dark History of Food Fraud, From Poisoned Candy to Counterfeit Coffee* (Princeton, NJ: Princeton University Press, 2008), 205–9.

35. Maria Parloa, *Miss Parloa's New Cook Book* (Boston: Estes and Lauriat, 1882), 345; Irma S. Rombauer, Marion Rombauer Becker, and Ethan Becker, *The Joy of Cooking* (New York: Scribner, 1997), 69.

36. Mary J. Lincoln et al., *Home Helps: A Pure Food Cook Book* (Chicago: N. K. Fairbank Company, 1910), 4.

37. Lincoln et al., *Home Helps*, 7.

38. Walter Weir, "Advertising Tells the Story," in *Food Marketing*, ed. Paul Sayres (New York: McGraw-Hill, 1950), 212.

39. Susan Marks, *Finding Betty Crocker: The Secret Life of America's First Lady of Food* (New York: Simon & Schuster, 2005), 11.

40. Marks, *Finding Betty Crocker*, 111.

41. Marks, *Finding Betty Crocker*, 114.

42. M. M. Manring, *Slave in a Box: The Strange Career of Aunt Jemima* (Charlottesville: University Press of Virginia, 1998), 60–61.

43. Manring, *Slave in a Box*, 76.

44. Manring, *Slave in a Box*, 75–78.

45. Marks, *Finding Betty Crocker*, 71.

46. Marks, *Finding Betty Crocker*, 181.

47. Quoted in Marks, *Finding Betty Crocker*, 30.

48. Kathleen Collins, *Watching What We Eat: The Evolution of Television Cooking Shows* (New York: Continuum, 2009), 16.

49. Tracey Deutsch, "Untangling Alliances: Social Tensions Surrounding Independent Grocery Stores and the Rise of Mass Retailing," in *Food Nations: Selling Taste in Consumer Societies*, ed. Warren Belasco and Philip Scranton (New York: Routledge, 2002), 166.

50. Quoted in Deutsch, "Untangling Alliances," 158–59.

51. Deutsch, "Untangling Alliances," 165.

52. Nancy Carlisle and Melinda Talbot Nasardinov with Jennifer Pustz, *America's Kitchens* (Boston: Historic New England, 2008), 153.

53. Leslie Land, "Counterintuitive: How the Marketing of Modernism Hijacked the Kitchen Stove," in *From Betty Crocker to Feminist Food Studies: Critical Perspectives on Women and Food*, ed. Arlene Voski Avakian and Barbara Haber (Amherst: University of Massachusetts Press, 2005), 41–61.

54. "Gas Stove Department," *American Kitchen*, October 1902, 43–44.

55. Andrew P. Haley, *Turning the Tables: Restaurants and the Rise of the American Middle Class, 1880–1920* (Chapel Hill: University of North Carolina Press, 2011), 76–82.

56. Haley, *Turning the Tables*, 110–11.

57. Haley, *Turning the Tables*, 141.

58. Robert D. Buzzell and Robert E. M. Nourse, *Product Innovation in Food Processing, 1954–1964* (Boston: Harvard University Press, 1967), 39.

4. 1945 TO THE EARLY 1970S

1. Clementine Paddleford, memo, August 29, 1956, file 1, box 82, Paddleford Collection.

2. Kelly Alexander and Cynthia Harris, *Hometown Appetites: The Story of Clementine Paddleford, the Forgotten Food Writer Who Chronicled How America Ate* (New York: Gotham Books, 2008), 1–2.

3. "The Press," *Time*, December 28, 1953, 45.

4. Emmett Davis, memo, July 10, 1959, file 9, box 1, Paddleford Collection.

5. Clementine Paddleford, biographical sketch, 1952, file 3, box 1, Paddleford Collection.

6. Clementine Paddleford to Mrs. J. Rattray, September 12, 1949, file 20, box 67, Paddleford Collection.

7. Robert D. Buzzell and Robert E. M. Nourse, *Product Innovation in Food Processing 1954–1964* (Boston: Harvard University Press, 1967), 79.

8. Buzzell and Nourse, *Product Innovation in Food Processing*, 286.

9. Buzzell and Nourse, *Product Innovation in Food Processing*, 50.

10. Buzzell and Nourse, *Product Innovation in Food Processing*, 50.

11. Katherine J. Parkin, *Food Is Love: Food Advertising and Gender Roles in Modern America* (Philadelphia: University of Pennsylvania Press, 2006), 2.

12. Clementine Paddleford, memo to staff, August 29, 1956, file 1, box 82, Paddleford Collection.

13. Clementine Paddleford, "Lemonade Soufflé," *How America Eats*, September 15, 1957.

14. Kay Ringe to Clementine Paddleford, July 2, 1956, file 5, box 87, Paddleford Collection.

15. Lou Scott to Mac Norris, August 7, 1958, file 18, box 89, Paddleford Collection.

16. Clementine Paddleford, *Clementine Paddleford's Cook Young Cookbook* (New York: Pocket Books, 1966), 1.

17. Anna Marie Doherty to Clementine Paddleford, memo, February 22, 1965, file 57, box 8, Paddleford Collection.

18. Memo to Clementine Paddleford, April 15, 1965, file 64, box 8, Paddleford Collection.

19. Anna Marie Doherty to Clementine Paddleford, memo, February 22, 1965, file 57, box 8, Paddleford Collection.

20. Raymond W. Hoecker and Dale Anderson, "The Modern Supermarket—America's Trademark," *Agricultural Marketing*, May 1963, 16–18.

21. Buzzell and Nourse, *Product Innovation in Food Processing*, 40.

22. James Beard and John Ferrone, ed., *Love and Kisses and a Halo of Truffles* (New York: Arcade Publishing, 1994), 12.

23. Beard and Ferrone, *Love and Kisses and a Halo of Truffles*, 156.

24. Beard and Ferrone, *Love and Kisses and a Halo of Truffles*, 170.

25. Beard and Ferrone, *Love and Kisses and a Halo of Truffles*, 152.

26. Beard and Ferrone, *Love and Kisses and a Halo of Truffles*, 167.

27. Beard and Ferrone, *Love and Kisses and a Halo of Truffles*, 122–23.

28. Beard and Ferrone, *Love and Kisses and a Halo of Truffles*, 255–56.

29. Beard and Ferrone, *Love and Kisses and a Halo of Truffles*, 257.

30. Beard and Ferrone, *Love and Kisses and a Halo of Truffles*, 66.

31. Ezra Taft Benson, "Address by Secretary of Agriculture Ezra Taft Benson at a dinner in honor of the 25th Anniversary Celebration of the Founding of the Frozen Food Industry," April 13, 1954, folder 15, box 277, Paddleford Collection.

32. *Adventures in Good Eating* (Ithaca, NY: Duncan Hines Institute, 1960), x.

33. Eric Schlosser, *Fast Food Nation: The Dark Side of the All-American Meal* (Boston: Houghton Mifflin, 2001), 197.

34. *Time*, March 18, 1946, 55.

35. Noël Riley Fitch, *Appetite for Life: The Biography of Julia Child* (New York: Doubleday, 1997), 196.

36. Elinor Parker, "Too Many Cooks: Cookbooks to Be Published This Spring," *Publisher's Weekly*, May 3, 1952, 1838.

37. Parker, "Too Many Cooks," 1838.

38. Parker, "Too Many Cooks," 1838.

39. Parker, "Too Many Cooks," 1839.

40. Kenneth T. Jackson, *Crabgrass Frontie: The Suburbanization of the United States* (New York: Oxford University Press, 1985), 232.

41. *Better Homes & Gardens Decorating Book* (Des Moines, IA: Meredith Publishing, 1956), 342.

42. *Better Homes & Gardens Decorating Book*, 343.

43. *Better Homes & Gardens Decorating Book*, 357.

44. *Better Homes & Gardens Decorating Book*, 336.

45. Fitch, *Appetite for Life*, 23.

46. Fitch, *Appetite for Life*, 84.

47. Fitch, *Appetite for Life*, 149.

48. Elizabeth David, *French Provincial Cooking* (New York: Harper & Row, 1960), 298–301.

49. Fitch, *Appetite for Life*, 241.

50. Quoted in Mary Drake McFeely, *Can She Bake a Cherry Pie? American Women and the Kitchen in the Twentieth Century* (Amherst: University of Massachusetts Press, 2000), 117.

51. McFeely, *Can She Bake a Cherry Pie?* 118.

52. Simone Beck, Louisette Bertholle, and Julia Child, *Mastering the Art of French Cooking* (New York: Alfred A. Knopf, 1965), vii.

53. Beck, Bertholle, and Child, *Mastering the Art of French Cooking*, viii.

54. Beck, Bertholle, and Child, *Mastering the Art of French Cooking*, 315–16.

55. Fitch, *Appetite for Life*, 207.

56. Kathleen Collins, *Watching What We Eat: The Evolution of Television Cooking Shows* (New York: Continuum, 2009), 52.

57. Collins, *Watching What We Eat*, 76.

58. Warren J. Belasco, *Appetite for Change: How the Counterculture Took on the Food Industry* (Ithaca, NY: Cornell University Press, 1989), 63.

59. Carla Emery, *Carla Emery's Old Fashioned Recipe Book* (New York: Bantam, 1977), unnumbered page.

60. Mrs. E. F. Haskell, *The Housekeeper's Encyclopedia* (New York: D. Appleton and Company, 1861), 296.

5. THE EARLY 1970S THROUGH TODAY

1. Julia Child, *The French Chef Cookbook* (New York: Alfred A. Knopf, 1968), vii.

2. Allen Salkin, *From Scratch: Inside the Food Network* (New York: Putnam, 2013), 50.

3. Trish Hall, "A New Spectator Sport: Looking, Not Cooking," *New York Times*, January 4, 1989.

4. Salkin, *From Scratch*, 19.

5. Salkin, *From Scratch*, 26, 168.

6. Sandra Lee, *Semi-Homemade Cooking* (New York: Hyperion, 2002), 93.

7. Kathleen Collins, *Watching What We Eat: The Evolution of Television Cooking Shows* (New York: Continuum, 2009), 120.

8. Collins, *Watching What We Eat*, 121–22.

9. Salkin, *From Scratch*, 106.

10. Salkin, *From Scratch*, 58, 90.

11. Florence Fabricant, "The Man Who Would Turn Chefs into Household Names," *New York Times*, March 17, 1993.

12. Salkin, *From Scratch*, 104.

13. Salkin, *From Scratch*, 85.

14. Mario Batali, *Simple Italian Food* (New York: Clarkson Potter, 1998), 9.

15. Batali, *Simple Italian Food*, 14.

16. Batali, *Simple Italian Food*, 13.

17. Jamie Oliver, *Jamie's Kitchen* (New York: Hyperion, 2002), 8.

18. Oliver, *Jamie's Kitchen*, 11.

19. William Cronan, *Nature's Metropolis: Chicago and the Great West* (New York: W. W. Norton, 1991).

20. See Dana Goodyear, "Mezcal Sunrise," *The New Yorker*, April 4, 2016, 40–47, for coverage of the growing popularity of mezcal.

21. Emma Callery, *House Beautiful Design and Decorate Kitchens* (New York: Hearst, 2007), 10.

22. Kenneth Jackson, *Crabgrass Frontier: The Suburbanization of the United States* (New York: Oxford University Press, 1985), 235.

23. U.S. Bureau of the Census, "Square Feet of Floor Area in New Single-Family Houses Completed," https://www.census.gov/construction/chars/pdf/squarefeet.pdf, accessed August 15, 2016.

24. Callery, *House Beautiful Design and Decorate Kitchens*, 26.

25. Callery, *House Beautiful Design and Decorate Kitchens*, 26.

26. Callery, *House Beautiful Design and Decorate Kitchens*, 6.

27. Kristina Shevory, "You Made the Meatloaf. You Just Didn't Make It at Home," *New York Times*, August 28, 2005.

28. Janet Lee, "Meal Delivery Services Put Dinner on Your Doorstep," *Consumer Reports*, August 24, 2016, 34.

29. Lee, "Meal Delivery Services Put Dinner on Your Doorstep," 40, 38.

30. Kim Severson, "It's Dinner in a Box. But Are Meal Delivery Kits Cooking?" *New York Times*, April 4, 2016.

31. Bee Wilson, *Consider the Fork: A History of How We Cook and Eat* (New York: Basic Books, 2012), 166.

32. Wilson, *Consider the Fork*, 174.

33. Wilson, *Consider the Fork*, 105–6.

34. Collins, *Watching What We Eat*, 140.

35. Barbara Kafka, *Microwave Gourmet* (New York: William Morrow, 1987), 229, 381, 336.

36. John P. Robinson and Geoffrey Godbey, *Time for Life: The Surprising Ways American Use Their Time* (University Park: Pennsylvania State University Press, 1997), 257.

37. Robinson and Godbey, *Time for Life*, 258.

38. Robinson and Godbey, *Time for Life*, 259.

39. BLS.gov, "Time Spent in Detailed Primary Activities and Percent of the Civilian Population Engaging in Each Activity, Averages Per Day by Sex, 2015 Annual Averages," at http://www.bls.gov/tus/tables/a1_2015.pdf, accessed September 3, 2016.

40. Robinson and Godbey, *Time for Life*, 95.

41. Robinson and Godbey, *Time for Life*, 105.

42. Robinson and Godbey, *Time for Life*, 135.

43. Robinson and Godbey, *Time for Life*, 38.

44. David Cutler, Edward Glaeser, and Jesse Shapiro, "Why Have Americans Become More Obese?" *Journal of Economic Perspectives* 17, no. 3 (2003): 100.

45. Emily K. Abel, "The Rise and Fall of Celiac Disease in the United States," *Journal of the History of Medicine and Allied Sciences* 65, no. 1 (January 2010): 81–105.

46. Jerome Groopman, "The Peanut Puzzle," *The New Yorker*, February 7, 2011, at http://www.newyorker.com/magazine/2011/02/07/the-peanut-puzzle, accessed September 5, 2016.

47. Stephanie Strom, "A Big Bet on Gluten-Free," *New York Times*, February 17, 2014.

48. Strom, "A Big Bet on Gluten-Free."

6. THE FUTURE OF HOME COOKING

1. Reay Tannahill, *Food in History* (New York: Stein and Day, 1973), 394.

2. Michael Pollan, "Out of the Kitchen, Onto the Couch," *New York Times*, July 29, 2009.

3. Pollan, "Out of the Kitchen, Onto the Couch."

4. Phyllis Korkki, "As Thanksgiving Goes, So Goes the Nation," *New York Times*, November 22, 2008.

5. USDA Economic Research Service, "Food Expenditures," "Percent of Consumer Expenditures Spent on Food, Alcoholic Beverages, and Tobacco That Were Consumed at Home, by Selected Countries, 2015," at http://www.ers.usda.gov/data-products/food-expenditures.aspx, accessed August 31, 2015.

BIBLIOGRAPHY

Abel, Emily K. "The Rise and Fall of Celiac Disease in the United States." *Journal of the History of Medicine and Allied Sciences* 65, no. 1 (January 2010): 81–105.

Accum, Fredrick. *A Treatise on Adulteration of Food, and Culinary Poisons*. London: Longman, 1820.

Adventures in Good Eating. Ithaca, NY: Duncan Hines Institute, 1960.

Alexander, Kelly, and Cynthia Harris. *Hometown Appetites: The Story of Clementine Paddleford, the Forgotten Food Writer Who Chronicled How America Ate*. New York: Gotham Books, 2008.

Batali, Mario. *Simple Italian Food*. New York: Clarkson Potter, 1998.

Beard, James, and John Ferrone, editor. *Love and Kisses and a Halo of Truffles*. New York: Arcade Publishing, 1994.

Beck, Simone, Louisette Bertholle, and Julia Child. *Mastering the Art of French Cooking*. New York: Alfred A. Knopf, 1965.

Beecher, Catharine E., and Harriet Beecher Stowe. *The American Woman's Home*. New York: J. B. Ford and Company, 1869.

Belasco, Warren J. *Appetite for Change: How the Counterculture Took on the Food Industry*. Ithaca, NY: Cornell University Press, 1989.

Beste, J. Richard. *The Wabash*. Freeport, NY: Books for Libraries Press, 1970.

Better Homes & Gardens Decorating Book. Des Moines, IA: Meredith Publishing, 1956.

Billings, John D. *Hardtack and Coffee*. Boston: George M. Smith & Co., 1888.

Bircher, William. *A Drummer-Boy's Diary*. St. Paul, MN: St. Paul Book and Stationery Co., 1889.

Buzzell, Robert D., and Robert E. M. Nourse. *Product Innovation in Food Processing, 1954–1964*. Boston: Harvard University Press, 1967.

Callery, Emma. *House Beautiful Design and Decorate Kitchens*. New York: Hearst, 2007.

Carlisle, Nancy, and Melinda Talbot Nasardinov with Jennifer Pustz. *America's Kitchens*. Boston: Historic New England, 2008.

Charles, Jeffrey. "Searching for Gold in Guacamole: California Growers Market the Avocado, 1910–1994." In *Food Nations: Selling Taste in Consumer Societies*, edited by Warren Belasco and Philip Scranton, 131–55. New York: Routledge, 2002.

Child, Julia. *The French Chef Cookbook*. New York: Alfred A. Knopf, 1968.

Collins, Kathleen. *Watching What We Eat: The Evolution of Television Cooking Shows*. New York: Continuum, 2009.

Cowan, Ruth Schwartz. *More Work for Mother: The Ironies of Household Technology from the Open Hearth to the Microwave*. New York: Basic Books, 1983.

Crayon, Geoffrey, Esq. (Washington Irving). *The Sketch-Book of Geoffrey Crayon, Esq.* Paris: Baudry's European Library, 1846.

Croly, Mrs. J. C. *Jennie June's American Cookery Book.* New York: The American News Company, 1870.

Cronan, William. *Nature's Metropolis: Chicago and the Great West.* New York: W. W. Norton, 1991.

Cutler, David, Edward Glaeser, and Jesse Shapiro. "Why Have Americans Become More Obese?" *Journal of Economic Perspectives* 17, no. 3 (2003): 93–118.

David, Elizabeth. *French Provincial Cooking.* New York: Harper & Row, 1960.

De Voe, Thomas F. *The Market Assistant.* New York: Hurd and Houghton, 1867.

Deutsch, Tracey. "Untangling Alliances: Social Tensions Surrounding Independent Grocery Stores and the Rise of Mass Retailing." In *Food Nations: Selling Taste in Consumer Societies,* edited by Warren Belasco and Philip Scranton, 156–74. New York: Routledge, 2002.

Dudden, Faye E. *Serving Women: Household Service in Nineteenth-Century America.* Middletown, CT: Wesleyan University Press, 1983.

Emery, Carla. *Carla Emery's Old Fashioned Recipe Book.* New York: Bantam, 1977.

An English Gentleman. *An Excursion Through the United States and Canada During the Years 1822–23.* London: Baldwin, Cradock, and Joy, 1824.

Fabricant, Florence. "The Man Who Would Turn Chefs into Household Names." *New York Times,* March 17, 1993.

Fitch, Noël Riley. *Appetite for Life: The Biography of Julia Child.* New York: Doubleday, 1997.

"Gas Stove Department." *American Kitchen,* October 1902.

Good Things to Eat from Wellville. Battle Creek, MI: Postum Cereal Company, 1916.

Goodyear, Dana. "Mezcal Sunrise." *The New Yorker,* April 4, 2016.

Groopman, Jerome. "The Peanut Puzzle." *The New Yorker,* February 7, 2011.

Haley, Andrew P. *Turning the Tables: Restaurants and the Rise of the American Middle Class, 1880–1920.* Chapel Hill: University of North Carolina Press, 2011.

Hall, Trish. "A New Spectator Sport: Looking, Not Cooking." *New York Times,* January 4, 1989.

Haskell, Mrs. E. F. *The Housekeeper's Encyclopedia.* New York: D. Appleton and Company, 1861.

Hines, Duncan. *Adventures in Good Eating.* Ithaca, NY: Duncan Hines Institute, 1957.

Hoecker, Raymond W., and Dale Anderson. "The Modern Supermarket—America's Trademark." *Agricultural Marketing,* May 1963.

Horowitz, Roger. *Putting Meat on the American Table: Taste, Technology, Transformation.* Baltimore: Johns Hopkins University Press, 2006.

Jackson, Kenneth T. *Crabgrass Frontier: The Suburbanization of the United States.* New York: Oxford University Press, 1985.

Kafka, Barbara. *Microwave Gourmet.* New York: William Morrow, 1987.

Kellogg, J. H., MD. *Battle Creek Sanitarium System: History, Organization, Methods.* Battle Creek, MI: Gage Printing Co., 1908.

Korkki, Phyllis. "As Thanksgiving Goes, So Goes the Nation." *New York Times,* November 22, 2008.

Land, Leslie. "Counterintuitive: How the Marketing of Modernism Hijacked the Kitchen Stove." In *From Betty Crocker to Feminist Food Studies: Critical Perspectives on Women and Food,* edited by Arlene Voski Avakian and Barbara Haber, 41–61. Amherst: University of Massachusetts Press, 2005.

Larkin, Jack. *The Reshaping of Everyday Life 1790–1840.* New York: HarperPerennial, 1989.

Lea, Elizabeth E. *Domestic Cookery.* Baltimore: Cushings and Bailey, 1869.

Lee, Janet. "Dinner on Your Doorstep." *Consumer Reports,* October 2016.

Lee, Sandra. *Semi-Homemade Cooking.* New York: Hyperion, 2002.

Levenstein, Harvey A. *Revolution at the Table: The Transformation of the American Diet.* New York: Oxford University Press, 1988.

Lincoln, Mary J., Sarah Tyson Rorer, Helen Armstrong, Lida Ames Willis, and Marion Harland. *Home Helps: A Pure Food Cook Book.* Chicago: N. K. Fairbank Company, 1910.

Manring, M. M. *Slave in a Box: The Strange Career of Aunt Jemima.* Charlottesville: University Press of Virginia, 1998.

Marks, Milton B. "The Longwood Co-Operative Kitchen." *Good Housekeeping,* February 1901.

Marks, Susan. *Finding Betty Crocker: The Secret Life of America's First Lady of Food.* New York: Simon & Schuster, 2005.

McFeely, Mary Drake. *Can She Bake a Cherry Pie? American Women and the Kitchen in the Twentieth Century.* Amherst: University of Massachusetts Press, 2000.

Melville, Herman. *Moby-Dick, Billy Budd, and Other Writings.* New York: The Library of America, 2000.

Nichola, A. "Easy Means of Relieving Pain." *Good Housekeeping,* March 1901.

Oliver, Jamie. *Jamie's Kitchen.* New York: Hyperion, 2002.

Paddleford, Clementine. *Clementine Paddleford's Cook Young Cookbook.* New York: Pocket Books, 1966.

———. "Lemonade Soufflé." *How America Eats,* September 15, 1957.

Parker, Elinor. "Too Many Cooks: Cookbooks to Be Published This Spring." *Publisher's Weekly,* May 3, 1952.

Parkin, Katherine J. *Food Is Love: Food Advertising and Gender Roles in Modern America.* Philadelphia: University of Pennsylvania Press, 2006.

Parloa, Maria. *Miss Parloa's New Cook Book.* Boston: Estes and Lauriat, 1882.

Peterson, Harold L. *Americans at Home: From the Colonists to the Late Victorians.* New York: Charles Scribner's Sons, 1971.

Pickard, Madge E., and R. Carlyle Buley. *The Midwest Pioneer: His Ills, Cures & Doctors.* New York: Henry Schuman, 1946.

Pollan, Michael. "Out of the Kitchen, Onto the Couch." *New York Times,* July 29, 2009.

"The Press." *Time,* December 28, 1953.

Randolph, Mary. *The Virginia Housewife.* Columbia: University of South Carolina Press, 1984.

"The Relative Cost of Home-Cooked and Purchased Food." *Massachusetts Labor Bulletin* 19 (August 1901): 67–98.

Richards, Ellen H. "The Eight Hour Day in Housekeeping." *The American Cooking Magazine,* April 1902.

Riely, Elizabeth. "Sylvester Graham and the Origins of the Breakfast Food Industry." In *Oxford Symposium on Food & Cookery 1989: Staple Foods.* London: Prospect Books, 1990.

Robinson, John P., and Geoffrey Godbey. *Time for Life: The Surprising Ways American Use Their Time.* University Park: Pennsylvania State University Press, 1997.

Rombauer, Irma S., Marion Rombauer Becker, and Ethan Becker. *The Joy of Cooking.* New York: Scribner, 1997.

Salkin, Allen. *From Scratch: Inside the Food Network.* New York: Putnam, 2013.

Schlosser, Eric. *Fast Food Nation: The Dark Side of the All-American Meal.* Boston: Houghton Mifflin, 2001.

Severson, Kim. "It's Dinner in a Box. But Are Meal Delivery Kits Cooking?" *New York Times,* April 4, 2016.

Shapiro, Laura. *Perfection Salad: Women and Cooking at the Turn of the Century.* New York: Farrar, Straus and Giroux, 1986.

Shephard, Sue. *Pickled, Potted and Canned: How the Art and Science of Food Preserving Changed the World.* New York: Simon & Schuster, 2000.

Shevory, Kristina. "You Made the Meatloaf. You Just Didn't Make It at Home." *New York Times,* August 28, 2005.

Shirreff, Patrick. *A Tour Through North America.* Edinburgh: Oliver and Boyd, 1835.

Simmons, Amelia. *American Cookery.* Hartford, CT: Simeon Butler, 1798.

Snodgrass, Mary Ellen. *Encyclopedia of Kitchen History.* New York: Fitzroy Dearborn, 2004.

Stanley, Hon. E. *Journal of a Tour in America.* London: Privately Printed, 1930.

Strom, Stephanie. "A Big Bet on Gluten-Free." *New York Times,* February 17, 2014.

Tannahill, Reay. *Food in History.* New York: Stein and Day, 1973.

Twain, Mark. *A Tramp Abroad.* New York: Oxford University Press, 1996.

U.S. Bureau of the Census. "Square Feet of Floor Area in New Single-Family Houses Completed." Accessed August 15, 2016. https://www.census.gov/construction/chars/pdf/squarefeet.pdf.

————. "Table 3. Population of the 33 Urban Places: 1800." Accessed December 14, 2015. https://www.census.gov/population/www/documentation/twps0027/tab03.txt.

USDA Economic Research Service. "Percent of Consumer Expenditures Spent on Food, Alcoholic Beverages, and Tobacco That Were Consumed at Home, by Selected Countries, 2015." Accessed August 31, 2015. http://www.ers.usda. gov/data-products/food-expenditures.aspx.

Weaver, William Woys. *A Quaker Woman's Cookbook: The Domestic Cookery of Elizabeth Ellicott Lea.* Philadelphia: University of Pennsylvania Press, 1982.

Weinstein, Bruce, and Mark Scarbrough. *The Ultimate Chocolate Cookie Book.* New York: William Morrow, 2004.

Weir, Walter. "Advertising Tells the Story." In *Food Marketing*, edited by Paul Sayres, 210–22. New York: McGraw-Hill, 1950.

Wilson, Bee. *Consider the Fork: A History of How We Cook and Eat.* New York: Basic Books, 2012.

————. *Swindled: The Dark History of Food Fraud, From Poisoned Candy to Counterfeit Coffee.* Princeton, NJ: Princeton University Press, 2008.

Wrangham, Richard. *Catching Fire: How Cooking Made Us Human.* New York: Basic Books, 2009.

Yoder, Paton. *Taverns and Travelers: Inns of the Early Midwest.* Bloomington: Indiana University Press, 1969.

INDEX

ABOUT THE AUTHOR

Tim Miller received a BA from Goshen College in Goshen, Indiana, and a PhD in history from the University of Kansas, where he wrote his dissertation about the foods eaten in American suburbs after World War II. He currently teaches history at Labette Community College in Parsons, Kansas, and lives in southeastern Kansas with his wife, Janet. He is the author of *Barbecue: A History* (2014).